JOURNEYS
ON THE
SILK ROAD

JOURNEYS
ON THE
SILK ROAD

*A desert explorer, Buddha's secret library, and the unearthing
of the world's oldest printed book*

JOYCE MORGAN & CONRAD WALTERS

LYONS PRESS
Guilford, Connecticut
An imprint of Globe Pequot Press

First published 2011 in Picador by Pan Macmillan Australia Pty Limited
First Lyons Press edition 2012

Copyright © Joyce Morgan and Conrad Walters 2011

Lyons Press is an imprint of Globe Pequot Press

Map by Pan Macmillan

Library of Congress Cataloging-in-Publication Data is available on file.

ISBN 978-0-7627-8297-0

Printed in the United States of America

10 9 8 7 6 5 4 3 2 1

The authors and publisher gratefully acknowledge permission to reproduce the following
copyright material. While every effort has been made to trace copyright holders, we regret any
inadvertent omissions.

Epigraphs from the Diamond Sutra are reprinted from *The Diamond that Cuts through
Illusion: Commentaries on the Prajñaparamita Diamond Sutra* (1992) by Thich Nhat Hanh with
permission of Parallax Press, Berkeley, California, www.parallax.org.

Quotations from Aurel Stein's letters are courtesy of the Bodleian Library, University of Oxford.

Quotations from *Ruins of Desert Cathay* and *Sand-Buried Ruins of Ancient Khotan* by Aurel
Stein, and C.E.A.W. Oldham's obituary of Aurel Stein, are courtesy of the British Academy.

Quotations from *Serindia* by Aurel Stein and *An English Lady in Chinese Turkestan* by
Catherine Macartney appear by permission of Oxford University Press.

Quotations from British Museum Central Archives are courtesy of the Trustees of the British
Museum.

Quotations from *Tun-huang Popular Narratives* by Victor H. Mair are courtesy of Professor Mair.

Quotations from *The Times* (London) are by permission of *The Times*.

Quotation from *The Manchester Guardian* is courtesy of *The Guardian* (London).

Cartographic art by Laurie Whiddon, Map Illustrations.

To our parents

Contents

Contents

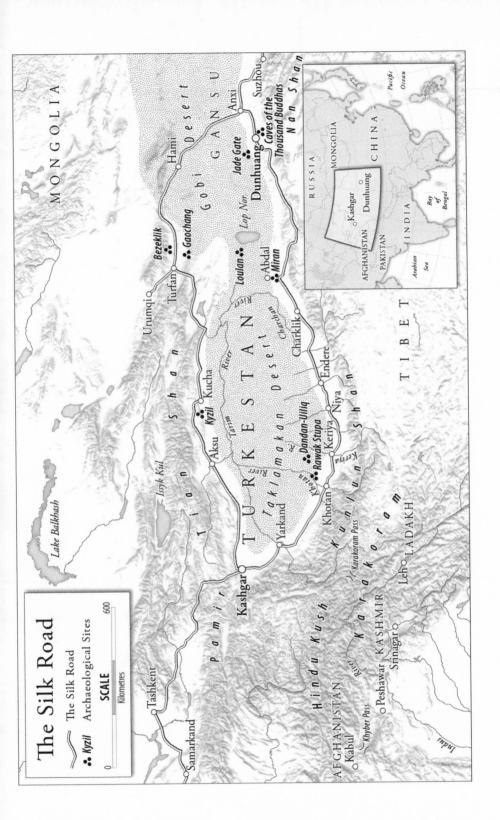

Prologue

For nearly a thousand years two attendants waited, sealed from the world in a hand-carved cave, while the sands of the great Gobi Desert crept forward. The figures, one with a topknot of black hair, the other robed in red, guarded the darkness with only a wooden staff for protection and a fan for comfort. Their cave was three paces wide by three paces deep, but they maintained a motionless vigil from the northern wall, where they merged with the room's arid earthy browns. Outside, the winds could howl, the sun could try to bake the sand into glass and the desert could encroach with each century until even a hidden doorway to the attendants' cave was buried. But inside, time had halted and everything was safe.

In front of the attendants were tens of thousands of manuscripts, piled as high as a man could reach. There were charts of the heavens, rules for monks, and deeds recording the ownership of slaves sold long ago. There were banners that could be unfurled from the cliffs outside and paintings on silk of enlightened beings. But outnumbering all of those were sutras—the words of the Buddha himself—piled into the black air, unheard, awaiting rebirth into a new realm.

Most were copies made with brushes dipped in lustrous charcoal ink by hands unknown, in kingdoms forgotten. But one paper sutra held special significance. It could confer spiritual blessings as no other. Where the rest were laboriously copied by long-dead scribes, this had been created with a wooden block and reproduced at a rate once unimaginable. It was the oldest printed book in the cave—the Diamond Sutra—and although no one outside knew it yet, this dated scroll was the oldest of its kind anywhere. The sutra taught that life is illusory and as fleeting as a bubble in a stream. True to its message, all who once knew the printed scroll was inside the cave had long since turned to dust, yet the Diamond Sutra itself remained intact.

Many copies of the sutra had preceded this one. Its words had been carried by man and beast through the wispy clouds of mountain passes, over the cracked earth of deserts, across the glacier-fed currents of surging rivers. In time this printed copy would cross the seas to reach lands unknown to its creators. One day it would even convey the Buddha's wisdom invisibly through the air.

While Christians fought the Crusades and Magellan circled the globe, while Shakespeare wrote *Hamlet* and Genghis Khan united nomadic tribes, while the Black Death consumed Europe and Galileo imagined the cosmos, while Joan of Arc answered the voices in her head and Michelangelo sculpted *David,* the two attendants stood in meditative silence. Then, at the cusp of a new century, sound returned to the Library Cave. It was 1900—the Year of the Rat—and a faint noise announced the painstaking sweeping of the sand outside the attendants' cave. Day by day, week by week, month by month, the level of the sand receded and the indistinct voices of laborers grew louder until their scrapings could be heard against the hidden door. For every moment across a millennium, the eyes of the two attendants had been open in anticipation. And, at last, a seam of light arrived.

1

The Great Race

An unforgiving wind blew clouds of dust and sand as if every grain were aimed at one tired man astride a weary pony. He urged his mount forward, determined to keep a promise. He had set out long before dawn, leaving behind his team of men and pack animals, knowing he would have to cover in one day ground that would typically take three. Traveling through the heat and glare of the Central Asian desert, he now looked on his vow—to arrive that day on the doorstep of friends in a distant oasis—as uncharacteristically rash. But for seventeen hours he pressed on across parched wastes of gravel and hard-baked earth.

As dusk approached, the sting of the day's heat eased, yet the failing light compounded his struggle to keep to the track amid the blinding sand. His destination of Kashgar could not be far away. But where? He was lost. He looked for someone—any-one—who could offer directions, but the locals knew better than to go into the desert at night during a howling wind storm. He found a farm worker in a dilapidated shack and appealed for help to set him back on the path. But the man had no desire to step outside and guide a dirt-caked foreigner back to the road, until enticed by a piece of silver.

The rider still had seven miles to go. He groped his way forward as the horse stumbled in ankle-deep dust. Eventually, he collided with a tree and felt his way along a familiar avenue until he reached the outskirts of the old town. Then, as if conceding defeat, the wind abated and lights could be glimpsed through the murky dark. He crossed a creaking wooden bridge to reach the mud walls that encircled the oasis. The guns that signaled the sunset closing of the iron gates to the old Muslim oasis had been fired hours ago. The only sound was the howling of dogs, alert to the clip-clopping of a stranger on horseback passing outside the high wall. He continued until he reached a laneway. He had covered more than sixty miles to reach Chini Bagh, the home of good friends and an unlikely outpost of British sensibilities on the edge of the Taklamakan Desert. Its gates were open in anticipation. He shouted to announce his arrival. For a moment, silence. Then surprised voices erupted in the darkness as servants recognized him. At last Aurel Stein had arrived. They moved closer to greet the man they had not seen for five years. At forty-three, he was no longer young, but his features were as angular as ever, and his body—though just five feet four inches tall—still deceptively strong.

Water was fetched so he could scrub away the sweat and grime etched into his skin. Only then did he present himself in the dining room. He eased into a chair, glad at last to sit on something other than his exhausted horse, and talked with his friends until well past midnight. At the dining table were Britain's representative in Kashgar, George Macartney, and his wife, Catherine Theodora, both eager to hear of Stein's journey so far and, equally important, his hopes for the trip ahead. The last time they had been together in Chini Bagh, in 1901, the explorer was at the end of his first expedition to Turkestan. He had been loaded with ancient treasures recovered from the desert, treasures that would stun scholars across Europe. Now he had returned, better equipped, better funded and better educated about the obstacles that lay ahead. George Macartney had been invaluable then, helping Stein assemble the crew that would pluck antiquities from beneath the sands. This time, the stakes were higher, the journey longer and the route more deadly.

As they talked into the night of June 8, 1906, Stein had much to tell of the two-month trip that had brought him to Chini Bagh's welcoming doorstep. His weather-beaten face had barely recovered from his trip over the mountains that separated Chinese Turkestan from northern India. The high-altitude sun left his face so blistered and swollen he had wondered if his friends would recognize him. But sunburn was the least of the hardships he encountered.

༄

His journey had begun on April 2, when he set out from northern India on a cold but sunny day. Spring had not yet greened the native chinar trees, nor had the irises sprouted as Stein left the alpine Kashmir Valley with a fox terrier named Dash at his heels. His intended route, at times following the footsteps of Alexander the Great, led up through the far north of present-day Pakistan, through lawless tribal territory, and briefly across Afghan terrain before descending to Turkestan. He knew robbery—or worse—was a risk and that at least one foreign explorer had been beheaded in the region, so he was armed with Lee-Enfield carbines and Webley revolvers. His path led over "the roof of the world," the Pamir Mountains whose jagged peaks are some of the highest on earth. The route was the quickest way to Kashgar, and he had every reason to hurry.

But the course was treacherous in the spring, as the arrival of Stein's faithful old caravan man, Muhammadju, attested. On the way to join Stein for this second, more audacious exploration of Central Asia, Muhammadju narrowly escaped an avalanche on a mountain pass. Seven of his companions had been swept to their deaths. Indeed Stein himself, after passing through the lower Swat Valley, was forced to spend two miserable days in a leaky, crumbling shelter near the foot of one of the most avalanche-prone passes, the Lowari, until a thunderstorm passed and the sky cleared.

The snow had been abnormally heavy the previous winter, and he had been warned not to attempt the crossing before June. But that was still a month off. If he waited until then, the gorges farther along his route would be rendered impassable by floodwaters from the melting snow. Stein knew the risks in early May could be reduced by crossing the 10,230-foot Lowari Pass at night, when plummeting temperatures firmed the snow fields into a hard crust. He divided his team of men and pack animals into three groups and spread his cargo so that each animal's burden was no more than forty pounds. Then, at 1 a.m., with only moonlight and their lamps to guide them, Stein led the first group on the slow ascent. The other teams followed at fifteen-minute intervals to reduce the weight on the snow. All were aware that somewhere beneath their feet lay the frozen bodies of seventeen ponies and two dozen men who had perished there five months earlier when attempting to cross in a snowstorm.

As dawn broke, Stein reached the wind-blown top of the Lowari Pass and saw that his frustrating wait had been justified. About halfway down he spotted the signs of an avalanche that had swept through on the previous afternoon. He watched anxiously as his porters zigzagged their way down the almost sheer descent. As he reached the bottom of the pass and looked back at his other teams, one sight cheered him: his incompetent, troublesome cook being carried down and looking "more like a log than an animate being," he later wrote. The useless cook (Stein had a string of them) was "incapable of facing prolonged hard travel, even when fortified by clandestine drink and doses of opium." Stein planned to offload him in Kashgar.

Stein and his men continued through the mountains for most of May. The thin "poisonous air" made breathing difficult and caused severe high-altitude headaches. At times men sank up to their armpits in the snow and had to be pulled out by ropes. When they reached the Wakhan Corridor, the narrow strip of Afghan terrain that sticks out like a pointed finger in the country's northeast, they supplemented their caravan with a team of yaks.

Dash, almost invisible against the snow except for his one black ear, crossed the mountains with only a single complaint: a rare, subdued whine uttered as he traversed the 16,152-foot Wakhjir Pass that separated Afghanistan from Turkestan. Stein felt his two-year-old fox terrier had more than earned the noble title he bestowed on him as a high-spirited puppy. His full name was Kardash Beg, Sir Snow Friend. As Stein descended the mountains into Turkestan he did so riding a yak with brave Dash mounted in front of him.

ﾝﾛ❡

George and Catherine Macartney knew what drove their stocky middle-aged visitor to embark on his dangerous journey. It was not a thirst for adventures, although there would be plenty of those. Ideas were what fired him. Stein spoke of lost worlds, ancient civilizations and early encounters between East and West. He craved to know how ideas and cultures spread. And one in particular: how had tolerant, compassionate Buddhism, born in the Indian Himalayas, reached China, transforming and shape-shifting along the way? He was convinced the answer lay just beyond Kashgar, beneath the Taklamakan Desert, the vast almond-shaped eye in the center of Chinese Turkestan.

But this was not a landscape that surrendered its answers readily. With dunes that can rise 1,000 feet, the Taklamakan is one of the most inhospitable places on earth. Even its local name has an ominous, if apocryphal, translation: Go in and you won't come out. Its shifting dunes, beside which the deserts of Arabia, Africa, and America seemed tame to Stein, are not the only formidable barriers to would-be explorers. To the east lies the legendary Gobi Desert. In the other three directions loom some of the world's highest mountain ranges: the Kunlun and Karakorams to the south, the Pamirs to the west and the Tian Shan, or Celestial Mountains, to the north. No divine protector could have conjured a more effective cosmic "keep out" sign.

Much depended on this latest expedition. Stein had only reached this point by the tenacious persuasion of his dual masters—the British Museum and the government of India—and each would demand tangible results in return. Soon after starting his journey he had met with the new Viceroy of India, Lord Minto. They spoke of Stein's lofty hopes for another Troy, the archaeological site excavated by the German Heinrich Schliemann less than forty years earlier. The expectations circulating around Stein were high. Minto was encouraging, even when Stein said he could not promise another set of Elgin Marbles, the classical Greek sculptures removed from the Parthenon and brought to Britain in the early nineteenth century. In fact, the treasures he brought back would in time invite comparisons as China's Elgin Marbles. What Stein's masters wanted were antiquities to fill their museums and add prestige to the Empire. Some fortunate archaeologists and adventurers could fund their own explorations, but Stein was a civil servant and obliged to plead and cajole for time away from desk-bound duties in steamy Calcutta. And he did so for what to many must have seemed dubious rewards. Although he lived in an era of exploration, Europe's attention was focused on the rich archaeological pickings closer to home—especially in Greece, Egypt and the biblical Middle East. These were places where the roots of Western culture could be discerned and where the showstopper hoards of gold, jewels, and tombs covered in hieroglyphics ignited the public's imagination. Few people gave more than a passing thought to the backblocks of Muslim Central Asia, let alone the possibility that lost Buddhist kingdoms might lie buried beneath its vast sands. Who even knew that long before the rise of Islam, a great Buddhist civilization had flourished across what we know today as Pakistan, Afghanistan, and the far west of China? Who even cared?

Stein knew—and cared—more than most. He had already completed his first successful foray into the southern part of the Taklamakan, returning from his yearlong trip with evidence of sophisticated and unknown cultures. Among his treasures were coins, statues, and murals, but to Stein, with his love of the written word, it was the documents that were most fascinating. He returned with records on wood, paper, and leather and in a range of languages: Chinese, Tibetan, and, most intriguingly, ancient Indian scripts. Documents can never compete with glittering jewels and golden statues for dramatic, visual appeal, but for Stein they could reveal so much more. To his trained eye, the written word exposed how language, people, and customs traveled and revealed the poignant details of ordinary life. Whether it recorded the daily duties of soldiers, the chores of monks or even the clumsy attempts of a child to complete his schoolwork, a document could reconstitute a life, and through that Stein could glimpse a civilization. Such discoveries had dazzled his colleagues and made his name as an archaeologist and explorer. They also made him hungry for more.

His first expedition laid essential groundwork. It was an apprenticeship during which he made vital contacts and friendships among the Muslim *begs* (headmen) and the Chinese *ambans* (high-ranking officials) along the desert's southern oases. He had assembled a trusted team of men, some of whom, like Muhammadju, rejoined him for his second expedition. His first trip had convinced him he could push much farther into the desert to uncover the secrets of the sands. If successful, he would cement his reputation and he could then devote his life to uncovering ancient knowledge. And if he failed? He risked forever being frustrated as a colonial wage slave and never again being allowed the freedom to explore.

He knew his intended route across the desert was feasible, if dangerous. The Swedish explorer Sven Hedin had proved it about a decade earlier. Hedin was the first European in living memory—and possibly the first since Marco Polo—to succeed. Younger and more gung-ho than Stein, Hedin had left two of his men dead from thirst—and nearly succumbed himself. Hedin had plucked long-buried items from the sands as he charged across the desert, but he was a geographer and cartographer, not an archaeologist. His interest was in the terrain, not what might lie below it. Even so, Hedin's example helped prompt Stein to mount his own more careful, systematic exploration.

ᢩᠣ

As Stein and the Macartneys conversed around the wooden dining table at Chini Bagh, the immediate concerns were practical. Stein's main task in Kashgar was to put together the team of men and animals for a two-year journey. The wise selection of both would be critical to its success. He had brought some supplies and men with him over the mountains, and he had spent all winter in India amassing the essentials he would need for the long road ahead. Among these were 2,000 fragile glass negatives to photograph the landscape, the finds and the faces he encountered along the way. A medicine chest held opium for pain relief, iodine for antiseptic, and quinine for malaria, from which he suffered repeatedly. He was equipped for minor surgery with forceps, suture needles, and silk. He imported quantities of dried food, including tins of Symington's pea soup and Captain Cookesley's Scotch broth and tomato soup, fifty pounds of tea, and ten pots of a nutritious new food, a salty yeast extract called Marmite. When Stein dispatched his shopping list to his London supplier, he penned a stiff letter to accompany the order: he wanted no repeat of the "regrettable" experience on his first expedition when the dried vegetables they supplied had spoiled within three months. He preferred bland English "sahib" food to local fare, even if he couldn't always find a cook able to prepare it. Stein was not a fussy eater, but perhaps only he could have thrived on a diet that included fifteen quarter-pound containers of desiccated cabbage.

He prepared for his expedition like a military chief mounting a campaign. No detail, however small, escaped him. He even ordered some lengths of Liberty silk brocade for gifts, which he knew would be appreciated in Turkestan and help smooth the path ahead. Stein was typically specific about what he wanted: good-quality pink and green floral and a cheaper length in yellow. If it seemed ironic to take silk back to the Silk Road, Stein gave no hint of this when he asked a friend in London to please mail some to him. His tent, which had been made for his first expedition and lined to withstand the cold, was repaired, felt boots and furs were sewn. His Jaeger wool blanket was packed, as was a canvas bath. Even Dash got his own custom-made fur coat. Stein had to prepare for all weathers, from baking desert heat to nights so cold he would sleep breathing through the sleeve of his coat.

The small party that started out with him from India included two men named Ram Singh. The older Ram Singh was an experienced Gurkha surveyor who had accompanied Stein's first expedition. The other was a thirty-two-year-old Indian Army handyman/ carpenter known as the Naik, or corporal. The Naik, who packed in his bags the uniform of his engineering regiment, would also sketch ancient ruins. Stein considered the Naik's youth an advantage in learning new skills such as photography and enduring the hardships ahead.

Macartney had been searching for months for other experienced hands to join the explorer in Kashgar, but this was no easy task. Macartney telegrammed Stein en route with an update on his efforts, including a few words about one unlikely caravan member. "Sadiq now in Chinese prison; but if you want him can probably get him out." Apparently Stein did not want him. Aside from being proof of Macartney's sway, the telegram suggests the lengths to which he was prepared to go to assist Stein. Now Stein needed Macartney's help to find the expedition's most crucial member: a Chinese assistant and interpreter. Of all the ways Macartney would help Stein—from arranging water tanks to organizing Stein's travel documents—finding the right man for this role would be the most vital. Stein planned to travel much farther east than on his first trip, this time into "China proper," as he called it. Although he was fluent in many languages, Chinese was not one of them. He needed an assistant who could not only speak the language, but who knew China's culture and protocols. He expected to uncover ancient Chinese written material and needed someone who could grasp its meaning on the spot. And he wanted someone who could teach him colloquial Chinese. Moreover, his assistant would need to be fit and have the temperament to withstand the rigors of desert travel. It was a tall order.

Chinese scholars were rare in far-flung Turkestan. The few who existed had been posted to sedentary, pen-pushing jobs in a local *yamen* or district office. They would hardly view as attractive a position that involved camping in a tent for months, with little more than Stein, a team of scruffy laborers and flatulent camels for company. Macartney had been keeping his eye out for a suitable candidate and had good news for Stein. He had learned of an educated Chinese man known as Chiang-ssu-yeh (Jiang Siye), or Secretary Chiang, who might be suitable. Chiang was believed to speak Turki, the local language. That would need to be their common tongue. Stein had learned Turki from a mullah during his first stay in Kashgar. Macartney would send for Chiang, but it would be ten days before he arrived.

Macartney knew all too well the reasons for Stein's race to Kashgar and his eagerness to get his caravan together as quickly as possible. Stein had fought long and hard to get this expedition under way. He had badgered and maneuvered, he had planned with meticulous care. But his masters had dragged their feet, delaying him a year. In that time formidable competition had mobilized. Others now had their eye on what Stein regarded as his stamping ground, among them teams from Germany and France. They were rivals for Turkestan's treasures who, gallingly, had been inspired by the success of Stein's first trip to mount their own expeditions. They had their eyes on the very places to which Stein was headed. The French were en route to the desert and the Germans had already arrived. Macartney had been quietly monitoring the latter's movements for months. It was a rare intruder who could slip into Turkestan without the knowledge of the ever-watchful George Macartney.

2

Signs of Wonder

Aurel Stein hardly looked the archetypal explorer. With his well-trimmed moustache and fastidiously parted dark hair, he appeared more dapper banker than a man who would cross desert wastes and rugged mountains and whose discoveries would transform our knowledge of the Silk Road. The man who would make off with the Silk Road's greatest treasure had prominent cheekbones, a high forehead and, even in old age, retained a firm, determined jaw. In photographs, he has a stiff, almost military air as he stands, hands in pockets, with his dark brown eyes more often fixed on a distant horizon than looking directly to camera. Whether posed in a pressed dark suit or bundled in a fur-lined coat to fend off the desert wind, a handkerchief often pokes jauntily from a breast pocket.

He was not driven by physical pleasure. Food and drink were simply fuel for long hours of work. Years of meager suppers eaten at midnight in his tent prompted few complaints, although these may not have helped the dyspepsia he suffered from throughout his life. A friend was so horrified by the state of Stein's kitchen that he marveled at the explorer's immunity to typhoid. Stein once served the same friend breakfast porridge that emitted a pungent odor. Impervious to gastronomic matters, Stein had stored his bag of oats in a chest that also contained mothballs.

He never married, never had a family and never appeared to have any romantic involvement with women or men. He had several long-lasting friendships, but there is nothing to suggest these were anything other than platonic. His friendships endured despite, or perhaps because of, long separations of time and distance. Although he mused repeatedly in his letters on the great joy he derived from his friends and how he wished he could be in their company, he chose a life that kept him from them for years at a time. Work, not romance, propelled him. And the work he valued was not easily undertaken with a wife and family in tow or abandoned while he disappeared into some of the world's most inaccessible and dangerous places. For this he chose to forgo a family, a home and material riches, although he may not have regarded this as a sacrifice. His reams of letters, written in a firm cursive hand—thousands of pages of which are now held at the Bodleian Library in Oxford—give no sense that the lack of these troubled him. Nor do they give more than a rare glimpse into his inner life. Even by the buttoned-down standards of the Victorian times through which he lived, Stein was the most private of men.

Few could follow a clue like Stein. His persistence in pursuing leads—often from seemingly unpromising sources—was extraordinary. One friend dubbed him Sherlock Holmes for his ability to infer much from scant information. He frequently consulted the centuries-old accounts by his heroes, the Venetian Marco Polo and China's great pilgrim monk Xuanzang, both of whom left detailed travel reports Stein could accurately cross-reference.

He had no permanent home. The closest he came was a canvas tent he pitched in a meadow in mountainous Kashmir, where he lived on and off for years. He retreated to Mohand Marg, north of the Kashmiri summer capital Srinagar, whenever he could. There he would walk, plan his expeditions or write. Surrounded by snow-capped mountains, he set his square wooden desk under pine trees, with vases of alpine flowers the only domestic flourish. He seems to most resemble the itinerant scholar-monks of China's Buddhist past, not least his "patron saint" Xuanzang. He was a lone wanderer.

But he did have one constant companion. He was rarely without a little dog at his side. He had a succession of seven over fifty years, all but one a fox terrier. Without exception, he named them Dash. Stein was not a man to waste time, not even on thinking up names for his dogs. The sturdy little fox terriers, known for their endurance and capacity for hard work, were an apt choice for a man with both traits in abundance. Stein's favorite by far was Dash II, his fellow traveler on what would be his greatest expedition. The smooth-haired terrier cleared mountain passes of more than 18,000 feet above sea level, quaffing saucers of tea along the way. He spent the days scampering alongside the caravan, and only occasionally joining Stein on "pony back." But each night was spent together in the relative comfort of Stein's tent. In time, Stein would confer an illustrious title on his intrepid canine: Dash the Great.

ၰ

Little in Stein's family background suggested the life he would lead. Born in Budapest into a middle-class Jewish family, he was baptized Lutheran. Such a practice was not uncommon then for the access it gave to education and the career doors it could open. Perhaps his name, Marc Aurel Stein, after the Roman emperor Marcus Aurelius, hinted at grand parental ambitions. He was a late, unexpected arrival for his mother Anna, then forty-five, and his struggling merchant father Nathan. They had already raised two children—Ernst was twenty-one and Theresa nineteen—when Stein was born on November 26, 1862. The age gap between himself and his parents and siblings may have prepared him for a solitary, self-reliant life. Certainly his education was overseen not so much by his parents but by Ernst and an uncle who was a pioneering ophthalmologist.

As a boy, Stein developed a lifelong fascination with Alexander the Great, the ancient Greek military leader whose marks on India and Central Asia remain today. Long before comic book heroes became a schoolboy staple, Alexander's ancient, and at times mythical, adventures had turned him into a sort of Superman. The young Stein read avidly of his hero's conquests through remote deserts and mountains, terrain he would himself one day cross. He heard the echoes of a long-forgotten past that cried out to be understood. And, consciously or not, he began acquiring the means to do so. Languages offered a key, and the young Stein had an aptitude for them. He studied Oriental languages in Vienna, Leipzig and Tübingen, where he received his PhD, and was proficient in Greek, Latin, Persian, and Sanskrit, as well as several European languages, including French, German, and English.

At twenty-one, he moved to Britain—whose nationality and Raj-era values he would later adopt—where, perhaps, there might be more opportunities than in Budapest for a young Oriental scholar. He undertook further studies, steeping himself in the great collections in the British Museum and at Oxford. His studies were interrupted for a year by military service in Hungary. Typically, he made good use of the time. He learned to ride a horse. He also studied surveying and mapmaking at Budapest's Ludovica Military Academy. They were skills that would prove invaluable in Central Asia, where he filled in some of the region's cartographic blanks.

He returned to London in 1886, but with his student days and his money running out, it was time to consider his next move. He seemed set on an academic career until an opportunity arose not, as he might have hoped, in a European university, but in the sprawling civil service of British-ruled India. For a young man versed in India's past, here was a chance to see first-hand the culture to which he was drawn and which, until then, he had studied only in books. For Stein, book learning alone would never satisfy. He accepted the dual role of registrar of Punjab University and principal of the Oriental College in Lahore. He said goodbye to his family and on the cusp of his twenty-sixth birthday set sail for India. He had begun to set his singular course.

ᎩᏯᎈ

Stein was sailing into uncharted waters. It was a time full of startling discoveries and possibilities for a young man with an interest in ancient cultures. The West was just beginning to learn about one of the world's oldest religions. The origins of Christianity, Islam, and Judaism had been known for centuries, but Buddhism's origins were a mystery to the West even into the nineteenth century. Some scholars thought that with his tight curly hair, flattened nose, and fleshy lips, the Buddha originated in Africa. The idea of a black Buddha persisted until the 1830s. Indeed early Orientalists could find no trace of Buddhism in India, so thoroughly had it vanished from its birthplace. Some wondered if the Buddha had ever lived or was simply a legend.

They might have saved themselves a lot of fruitless effort and theorizing if they had been able to read the tales of the ancient Chinese pilgrims. It was no mystery to these wandering monks where Buddhism came from. Traveling along the Silk Road from China into India and back, these monks had seen the Buddhist holy land with their own eyes and left accounts. They knew Buddhism came from northern India. It was the reason the monk Faxian had ventured there at the turn of the fifth century and the even more observant Xuanzang two centuries later.

But few Europeans could read of their travels until the mid-nineteenth century, when the ancient writings were finally translated, first into French and then English. When a two-volume account of Xuanzang's travels was published, it prompted a lengthy article in *The Times* in April 1857 that stated: "He describes some parts of the world which no one has explored since."

They soon would be. These accounts were seized on by a handful of Raj-era soldiers, adventurers and others who began to retrace the pilgrims' steps. It was as if they had been handed a long-lost map of an ancient maze. The writings of these wandering Chinese monks helped unlock Buddhism's forgotten Indian origins. It is hard to overestimate their significance: China's ancient pilgrims held the cultural memories India had forgotten and Britain would help recover.

A British army engineer and archaeologist, Alexander Cunningham, played a central role. In the 1860s, using the pilgrims' accounts as his guide, he rediscovered many of the key sites of Buddhism's beginnings. Today those places draw pilgrims from around the globe, but just 150 years ago they had been forgotten and overgrown for centuries. Cunningham identified the once-great monastic university of Nalanda, the city of Sravasti and the ruins of Jetavana Vihara, the garden where the Buddha taught the Diamond Sutra. Cunningham also restored Buddhism's most sacred site, the Mahabodhi Temple in Bodhgaya, near where the Buddha attained enlightenment. Stein closely followed the accounts of such discoveries. He arrived in India keen to make his own.

ﾁﾀ

Stein found a city filled with Moghul-era splendors when he reached Lahore at the beginning of 1888. The fort of its old walled city was a forty-nine acre citadel; the Badshahi Mosque dwarfed even the Taj Mahal; and the Shalimar Gardens featured more than 400 marble fountains. But it was inside the old Lahore Museum where Stein's eyes were opened to much earlier treasures. The curator was John Lockwood Kipling, whose son Rudyard Kipling described the museum in his novel *Kim* and gave the building its moniker—the Wonder House. And the museum soon worked its wonders on Stein. Never before had he seen such an extraordinary collection of ancient Buddhist statues. Some had features more European than Asian, indeed many resembled Greek gods. Here were Buddhas with round eyes and wavy hair and moustaches, wearing what looked more like Roman togas than the patched robes of monks.

The figures were from Gandhara, an ancient Buddhist kingdom that flourished for centuries around the Peshawar Valley in northwest Pakistan and Afghanistan. Its boundaries moved over the centuries, but it produced a rich vein of art, especially from the first century BC to the fifth century AD. Gandhara was where Eastern ideas met Western art, where Buddhism, migrating west from its Himalayan birthplace, encountered the legacy of Alexander the Great. His armies marched east and conquered the region. The soldiers departed, but the influence of classical art remained. Gandhara also produced some of the oldest surviving images of the Buddha as a human figure. Because of this unique meeting of cultures, the Gandharan depictions of the Buddha have decidedly Western features.

For Stein, fascinated by the journey and the changing face of Buddhism and liminal places where cultures merged, these strange Buddhas were intriguing. He was as enchanted as the Tibetan lama in *Kim's* opening pages who stands awestruck on entering the Wonder House. Stein saw the figures when few Westerners were aware of Gandharan art. Lockwood Kipling, the model for *Kim's* white-bearded curator of the Wonder House, was an expert on Gandharan art and no doubt shared his knowledge with Stein in the many evenings they spent at Kipling's home. They also appeared to share a familiarity with the man who inspired English literature's first Buddhist character, for after *Kim's* publication, Lockwood Kipling wrote to Stein: "I wonder whether you have seen my son's *Kim* & recognized the old Lama whom you saw at the old Museum."

Through Lockwood Kipling, Stein met Fred Andrews, the first of his lifelong Lahore friends who would provide intellectual sustenance and logistical support throughout his travels. Andrews was a friend of Rudyard Kipling and was Lockwood Kipling's deputy at Lahore's Mayo School of Art. Andrews was an artistic young man, whose brother George Arliss became a filmmaker and an Academy Award–winning actor who helped launch Bette Davis's career. Andrews would never achieve the fame of his brother—or that of his friend Rudyard—but he would become Stein's right-hand man.

Stein moved into Mayo Lodge, a large bungalow where Andrews lived with his wife and young daughter. In 1890 the two young men took a short trip to the Salt Range hills of Punjab, where Andrews introduced Stein to the new-fangled art of photography, which, like his mapmaking skills, Stein would put to good use in Central Asia.

The Mayo Lodge circle was widened to include Percy Stafford Allen, a young history professor, and Thomas Arnold, a philosophy professor. For a reticent man such as Stein, it was a sociable life with picnics, costume parties, and tennis games, although Stein avoided the latter. The four men soon developed chummy nicknames for each other. The names stuck and they addressed each other by them in letters throughout their lives. Andrews was the Baron, Arnold the Saint, and Allen, who would become Stein's closest friend and confidant, was Publius for sharing the three initials of Publius Scipio Africanus, the Roman tactician who defeated Hannibal and his elephants. Stein himself became the General, a hint that the more commanding of his traits were already evident. Also apparent was Stein's appetite for work, especially pursuing his own scholarly interests in the hours before and after his official day job. He rose before 6 a.m. and worked until dinner time. It was a prelude to his years as an explorer which invariably saw him up before dawn, traveling or exploring all day, and writing copious notes, diaries, and long letters to officials and friends for hours after his men were asleep around their campfires. His focus on his work was such that when a house in which he was a guest threatened to burn down one night, Stein's first response was not to save himself but to pile his books and papers into a blanket ready to toss them out the window.

As Stein was settling into his Lahore life, a gruesome murder in the mountains that separate Turkestan from Ladakh would inadvertently set the trajectory for his future. Andrew Dalgleish, a young Scottish adventurer and trader, was hacked to death with a scimitar—along with his little dog—while crossing the Karakoram Pass in 1888. News of the Scotsman's murder was reported widely. Why Dalgleish was slain was not known, but the identity of his attacker was. The killer was a bankrupt Afghan named Daud Mohammed. A British army officer, Lieutenant Hamilton Bower, was sent to arrest the culprit. The Afghan was eventually tracked by the Russians to a bazaar in distant Samarkand, where he was arrested and died (suicide, allegedly) before he could be brought to justice.

As a murder hunt it was a failure. But it sparked a different kind of chase—for buried treasures. During the pursuit for Dalgleish's killer, Lieutenant Bower arrived in the Turkestan oasis of Kucha, where he bought an ancient manuscript on birch-bark leaves that local treasure hunters had found in a ruined tower. He sent the fifty-one leaves to Calcutta, where they were eventually deciphered by Oriental scholar Dr. Rudolf Hoernle. The Bower Manuscript, as it came to be known, dealt with oddities such as therapeutic uses of garlic, necromancy—communing with the dead—and care of the mouth and teeth. But it wasn't the ancient tips on dental hygiene that set the scholarly world alight. Experts were intrigued by its Indian script, ancient Brahmi from around the fifth century. It was older than any other known Indian document, but it had been found in far-off Chinese Turkestan, across the Taklamakan Desert on the old northern Silk Road. Its isolation, far from humid, monsoonal India, was the very reason the document had survived. But how had it got there and what else was buried under the desert sands? Other fragments and artifacts soon began appearing in the oases that fringe the Taklamakan, making their way from the hands of locals to collectors in European capitals. It prompted some in Europe to wonder about the influence of India on this then little-known region in Central Asia. The more adventurous packed their bags, hired camels and went to find out.

ᗡᗅ

Stein started planning his first expedition to Turkestan when, after more than a decade in Lahore, he moved to Calcutta to become principal of a Muslim boys college in May 1899. He loathed the city's steamy climate but made the most of its proximity to Buddhism's birthplace and sacred sites. One of his first journeys out of Calcutta was to the ruins of Bodhgaya, where the Buddha attained enlightenment. Although Stein wandered from early morning until dusk, the day was too short. Within months of arriving in India's northeast he embarked on a longer tour of ancient Buddhist sites, traveling partly on an elephant.

The trips equipped him with first-hand knowledge of Buddhism's roots when he left India for Turkestan in May 1900. He was then thirty-seven and planned to travel for a year. His sights were set on an area around Khotan on the southern edge of the Taklamakan Desert. The oasis, known today as both Hotan and Hetian, had for centuries been famed for its exquisite jade and its carpets. But these were not what interested Stein. He knew local treasure seekers had recently found fragments of ancient Indian manuscripts in the region.

He had read the works of ancient Chinese pilgrims who told of a flourishing Buddhist kingdom centered around Khotan. Stein had also read Swedish explorer Sven Hedin's accounts of his travels through the desert near Khotan and gleaned practical information about surviving the brutal desert climate. From the Swede's descriptions of ruined wall paintings encountered on his hasty trip, Stein was in no doubt that these were ancient Buddhist images. A thorough search, he believed, could reveal how far Indian culture had spread into Turkestan.

Stein was the first archaeologist to dig methodically into Turkestan's pre-Muslim past. Nearly a hundred miles northeast of Khotan was Dandan-Uiliq, or the Place of Houses of Ivory, where the bleached wooden posts of ruined houses stuck out of the sand dunes like ghostly fingers—fingers that beckoned to Stein on his first desert foray. This dig would be the training ground for the years ahead. He arrived amid the dunes in December 1900 with a team of camels, donkeys, laborers, and enough supplies to last a month. It meant he could stay longer and dig more thoroughly than any of the poorly equipped locals. He could see where they had worked, but much remained untouched. From murals on the walls, he quickly realized this had been a Buddhist settlement. In one temple, he found a pedestal where a colossal Buddha statue once stood. But all that remained were the feet. He found painted wooden panels that reflected the range of influences, including Gandhara, and even a black-bearded Persian-style Buddhist image. Never before had he seen such a feature on any Buddhist figure. It pointed to the influence of distant Persia across the Taklamakan Desert. In the ruins of a monastic library he found fragments of ancient Indian scripts.

In early January 1901, Stein resupplied his caravan in an oasis and moved to other sites. At one he found remarkable proof of the links with the classical world. Amid ruins in the Turkestan desert, he found clay seals with images of the gods of ancient Greece: Eros, Heracles, and Athena. Stein was so taken with the image of the goddess of wisdom and strategy that he adapted her image from the seal and used it in the front of his published works. At another site, he uncovered what were then the oldest known Tibetan documents. And at a solitary sacred mound, or stupa, named Rawak he found the remains of nearly a hundred large Buddhist statues, some with traces of gold leaf and their once-vivid color. The stucco figures were depicted wearing embroidered coats and large boots into which were tucked baggy trousers. Stein excavated and photographed the figures, some more than nine feet tall, but they were too fragile to remove and so he returned them to the sand. "It was a melancholy duty to perform, strangely reminding me of a true burial," he wrote. He hoped this would keep them safe until one day Khotan had its own museum.

His final task before leaving Turkestan on his first expedition involved uncovering material of a different sort. For several years Stein had been suspicious about some woodblock-printed books that had supposedly been found in the desert near Khotan.

George Macartney had bought them in Kashgar and sent them to Calcutta to Hoernle, the eminent scholar who had deciphered the Bower Manuscript. The Orientalist labored long over these strange Khotanese books, but their printed script baffled him. Hoernle raised the possibility that they were fakes before he cast scholarly caution to the wind and dismissed the idea.

Stein was more skeptical. As he dug his way around the Taklamakan Desert, his suspicions grew. He had uncovered fragments of ancient documents in the desert sands—in Chinese, Tibetan, and ancient Indian scripts. But not the tiniest fragment was in an unknown script. He knew the common link between Hoernle's mysterious old books and others that had turned up in London and Moscow was a Turkestan man. Stein resolved to confront him.

Islam Akhun had a checkered past. For years, he had survived by collecting coins, seals, and other antiques from around Khotan. But by the time Stein arrived in Turkestan, Islam Akhun had reinvented himself as a *hakim*, or medicine man. His therapeutic skills somehow involved the use of several pages of a French novel. Whether these were read aloud or administered internally, Stein quipped, he could not say.

Islam Akhun strenuously denied forging the documents when he was first brought before Stein in Khotan. He was simply a middleman for others who had since died or disappeared. He had never even seen the sites where these finds were made, he protested. But then Stein confronted him with the account Islam Akhun had previously given Macartney of exactly how and where he had found the old books. Islam Akhun was outfoxed and oddly flattered that his fanciful tales had been recorded—and he confessed.

He said he knew Europeans were prepared to pay for old manuscripts, but he had no wish to engage in back-breaking digging in the desert to uncover them. The enterprising scoundrel had a better idea. His first "old books" were handwritten imitations of genuine fragments. However, as his European buyers couldn't read them anyway, the effort in copying real script seemed needless. Documents in "unknown scripts" began appearing. Business was brisk and soon supply of the handwritten documents couldn't keep up with demand. By 1896 he turned to mass production using woodblock printing. Sheets of paper were dyed yellow and hung over a fireplace to "age" them. At times this was done too enthusiastically and Stein noted some of the old books sent to Calcutta were scorched. They had been bound so as to imitate European volumes—which should have rung alarm bells—and their pages sprinkled with sand.

Stein had solved a mystery which had fooled a brilliant scholar. Even so, he had no wish to see Islam Akhun punished. The man was no stranger to harsh local justice. For past misdeeds, including fraud, he had been imprisoned, flogged, and forced to wear a wooden collar or *cangue*, similar to a portable pillory, which renders the offender unable to feed himself or lie down. Stein even developed a grudging respect for the "versatile rogue," whom he found witty and highly intelligent. Too intelligent to waste his not inconsiderable talents in Khotan, Stein told him in jest. And in this throwaway line, Islam Akhun was quick to sniff fresh opportunity. He begged Stein to take him to Europe where he could, no doubt, find a bigger market for his unique skills. Stein declined the rogue's entreaty.

A year after he arrived in Turkestan, Stein departed Kashgar with his treasures destined for the British Museum and his baggage loaded onto eight ponies. Flushed with success, Stein accompanied his cargo west across the border to the Russian railhead and on to London. He had learned how to work in the desert, uncovered a forgery and gathered a wealth of antiquities from a forgotten civilization.

〜୭

Stein was never going to be content as a cog in the civil service. Soon after he returned to India from his first expedition into Turkestan, he began lobbying for another trip that would again take him away from the confines of desk work. Initially, it wasn't a return to Turkestan that called him but new ground, Tibet. He was keen to join a mission being led by British army officer Francis Younghusband, a man destined to become known as much for his eccentric, free-loving beliefs and a mystical vision in Tibet as for his daring military leadership.

Stein's bid to go to Tibet was rejected because he lacked the language skills required. Undeterred, he switched his attention back to Turkestan, where there remained much more he could do. His first expedition had barely scratched the surface. Just think what he might achieve with more time and money. He set about getting both. He wanted to travel beyond Turkestan to the edge of China proper—as the neighboring province of Gansu was thought of—to explore the ancient route between China and the West.

He presented his masters with his grand plan in September 1904. He began by reminding them of what he had achieved in his first endeavor. The artifacts he had already unearthed in the desert showed how far Indian culture had spread. He also revealed that the area around Khotan had been a previously unknown meeting place between the great ancient civilizations of China, Persia, India, and the classical West. And for those not impressed with scholarship, he drew attention to practical realities: he had done it within the time and budget allotted.

He wanted to return to Khotan, where he expected the ever-shifting dunes would have surrendered more ruins in the years since his first visit. Then he would strike out across the desert to the Lop Nor region in the Taklamakan's far east, where Sven Hedin had discovered an ancient settlement called Loulan. Just beyond the desert in Gansu was the oasis of Dunhuang, or Sha-zhou—the City of Sands. This was the ancient gateway between China and Central Asia through which all Silk Road travelers once passed. Nearby were caves filled with murals and sculptures he wanted to explore. "A great many of the grottos are now filled more or less with drift sand and hence likely to have preserved also other interesting remains," he wrote with greater prescience than he could have imagined.

The urgency was obvious. The Bower Manuscript had drawn attention to the riches of the desert's sands. Local treasure seekers were destroying archaeological evidence, and rival European expeditions were likely. Stein's successes had already prompted a German team to head to Turkestan and return with forty-four crates of antiquities. And, he noted pointedly, they had three times his budget. The Russians, too, were considering mounting an expedition. The implications would not be lost on the British government. Stein was working against a backdrop of the Great Game, a phrase popularized by Rudyard Kipling to describe the nineteenth-century equivalent of the Cold War.

Political uncertainties within China were also a factor, he argued. Local Chinese authorities had been helpful so far, but that could change. "It seems scarcely possible to foresee whether . . . political changes may not arise which would close that field to researches from the British side." Nor could he foresee that when the political winds did change, he would be at their center. Having already applied for British citizenship, he appealed to national and imperial pride. "The wide-spread interest thus awakened makes it doubly desirable that the leading part so far taken in these explorations by British enterprise and from the side of India should be worthily maintained."

To add further muscle to his application, he lobbied influential scholars and associates—Stein was a great networker—for their support. He had characteristically argued his case from all directions: scholarship, patriotism, politics, and economics. He knew he needed to if he was to avoid a refusal by the bureaucracy, that "centre of intellectual sunshine," as he dubbed it.

The bottom line was he wanted to leave India in the spring of 1905 for two and a half years—more than twice the duration of his first expedition—and wanted a corresponding increase in funds to do so. It was an audacious request, as he well knew. "A bold demand which possibly may make an impression—or frighten," he admitted in a letter to his friend Fred Andrews. It did both. And the effect in certain quarters was not what he hoped. Some were miffed that within a year of a role being created for him Stein was lobbying to take off. The title Archaeological Inspector had been added to his already long-winded one of Inspector General of Education for North-West Frontier Province and Baluchistan. The authorities were annoyed that he wanted to depart before he had completed a detailed report on his first Turkestan trip and helped settle how the antiquities he brought back should be divided between museums in Britain, Lahore, and Calcutta. Stein realized he would have to delay his trip for a year to do this.

Behind the scenes, other objections were raised too. There were hidden costs, argued one official. Although Stein had prepared a detailed budget—even including the cost of presents to local officials—he had neglected a vital element: he hadn't allowed for his onward travel to Europe to accompany his finds and time in London to work on them. Meanwhile, another bean counter, scrutinizing the itinerary itself, pondered whether Stein couldn't perhaps reduce his traveling time by cutting the Dunhuang leg of his journey. Had he done so, Stein would have missed out on the site of the Silk Road's most remarkable discovery.

As officialdom dragged its wearying chain, Stein waited to hear the fate of his proposal. Then, unexpectedly, in April 1905, a telegram arrived from his old friend Thomas "the Saint" Arnold.

It must have seemed like news from the gods. Arnold, now back in London and working in the India Office, tipped Stein off that a decision on his proposal had finally been made. Arnold's one-word cable to Stein read simply: "Rejoice."

If daughters or sons of good family want to give rise to the highest, most fulfilled, awakened mind, what should they rely on and what should they do to master their thinking?
—VERSE 17, THE DIAMOND SUTRA

3

The Listening Post

Stein did indeed rejoice, but even before his pots of Marmite and desiccated cabbage reached him in India he was receiving unsettling news from Kashgar. Macartney regularly updated Stein about goings-on in the oasis, proudly boastful of his son Eric and quietly amused by the activities of a mutual friend there, an eccentric but much-loved Dutch priest named Father Hendricks. But Macartney's letters went well beyond domestic chit-chat.

"There is a piece of news which should interest you," he wrote with typical British understatement. "A German expedition is now at Turfan. I had a letter from them only this week . . . I don't know how many Germans there are. But the man who wrote me signed himself Albert von Lecoq [sic]; and he mentions a companion of his under the name of Bartus." Exactly what they were up to at Turfan, more than 800 miles east of Kashgar, Macartney wasn't sure; he suspected they might be geologists or intruders on Stein's archaeological terrain. However, he did know they were heading for Kashgar. And the Germans were not the only ones bringing their buckets and spades to Turkestan. Macartney had learned of "another poacher on your preserves."

An American named Ellsworth Huntington had asked Macartney if he knew anything about old manuscripts discovered in the desert. "The sooner you are on the field, the better," Macartney warned Stein.

Having been forced to postpone his trip by a year, Stein's frustration grew the more he learned of these rivals. As his departure day drew closer, the news from Kashgar became increasingly alarming. The two Germans had arrived in Kashgar in October 1905 and were staying under Macartney's roof. Even as Macartney was enjoying the lively companionship of some new European faces in town—and a gregarious pair at that—he was gleaning information about their plans and quietly passing the news to Stein, along with the confidential reports prepared for his own political masters in India. The Germans represented rival ambitions. Nothing personal, of course.

Albert von Le Coq, two years older than Stein, was an assistant at Berlin's Ethnological Museum. It was the first time von Le Coq, who studied medicine and languages before joining the museum, had led an expedition or journeyed to Turkestan. He was the wealthy heir to a wine and brewing fortune, and judging by the contents of his baggage he had a very different temperament to the reserved and stoic Stein. Von Le Coq ventured into the desert with twelve bottles of Veuve Clicquot champagne, a farewell gift from his sisters. He chilled the bubbly by wrapping the bottles in wet felt and leaving them in a breeze. After a hard day's digging, he found it a most refreshing drink.

He had set out from Germany with Theodor Bartus, the museum's knockabout handyman. Bartus had no formal education but knew his way around Turkestan, having accompanied the first German expedition to Turfan three years earlier. In Kashgar, the two men were waiting impatiently for the arrival of their museum boss and Indian scholar Professor Albert Grünwedel. Traveling overland from Europe, the professor had been stuck for more than a month in Russian Turkestan waiting for baggage that had gone astray. Until Grünwedel turned up, von Le Coq's movements were stymied.

"The absence of the Professor seems to have disconcerted Mr. Lecoq considerably," Macartney wrote in mid-October. Exactly why would not be known until much later. But Macartney did learn that von Le Coq appeared to have his eye on the very places Stein was aiming for: Lop Nor and Dunhuang. Moreover, Macartney also learned von Le Coq was not looking forward to the arrival of Grünwedel, who would take over as expedition leader. Von Le Coq and Bartus worked well together; they moved quickly and traveled light. Grünwedel, by contrast, was slow and meticulous. Their different methods were not the only reason for disharmony. "There is a good deal of jealousy between Grünwedel & Lecoq, and Lecoq tells me that he is not anxious to work with Grünwedel with whom he is rather afraid of having misunderstandings. Bartus is a splendid man," Macartney reported three weeks later.

Indeed Bartus was a garrulous sidekick. The former sailor had washed up in Australia at one stage, where he had learned to ride a horse, lost his money in a Melbourne bank collapse and returned to Europe. He was a man with a mischievous sense of humor. When Turkestan officials once asked him to teach them a polite German greeting, he kept a straight face as he instructed them to say: "Good morning, old fat-head." Bartus taught them well. When Grünwedel returned six years later, that was how he was greeted.

Macartney kept silent about Stein's plans to his lively German guests. But he suggested that perhaps Stein should write to von Le Coq, whom he found a "pucca" well-read man, and make clear his intentions. After all, Stein's movements could not remain a secret for much longer. What prompted Macartney's suggestion isn't known. Perhaps it was made out of the respect Macartney developed for von Le Coq in the two months the German spent under Chini Bagh's roof. Or maybe he saw it as a way for Stein to explicitly stake out his territory. But declaring his hand was against Stein's instincts. He had gone to great lengths to keep his plans secret and did not want his rivals tipped off. "I have never believed in the advantage of grand announcements beforehand," Stein wrote back.

Meanwhile, Grünwedel and his young offsider, Referendar Pohrt, eventually overcame their problems with the Russian railways and reached Kashgar. They no sooner arrived than Macartney penned a candid sketch from which Stein, still busily making preparations in India, could draw some cheer. "Grünwedel is ill, can't go on horseback & has to be looked after like a big baby. Pohrt is a young fellow with no experience, and at present finds the Turki girls far more interesting than archaeology . . . The Germans have certainly not shown much despatch in their movements. No doubt had they known that you also were on the war path, they would have dragged Grünwedel off, ill or not, long before now."

The latter point would reinforce Stein's belief in the value of keeping plans secret. But even with the welcome news of the German party's dithering, Stein could not relax. A French expedition was to get under way in the spring of 1906, around the same time as his own. It would be headed by a precociously brilliant young Sinologist, twenty-seven-year-old Paul Pelliot. Like Stein, he was an accomplished linguist but with a key difference: he was fluent in Chinese. In January 1906, Stein confided his intentions to his friend Percy Allen, writing, "My own plan now is to keep council [sic] to myself & to be on the ground before either Germans or Frenchmen know exactly of my start."

Stein hoped Grünwedel's slow, thorough approach would keep the Germans out of his way in distant parts of the desert. When Grünwedel left Kashgar his progress was even slower than usual. Still too sick to ride, he made an inglorious exit, bumping his way along the oasis's dusty, rutted road atop a cart filled with hay. Of Pelliot's movements there was no news. Stein confessed to feeling wicked enough to hope the Frenchman and his party might get stuck in transit. He wasn't sure how Pelliot would travel to Turkestan. If he came via India, with a word in the right ear Stein could even help engineer a delay. As it turned out, he didn't need to. Pelliot came via train from Europe and got stuck in Tashkent for two months waiting for his bags to arrive. Ever the acquisitive linguist, Pelliot used the time to learn Turki, the main language of Turkestan. "The true race will be with the Frenchmen," Stein told Allen.

Yet the Germans were not simply sipping champagne. Albert von Le Coq had chanced upon a curious piece of information that Stein would not learn until reaching Dunhuang. Had he known, Stein might not have been quite so dismissive of the Germans in the months before he reached Kashgar.

さ9

Chini Bagh, meaning Chinese garden, was a single-story mud-brick home built around three sides of a courtyard. Situated atop a cliff, its terraces overlooked a river where naked boys riding bareback would water their horses and where lengths of cloth were dyed deep red with hollyhock flowers. On clear days, the snow-capped Tian Shan mountains were visible in the distance.

The Macartneys presided over one of the most hospitable and unconventional houses in Central Asia. Through its gates passed an unusual cast of characters: adventurers, oddballs and journalists, aristocrats and missionaries, Chinese dignitaries in sedan chairs and fleeing refugees. The Macartneys were themselves an unusual couple. George Macartney was the son of a Scottish father, who had served in China, and a Chinese mother. He never spoke of his mother, not even to his children, yet his Chinese heritage was apparent in his features. He was fluent in Chinese, having spent his childhood in Nanjing, and was educated in England.

Early in his career, he was the translator for Francis Younghusband, then a young army officer, when the pair arrived at Kashgar in 1890 and the two men moved into Chini Bagh. Younghusband departed the following year and continued his controversial career, most notably leading the British invasion of Tibet in 1904. Macartney, who remained in Kashgar, could hardly have predicted Chini Bagh would be his home for the next twenty-eight years.

He briefly returned to Britain on leave in 1898. His Scottish fiancée, twenty-one-year-old Catherine Theodora Borland, had not been expecting him when he arrived on her doorstep, but nonetheless married him a week later. Their parents were friends, and the pair had known one another since childhood, but George and Catherine were opposites. He was a man of few words—his talent was for listening. In group photographs he invariably appears off to one side or in the background, as though quietly assessing the scene before him. Mrs. Macartney was a warm, sociable figure. She began her marriage as "the most timid, unenterprising girl in the world . . . and certainly had no qualifications for a pioneer's life, beyond being able to make a cake." She soon proved otherwise. Within weeks of her hastily arranged wedding, she cheerfully made the rugged overland trek to Kashgar via Russia on horse and camel, picking up a harmonium along the way to accompany her singing.

Kashgar has long been one of Central Asia's great crossroads. In Stein's day, it drew Muslim merchants from Tashkent and Samarkand, Jews from Bokhara, fierce Pashtuns from Afghanistan, and Kashmiris and Ladakhis from across the Himalayas to the south. Remote as it was from Europe's salons and drawing rooms, few places have been more strategically significant, especially at the height of the Great Game rivalry when the Russian and British empires jostled for influence in Central Asia. Turkestan, like Afghanistan, was seen as a buffer against Russian expansion that might threaten the jewel in Britain's imperial crown, India. As a result, Kashgar was home to two European outposts: Chini Bagh and the Russian consulate. Both were just outside the old Muslim city and a few miles north of the newer Chinese city. The Chinese administered the oasis and raised taxes, but the Muslims had their own leaders. China's influence had waxed and waned in Turkestan, which has been known by many names. The West has variously called it Chinese or Eastern Turkestan, High Tartary, Kashgaria, and Sinkiang. China has called it the Western Regions and New Dominions. Today it is known as the Xinjiang Uyghur Autonomous Region.

When Stein first visited Kashgar, the effects of its shifting fortunes were still apparent. An unlikely Muslim leader named Yakub Beg, a Tajik adventurer and former dancing boy, had seized control of Kashgar and most of Eastern Turkestan and proclaimed himself King of Kashgaria in the 1860s. Yakub Beg claimed descent from the great Central Asian conqueror Tamerlane and was adept at playing off one Great Gamer against another. The Russians shed no tears when, in 1877, the wily despot died, Kashgaria unraveled and China regained control. But Britain had cozied up to Yakub Beg and Macartney felt the aftermath of China's displeasure. Although China had promptly allowed Russia to establish a consulate in Kashgar in 1882, Britain wasn't allowed to do so for more than twenty years. Until then, Macartney was outranked by the Russian consul. For much of that time, Russian authority was wielded by the formidable and capricious Nikolai Petrovsky. Relations between Petrovsky and Macartney were cordial for a while. Petrovsky even sent a Cossack guard to escort Macartney and his new bride into Kashgar, and the two representatives of the rival empires celebrated Christmas together. But the mood so chilled at one stage that Petrovsky, who had lent Macartney a pane of window glass—a rare commodity in Kashgar—demanded it back. On another occasion, the Russians diverted Chini Bagh's water supply. For about three years, including during Stein's first visit in the summer of 1900, Macartney and Petrovsky did not speak to each other. Perhaps an uneasy relationship was no surprise given their roles. But with just a handful of Europeans in the oasis—missionaries and medics mostly—such a falling-out could only increase Macartney's sense of isolation in his remote posting.

The social glue in Kashgar was provided by the cheerful Father Hendricks, a Roman Catholic priest welcomed by Chinese and Europeans alike. In his well-worn Chinese coat topped with a black clerical hat, Hendricks was a familiar sight as he scurried around the oasis—he was always in a hurry—collecting and relaying the latest news. So well informed was the entertaining Father Hendricks that Stein dubbed him a "living newspaper." Hendricks had arrived in 1885, but his past was a mystery. He never spoke of it, and in all his years in Kashgar he never received a letter. In two decades at the oasis, he made few converts, other than a Chinese shoemaker. Yet he celebrated Mass each day alone in his dingy hovel on an altar made from a packing case and covered with a soiled lace cloth. His chief talent, aside from socializing, was turning the abundant supply of local grapes each autumn into wine. Hendricks had no income and survived on charity. The bearded, bespectacled priest lived on scraps of bread and vegetables until Macartney arrived in Kashgar and began sharing his meals with him. Hendricks eventually moved into Chini Bagh, but insisted on moving out when Macartney married, though he remained a frequent visitor.

From his Kashgar listening post of Chini Bagh, Macartney represented British interests and subjects in the region. The latter were mostly Hindu money-lenders from distant Shikarpur in India's Sindh province who had spread across Turkestan plying a trade prohibited to Muslims. About the money-lenders, few had a good word to say. Their interest rates were exorbitant and locals unable to repay their debts risked becoming virtual slaves. So it was little wonder there were tensions between the two groups that Macartney had to smooth out. These had political implications as British prestige and influence could suffer because of the behavior of its subjects.

Macartney regularly sent his masters secret bulletins apprising them of incidents around the oases. They learned, for example, how a Muslim woman had been caught in the room of a Hindu cook. A 500-strong mob of men wanted her stoned and the cook's face blackened. Peace was eventually restored and the cook fined fifty rupees—the woman's fate is unknown.

As George Macartney kept his eye on British interests and Russian movements, his wife transformed the modest house, which until her arrival had been inhabited by single men, into an oasis within an oasis. The more exotic pets of Macartney's bachelor days departed. "Wolves, leopards, and foxes did not appeal to me," Mrs. Macartney commented. Instead, a pair of geese took up residence within the house, and one could often be found nestled beside Mrs. Macartney in the drawing room. Despite the livestock, Stein described Chini Bagh as having all the comforts of an English home. Mrs. Macartney installed lamps and rugs and even a well-traveled Cramer piano that survived at least one soaking in a river on its way across Russia. The couple's first child, Eric, also survived the accident-prone trip. Born while his parents were on leave in England in the autumn of 1903, the boy was just five months old when he was wrapped in bedding and carried on horseback over mountains. "Baby had three falls, two on the snow . . . & another on the hard ground . . . [but he] did not even wake during these mishaps," Macartney wrote to Stein. By the time Stein returned to Kashgar in 1906, Mrs. Macartney had just given birth to Sylvia, the second of her three children.

Mrs. Macartney soon got to grips with local customs, at times to her own embarrassment. She quickly learned that the Hindu guard of honor who greeted her arrival with rupees in the palms of their hands were offering respect. She was expected to touch the money, not pocket it. She created a shady garden and an orchard of peaches, apricots, figs, and mulberries. She took charge of the staff, including three Indian servants in red and gold uniforms topped with white turbans. And she oversaw the gardener, a man who appeared to have direct communication with his vegetables. When she once asked him when the peas would sprout, he replied: "They tell me they will be coming out tomorrow."

Although she lacked female compatriots—she was visited by only three English women in all her years there—she observed, and at times entertained, local women, including Chinese women with bound feet. Barbaric as the practice seemed, she wondered if it was any worse than the tight corseting in vogue among their European counterparts. She also observed the rituals under way at a shrine just opposite Chini Bagh, where young Muslim women came to pray for husbands. "I sometimes suspected that their prayers were answered pretty quickly, for I often saw youths wandering about near the shrine, furtively inspecting the supplicants."

༄

As the nights warmed during his two weeks at Kashgar in June 1906, Stein pitched his tent under the trees in Chini Bagh's garden. Although the walls of the residence were two feet thick, to insulate against the winter cold and summer heat, Stein preferred to sleep under canvas. He liked the relative cool—and perhaps the solitude. Some nights the sounds of the Cossacks singing Russian airs carried to Chini Bagh, where they mingled with the call to prayer from the nearby Id Kah mosque and Kashgar families returning from their orchards singing melodies that reminded Stein of Hungarian songs he knew from his childhood.

The capricious Petrovsky had been replaced since Stein's previous visit by a more amiable Russian consul, Colonel Kolokoloff. Father Hendricks still paid his regular visits, although he was a less robust figure than before. Elsewhere in Kashgar, little had changed. Thursday was market day in the old city of about 40,000 people. Women in their finery paraded in loose red gowns, matrons wore pork pie hats atop their long plaits and young women tucked a marigold or pomegranate flower behind their ears. Stalls in the market square were piled with the summer fruits that had ripened just as Stein arrived. The narrow side streets were filled with specialist bazaars. Cotton merchants filled one section, grain merchants another. The sounds of blacksmiths and silversmiths rang out. Hatmakers stitched velvet caps with fur for winter or embroidered them for summer. In the tea shops, people rested from the heat as musicians plucked instruments and storytellers spun their yarns.

But the leisurely life in the fertile oasis frustrated Stein, who grumbled to Allen about its "easy-going slackness" and the difficulty in hiring artisans during summer when picnics and garden parties were the main occupation. For a man in a hurry, he had arrived in Kashgar at the worst time. "It cost great efforts to catch the carpenter, smither, [and] leather-worker I needed and still greater ones to keep them at work." Saddles needed repairing, clothes needed sewing and, most importantly, animals needed purchasing—camels especially, as these would be the core of his desert caravan. Stein was alarmed to discover how much prices had increased in the thriving oasis. He bought eight well-seasoned camels within a week of arriving. They were double-humped Bactrian camels whose thick seasonal coats can withstand the region's extreme temperatures. It pained Stein to shell out triple the amount for each beast that he paid on his first expedition. At least ponies were still a bargain, about a tenth of the cost of his camels. In Kashgar's weekly animal market he snapped up a dozen of them to convey his team and some of the lighter baggage. Although never reckless with money, Stein had to administer his meager government budget carefully.

He also had formal visits to pay. His first call on a well-heeled Chinese official turned into an impromptu feast of eighteen courses. It was accompanied by knives and forks rather than chopsticks, but the food itself was so mystifying that even Macartney struggled to identify some of the dishes. Such prolonged banquets could be wearing to the dyspeptic Stein, not least because he preferred a simple diet, but they helped forge useful friendships.

Stein needed more men, too, so he was overjoyed when his former camel man, Hassan Akhun, signed on. Stein admired the camel man's inquisitiveness. Hassan Akhun knew his own mind and took great care of his camels. Stein sensed in him a kindred spirit, a man who welcomed adventure. In Stein's view these traits outweighed an explosive temper. On their first trip together, Hassan Akhun had become so embroiled in a fight with another man that the explorer had been forced to separate the combatants with his antique walking stick.

Stein was less thrilled to see his former interpreter, Niaz Akhun. Stein knew more than he cared to of this worker's shortcomings, which included an "inordinate addiction to opium and gambling, and his strong inclination to qualified looting." Not to mention womanizing. Niaz Akhun's amorous encounters during the first expedition had so outraged locals and Stein's Muslim workers that he had to be isolated for his own safety. The philanderer had become so enamored with a "captivating Khotan damsel of easy virtue," as Stein coyly described her, that he abandoned his family and divorced his wife. Inevitably the romance soured and Niaz Akhun had gambled and drifted his way back to Kashgar. Stein did not offer him his old job, but gave him some silver, which was soon sacrificed to the "God of the Dice." Stein also needed to replace his troublesome cook, whose abilities had "shrivelled up with the cold" as they had crossed the mountains.

He settled for a rough Kashmiri named Ramzan, "a hardy plant though not sweet to look at."

Chiang, the man Macartney had recommended as Stein's secretary, arrived. Like many of the Chinese who filled the civil offices in Turkestan, Chiang hailed from Hunan, nearly 3,000 miles to the southeast. He had left behind his home, wife and son seventeen years earlier and had been engaged in the *yamen* in the oasis of Yarkand, 120 miles from Kashgar. Clearly, Chiang was a man able to cope with long separation from family.

But he also knew his own worth. His terms were high—120 rupees a month and his own servant—but made in the knowledge that Chinese gentleman clerks in the remote province were well rewarded. And unlike most of Stein's other men, he had no fear of the "Great Gobi" (the blanket term was used to cover the Taklamakan Desert as well). The only problem was that Chiang's grasp of Turki, the language intended as their shared tongue, was shaky. He spoke little of it despite his many years in Turkestan, and his accent was almost impenetrable. But Chiang impressed Stein with his engaging manner and his "lively ways, frank and kindly look, and an unmistakable air of genial reasonability . . . Something in his round jovial face and in the alert gait of his slight but wiry body gave me hope that he would know how to shift for himself even on rough marches and among the discomforts of desert camps," Stein wrote. Hiring Chiang would prove one of the wisest decisions Stein ever made.

As the days were filled amassing his caravan, Stein had little time to unwind in the evening with his friends on Chini Bagh's flat roof. He was juggling another deadline. He needed to finish proofreading his account of his first expedition, *Ancient Khotan*, and get the corrections in the mail. From Kashgar he could get the proofs back to England relatively quickly, within about twenty days, using the overland Russian mail route. He also wrote many letters to friends in Europe. It was his last chance to avail himself of this postal system. Once he left Kashgar, his mail would have to be relayed by "*dak* runners." These formed a network of hardy native postmen who carried their mailbags across the desert and over the mountains to India. Three times a month, *dak* runners crossed between Kashgar and Hunza. When camped in the desert, Stein allowed up to three months for his mail to reach Europe. A telegraph line existed between Kashgar and Beijing, but the poles were sometimes knocked over by fierce storms and even bears. The animals mistook the humming of the wires for bees.

Meanwhile, Macartney had an update on the Germans. They had crossed to Kucha, far away on the northern Silk Road, and were still undecided about where to go next, India or China. Stein feared the latter and that they might head for Lop Nor and Dunhuang. Of Pelliot's team, there was no news, only vague rumors among the Russians. "They may turn up any day—or a month hence," he speculated to Allen.

He believed he could still keep ahead of the Frenchman, who would need most of a month to put his caravan together in Kashgar while Stein's was nearly ready. But if Pelliot did arrive, Stein would have to consider crossing the desert in the baking summer heat, an extremely risky prospect. He hated having to work in such haste, constantly looking over his shoulder, fearful he might find a rival behind every sand dune. "The rush past places which might still yield something to me is by no means an attractive idea for me, and the heat will be trying . . . You will understand, with your infinite sympathy, how weary work it is to have to watch for others' moves, instead of being free to follow one's own plans straight," he wrote.

꩜

At last Stein's caravan was ready. Ahead of an early morning departure, he bid farewell to his Kashgar friends, except one.

Stein had not seen Father Hendricks in those final busy days. But Mrs. Macartney had and thought he looked particularly frail, although he still managed a cheerful word for her baby daughter. She had previously offered to take the old priest in and nurse him. Typically, he had refused and was determined to remain alone. So as Stein was occupied with last-minute preparations on his final day in Kashgar, Macartney decided to visit Hendricks' hovel within the old city walls. There he discovered that his friend, the purveyor of gossip and good spirits, lay dead. The priest had been ailing for months, but his lonely death, apparently of throat cancer, had come more quickly than anyone expected.

The funeral was set for the next day, the day of Stein's departure. Stein delayed his start so he could attend. But in Kashgar, even the rituals of death assumed a leisurely air. The local carpenter was in no hurry to finish making the coffin when Macartney and Stein arrived at his shop on the morning of the funeral. There they found the Russian consul, who had taken charge of the burial arrangements, waiting impatiently for the coffin that should have been finished the previous evening. As the hours passed with little progress, the coffin was eventually completed with the aid of the consul's Cossacks. Around noon, Stein, together with Kashgar's few European residents, followed the empty coffin as it was carried through the dusty lanes to Father Hendricks' shabby home where the Chinese shoemaker convert had kept vigil. The tiny place was crammed with books, maps and the priest's altar, beside which was a trapdoor leading to his wine cellar. It resembled, Stein said, "a cave by the seashore where the play of the waves had deposited strange debris from distant coasts."

The Cossacks eased the priest's body into the coffin and, bareheaded in the midday heat, carried it to the Christian graveyard about a mile away, between the river and Chini Bagh. The Russian consulate guard marched in front of the coffin and the rest of

Kashgar's Europeans behind, though they were not the only people to mourn the much-loved priest. For months after Hendricks' death, Chinese friends kept a light burning nightly on his grave.

4

The Moon and the Mail

Stein passed beyond Chini Bagh's avenue of poplars late in the hot afternoon a few hours after Father Hendricks was laid to rest. The heat in late June was so intense—with temperatures of 105 degrees Fahrenheit in the shade—he and his caravan traveled mostly by night. They would set off well before dawn, usually around 2 a.m., and cover up to twenty-five miles before the sun forced them to seek refuge. Sleeping in a tent during the day was impossible, so Stein reluctantly slept under more solid shelter. It wasn't just the dirt that bothered him in the Chinese rest houses, but the inquisitive caretakers and other travelers who gave him little peace as he attempted to rest, attend to his caravan and read the remaining proofs of his book—a task unfinished in Kashgar. The buildings were also almost as hot as his tent since they faced the midday sun.

He soon availed himself of the local rules of hospitality among the oases which allowed him to lodge pretty much wherever he liked. "One may invade the house of any one, high or low, sure to find a courteous reception, whether the visit is expected or otherwise." He stayed with well-to-do villagers, enjoying their orchards where the trees, heavy with apricots and mulberries, splattered the ground with their ripe fruit.

These were the first days of their long journey together, but Chiang was already proving a worthy companion. As the caravan moved along in the pre-dawn light, Chiang began to teach Stein some Mandarin. The explorer, with his ear for languages, picked it up quickly. He also picked up Chiang's strong Hunan accent. But at least they could talk together in a language other than Chiang's impenetrable Turki. Stein found Chiang a ready source of gossip and amusing anecdotes, a keen observer of human foibles. "He has told me many little secrets of the official machinery of the chequered careers of proud Ambans & their unholy profits. 'The New Dominions' are a sort of India for Chinese officials, where everybody knows everybody else," Stein wrote.

Chiang's dress was as colorful as his stories. He wore either a dark blue or maroon silk jacket, which he teamed with bright yellow overalls when he rode on horseback. On his pigtailed head he added a light blue silk cloth under his traveling cap to shield him from the heat, and he shaded his eyes with a detachable peak of rainbow-colored paper. Even his black horse had colorful flourishes. Atop its saddle Chiang placed a vivid scarlet cushion, and the saddle itself had leather flaps decorated with yellow and green embroidery. But Chiang's preference for heavy old-fashioned stirrups worried Stein. "I never could look at this heavy horse millinery and the terribly massive stirrups, each weighing some three pounds and of truly archaic type, without feeling sorrow for his mount," Stein noted. Consequently, Stein gave Chiang the hardiest of the horses.

Chiang had planned to set out with an alarming amount of baggage, including most of his library, but was convinced to leave much behind. As he became accustomed to desert travel, he willingly began to shed more. He took to rough travel with gusto, showing an indifference to its hardships. He even shared Stein's curiosity about the past. Certainly Chiang was a far cry from the pugnacious, womanizing interpreter who had accompanied Stein's first Turkestan expedition. "It was a piece of real good fortune which gave me in Chiang, not merely an excellent teacher and secretary, but a devoted helpmate ever ready to face hardships for the sake of scientific interests," he wrote. "With all his scholarly interests in matters of a dead past, he proved to have a keen eye also for things and people of this world, and his ever-ready flow of humorous observations lightened many a weary hour for us both."

After some hard bargaining in the oasis of Yarkand, where Chiang had long worked, Stein secured for himself a fine young horse he named Badakhshi after what he believed were its blood-lines from Badakhshan. Clearly Stein spent no more time naming his horse than he did his dynasty of dogs. Badakhshi was to prove a perfect mount for Stein and for Dash II, who taught himself to leap to the stirrup and then up to the saddle, where he would sit on the pommel. Badakhshi was hardy and unsociable, not unlike his master.

ﻭﺨ

Stein was at last doing exactly what he loved. He was on the move in Turkestan, where he felt more at home than almost anywhere; certainly more so than in India—despite living almost twenty years there—with its caste rules and stultifying bureaucracy. As his camels, his ponies and his men moved steadily along, in the same way travelers had done for centuries, he could forget for a while the modern world with its bustle of speeding trains and alienating cities. "To peep into every house & hut along the road is better than to see towns in electric illumination flit past like fireflies," he wrote.

He loved the sense of being transported to an earlier era. And that feeling recurred when he encountered a caravan of traders heading over the mountains to Ladakh. He entrusted their jovial leader with a letter to a friend there and felt cheered to

53

be reminded that long-distance communication was possible well before the existence of a postal service. The traders' cargo was likely to transport in an altogether different way; it consisted of "that precious but mischievous" drug *charas,* or hashish.

Only his relationship with the elder Ram Singh intruded on the joy of returning to his Turkestan. The surveyor had become unaccountably sullen. This reached a peak when, as the caravan was readying to depart one morning before dawn, the surveyor sent a message to say he was not prepared to move unless he was given a couple of assistants of his own. When Stein went to see him, the surveyor had other complaints. Among them, he did not want to start at such an early hour, even though it was when Stein often broke camp. Stein did not know what precipitated the surveyor's demands and was not about to acquiesce to them. Instead, he criticized Ram Singh for setting a bad example.

Stein was impatient with delays. When a rare late start was made, he grumbled about his men's reluctance to tear themselves away from the "fleshpots" of a local oasis. For Stein it was the desert, not the oases, that attracted him. One night during his first expedition, he became entranced watching the full moon ascend over the desert.

She looked as if rising from the sea when first emerging from the haze of dust that hid the plains, and her light shimmered on the surface. But when she climbed high up in the sky it was no longer a meek reflection that lit up the plain below. It seemed as if I were looking at the lights of a vast city lying below me in the endless plains. Could it really be that terrible desert where there was no life and no hope of human existence? I knew that I should never see it again in this alluring splendour.

Now, six years on and under another full moon, he was back in the desert whose terrifying beauty haunted him. He camped amid the rolling dunes beside a Muslim shrine inhabited by thousands of sacred pigeons to whom grateful travelers made offerings. The shrine was near what Stein called "my kingdom" of Khotan, once the center of a Buddhist civilization. He was intrigued by its legend. Locals said the birds were the descendants of a pair of doves that had sprung from the heart of a Muslim martyr killed as his army battled Khotan's Buddhist infidels. But to Stein, the tale recalled a similar, though much older legend encountered by Xuanzang as he journeyed through the kingdom. In this version, the sacred animals weren't birds but rats—giant rodents the size of hedgehogs with hair of gold and silver—and they had saved Khotan's Buddhist king from invading Huns by chewing through the enemy's leather armor and harnesses in the night. Stein suspected that with the spread of Islam through the region, the Buddhist rats had evolved into Muslim birds. The legend had been appropriated rather than eliminated. It was the sort of cultural shape-shifting that appealed to Stein. It also suggested that beneath the Muslim surface were the remains of an earlier Buddhist mythology.

Whatever the basis of the story, some help for the journey ahead wouldn't go astray. Stein's men had brought along extra grain for the pigeons and they insisted he, too, pay homage. While the caravan was getting ready before dawn, Stein entered the wooden sheds where the birds were nesting. Carefully avoiding crushing any eggs, he scattered grain for the fluttering birds. His offerings would be richly rewarded.

∽◦

Stein's sights were set on two places far across the desert. He wanted to find the mysterious settlement of Loulan that Sven Hedin had discovered in 1899. Amid the ruined buildings of the ancient Chinese garrison town, Hedin had uncovered fragments of early paper, wooden documents, and Buddhist images. One of these, a fragment made between AD 150 and 200, was then the world's oldest known piece of paper and the earliest example of handwriting on paper. Hedin had observed that the door to one house stood open just as it had when it was abandoned 1,500 years earlier.

Beyond Loulan was Dunhuang and the painted caves, but all of these would have to wait for winter. Only then would it be safe to cross that part of the desert, and it would require a resourceful method to overcome the lack of water. Stein's more immediate goal was to travel southeast from Kashgar to the Kunlun Shan, the vast mountain range on the northern border of the Tibetan plateau. There he would undertake surveying work before returning to the desert in the cooler weather. Mapping in this region was politically sensitive and dangerous. Some servants of the Raj went to extraordinary lengths to carry out their clandestine activities. Several Indian surveyors disguised themselves as Tibetan pilgrims and carried specially adapted prayer wheels and Buddhist rosary beads. The number of beads was reduced from the traditional 108 to 100 so the surveyors could easily count their steps. They recorded their tally on tiny paper scrolls which they hid inside the hollow prayer wheels, some of which also contained compasses. James Bond's Q could hardly have developed a more ingenious solution.

Stein never adopted such a disguise himself. He left behind his camels and some of his men and headed into the Kunlun Mountains in August 1906. With its bluebells and edelweiss the alpine landscape was a verdant relief after the barren desert and recalled his beloved Kashmir. Surrounded by snow-capped peaks, he found an idyllic camp where he could put the final touches to his book about his first expedition. As he continued through the mountains, Stein was eager to solve a mystery more than forty years old. It concerned the difficult and long-abandoned route by which British surveyor William Johnson crossed from Leh to Khotan in 1865. Stein had been puzzled by discrepancies between Johnson's hand-drawn sketch and the topography of the mountains. Despite the existence of the sketch, local hill men denied knowledge of such a path. Stein suspected such denials stemmed from a fear that rediscovery would expose the inhabitants to unwanted intruders. He had tried to determine the route during his first expedition without success, and once again he was unable to do so.

Nonetheless, after nearly a month amid mountain rivers, glaciers, rugged gorges and alpine valleys, he was in good spirits as he returned to the lower ground of Khotan, where early autumn hues colored the oasis's poplars. He camped, as he had in 1900, in the garden of his prosperous friend Akhun Beg. But the elderly man had left two days earlier on a pilgrimage to Mecca, from which Stein and the landowner's family feared he might not return. Khotan's new Chinese *amban* organized a lavish garden party in Stein's honor. He was led in procession along an avenue of shady vines in the old garden palace known as Narbagh to a pavilion filled with red felt rugs and carpets. The young handyman, Naik Ram Singh, was an imposing presence in his scarlet and blue army uniform and carefully wound turban. The guests, including Chinese officials and Muslim leaders, feasted for hours, although on what Stein did not say. He admitted only that it was a challenge to his European digestion and that he was glad when the rice arrived—a signal of the feast's end. But he enjoyed the musicians who performed throughout on stringed instruments, tambourines and flutes. Khotan's reputation for musicianship was well justified, he felt. "After an event like that Wagner is hardly likely to have any charms for you," a friend later commented to Stein.

But the celebratory mood was short-lived. He returned to the Buddhist stupa of Rawak, where on his 1900 expedition he had found and reburied fragile statues. He was devastated to discover that in the intervening years treasure hunters had destroyed the figures in their search for hidden jade. "My care in burying these again under the sand, just as I had found them, had proved in vain," he wrote. "All that survives now, I fear, are my photographs."

That was not the only loss Stein faced. Of the eight camels he had bought at great expense in Kashgar, five were dead soon after Stein rejoined his caravan to travel east. The cause was a mystery. They had been well tended in Stein's absence by his trusted camel man Hassan Akhun, who was distraught at their loss. It was a major setback, and they would have to be replaced. This would dent his already tight budget, although the cost was not the only reason for his anguish. He prided himself on the fact that, unlike Hedin, he lost few animals and genuinely cared about their welfare. Finding replacements would be difficult more than 400 miles from the bustling crossroads of Kashgar. For two days the camel owners of Keriya produced a dispiriting array of dubious beasts they hoped to offload. Finally, seven strong camels were secured with the aid of Hassan Akhun's knowledge and his sharp tongue. These would not only survive but more than earn their keep.

The loss of his camels was compounded by more bad news. Macartney reported that Pelliot had just arrived in Kashgar. Stein was convinced the Frenchman would aim for Lop Nor and Dunhuang. "There is thus every reason to push on eastwards with as little delay as the work en route allows. [Pelliot] intends to explore the Kucha caves and other places on the northern route, and this gives me a fair chance, I think, for arriving in time. But how glad I should have been if all this hustle could have been spared to me by my start as originally intended!" he wrote to Allen.

Stein spent the autumn months of 1906 digging at desert sites as he made his way east. The siren call of the desert drew him on.

The expanse of yellow dunes lay before me, with nothing to break their wavy monotony but the bleached trunks of trees or the rows of splintered posts marking houses which rose here and there above the sand crests. The feeling of being in an open sea was ever present, and more than once those remains seen from a distance suggested the picture of a wreck reduced to the mere ribs of its timber.

After a couple of months revisiting some of the sites from his first expedition, the temperature dropped, and in December his caravan pulled into Charklik. The remote oasis of about 500 homesteads was inhabited mostly by semi-nomadic herders and fishermen known as Lopliks. This was new terrain for Stein. Charklik was the most easterly oasis on the southern Silk Road, and from here he launched his winter search for Hedin's Lou-lan. The ancient garrison lay in the fearsome Lop Desert at the eastern extreme of the Taklamakan. Lop is not a place of rolling sand dunes but hard clay terraces, salt marshes and the massive, moving Lop Nor salt lake. (In recent decades, China has tested its nuclear weapons in this desolate region.)

Stein hired extra camels and donkeys for what lay ahead. "All Charklik is being ransacked for the supplies," he wrote. He needed thirty-five laborers, but the locals were understandably reluctant to head off on a long journey into a waterless desert in the middle of winter, no matter how much they were to be paid. Their relatives feared it was a death sentence. However, Stein had a stroke of good luck when two hunters who had accompanied Sven Hedin turned up from the neighboring hamlet of Abdal.

Wiry Old Mullah had spent his life chasing wild camels and selling their meat. Aged nearly sixty and with a high-pitched voice, he may have looked and sounded unpromising, but he knew the desert like the back of his wrinkled hands. He had even rediscovered a long-forgotten caravan route from Abdal to Dunhuang— a route Stein was keen to eventually follow. The younger man, burly Tokhta Akhun, was about thirty-five and arrived with an intriguing scrap of old paper. It was written in Tibetan and he had found it in the desert not far away at a place known as Miran. Stein decided it just might be worth a look. It would not be the last time he would follow up a tip with extraordinary results.

Cries of *yol bolsun*—"may there be a way"—from the laborers' anxious relatives accompanied the party as they left Charklik on

December 6. Despite the promise of fresh terrain, Stein could not shed his familiar apprehensions. "I shall make a depot at Abdal, the easternmost inhabited place, so as to be ready for the rush to [Dunhuang] if the appearance of Pelliot's party should force me to hurry on. In this way I hope to secure the advantage of a nearer base & quicker start if fate wills that we should meet at the ruins."

Stein pulled into Abdal, a wretched village of gouty octogenarians, where he established his base beside the Tarim River. There he left everything not needed in his search for Loulan. He assigned one of his most reliable men, Tila Bai, to guard the finds collected so far and a large quantity of uncoined silver he would need when journeying in China, where the coins of Turkestan were not accepted. Reluctantly, he left Chiang at Abdal too. Stein feared his secretary would not cope with long tramps on foot and he could not spare him an extra camel. Chiang would winter in what passed for comparative comfort: the best reed hut in the cheerless hamlet.

Meanwhile, Stein prepared his caravan for the hunt. The camels were each given seven buckets of water—it would have to last them several weeks. There would be no water ahead other than what could be carried as blocks of ice. Working until midnight under the light of giant bonfires, the men hacked ice from a frozen freshwater lagoon and stored the chunks in woolen bags. Each camel was loaded with more than 400 pounds of ice. They could expect no fodder save some foul-smelling rapeseed oil, "camel's tea" as Hassan Akhun called it. Thirty donkeys were loaded with smaller amounts of ice. The donkeys were used in relay, traveling two days beyond the furthest ice supply to deposit their loads and return for more. It was a hugely complicated arrangement and required military precision. However, it would enable Stein and his men to stay longer in the desert than had Hedin.

The route back had to be marked with the remains of bleached, dead trees and blocks of clay since the caravan would leave few footprints in the hard ground. Even those they did leave would be obliterated by the first gale in the windswept region. The terrain consisted of rocky outcrops known as yardangs. Separated by parallel trenches, the sculpted forms ran northeast to southwest. The ground was so hard that even knocking in iron tent pegs was difficult. Travel was slow going and the heavily laden camels could cover only a mile and a half an hour. Their feet cracked on the salt-encrusted ground. At night Stein could hear the footsore beasts bellow as Hassan Akhun and his helpers resoled the camels by the painful local method: sewing ox hide onto their foot pads. It took half a dozen men to hold down each camel and the process took hours. Even Dash grew footsore. But the wiry fox terrier at least found a warm nightly refuge curled up in Stein's tent under camelhair blankets.

Seven days passed without a sign of Loulan. To raise flagging spirits, Stein promised a reward of silver to the first man to sight a ruin. The party had covered about eight miles on a particularly bitter day when one of his keen-eyed men spotted the distant knob of a ruined stupa on the horizon. Stein had at last found what he was looking for. He had used Hedin's map to guide him to Loulan, and it had proved remarkably accurate.

The dispirited Charklik laborers were buoyed and so too was Hassan Akhun, who instantly forgot his own dejection. In his bright red cloak and purple high-peaked cap, he stood on top of a yardang to address the weary laborers. An amused Stein watched as the camel handler stood with his arms outstretched like an ancient prophet. "Had he not always tried to drum it into their thick heads that under the guidance of *his* Sahib, who could fathom all hidden places of the dreaded Taklamakan with 'his paper and Mecca-pointer,' i.e. map and compass, all things were bound to come right?"

Despite the quick-witted camel man's fiery temper and bouts of petulance—"a handful when things are easy, & a man of resource when given a hard task"—perhaps Stein felt more than ever that the mercurial camel man was not driven by money alone. "I felt the instinctive assurance that Hassan Akhun's was the only human soul with me for whom this desert adventure had a real attraction," Stein wrote. He put it more bluntly in a letter to his friend Percy Allen. "One longs for helpers really interested in the work and not mainly longing for fleshpots."

He was overjoyed to find no trace of the Germans or French at Loulan. Nor were there any signs of local treasure hunters. Hedin, who had only five men and six days in which to work, had left plenty for Stein to uncover in the next eleven days.

Loulan was once on the edge of the Lop Nor lake, but the lake had long since shifted course and the town was abandoned in the fourth century. The town had once helped protect trade along the ancient Silk Road, and one of the first items Stein uncovered was a roll of brittle yellow silk. The men dug among ruined dwellings and in ancient rubbish dumps while winds gusting up to fifty miles an hour scattered filth in their faces. "The odours were still pungent, with the icy northeast wind driving fine particles impregnated with ammonia into one's throat and nose."

He uncovered not gold and jewels but humble relics of everyday life: beads, coins, fragments of carpet, an embroidered slipper, and military records. He found woodcarvings and writing on paper and wood, including an ancient script used in Gandhara, known as Kharosthi. Here, on China's edge, was evidence of the influence of far-off Gandhara. He also found the first fragment of the lost language of Sogdian, the ancient tongue widely spoken along the Silk Road.

His dig at Loulan was punctuated by two unusual events on consecutive days. The first was his discovery of a "relic" left by the site's only other recent Western visitor—a metal tape measure that Hedin had dropped in 1901. Stein returned it to the Swede at a Royal Geographic Society dinner in London two years later. The well-traveled metal tape measure remains in the society's collection.

Santa Claus with mail

The next day, as dusk fell on what Stein expected would be a cold, lonely Christmas Eve, a commotion erupted among his men. He looked up to see that his weary *dak* runner, Turdi, had trudged into camp with a huge bag of letters. Stein could hardly have been more astonished if Santa Claus had arrived pulled by a team of reindeer. Stein had last seen Turdi six weeks earlier on November 15, when he had dispatched him to Khotan with his mail. Turdi had reached the oasis twelve days later. There he had been given a pony and a fur coat for the long journey back east, together with a big bag of mail sent by Macartney in Kashgar. Meanwhile, Stein had moved more than 500 miles farther east.

Turdi had reached Abdal but could not find anyone there who knew which direction Stein had gone. So determined, foolhardy Turdi had abandoned his pony and headed on foot into the desert carrying his heavy mail bag. He followed Stein's tracks as best he could but ran out of ice five days later. The thirsty *dak* runner pressed on, not knowing how far ahead Stein had traveled. He simply hoped the chances of finding Stein—somewhere ahead, sometime soon—were greater than the certainty of a slow death in the waterless waste if he turned back. Turdi's terrible gamble paid off. When he staggered toward Stein on the sixth day, Turdi's demand was not for water but for Stein to check that the seals were intact—and hence his own integrity—on the mail bags he had carried from Khotan. How Turdi had covered an astonishing 1,200 miles in thirty-nine days, an average of thirty miles a day, was a mystery.

Stein devoured the letters and although their news was four months old it helped dissolve his sense of isolation. Wrapped in his rugs and furs, he sat in his tent reading and replying to his letters by candlelight late into the bitter night. To Allen he wrote: "The ink is beginning to freeze in my fountain pen, though I have sacrificed an extra cake of compressed fuel to keep up the temperatures in the tent for this long chat with you."

If there were as many Ganges Rivers as the number of grains of sand in the Ganges, would you say that the number of grains of sand in all those Ganges Rivers is very many?

—VERSE 11, THE DIAMOND SUTRA

5

The Angels' Sanctuary

New Year's Day dawned brightly and the wind dropped as Stein headed away from Loulan and southwest toward the Tarim River. The terrain changed from clay terraces to sand dunes that grew in height as he continued. Fuel was scarce. Just a few armfuls had been gathered by the time his party halted for the evening. There was enough to make tea and cook a meal, but too little to sustain a warming fire. That night was the coldest of the winter and the temperature fell to minus sixteen degrees Fahrenheit. It was a cheerless start to what would become the greatest year of Stein's life, though one that would cost him dearly.

With his ice supply dwindling, he was pleased to see the droppings of hares and deer since this signaled water was near. That meant there would be fuel for a fire and grazing for the hungry camels, who by then had been ten days without food. The joy of the party was palpable when at last they encountered a glittering frozen lake. The ice was a foot thick but so clear Stein could see fish swimming below. "How sorry I am for having withstood the temptation of bringing skates with me!" Stein wrote. Hedin too had been tempted by a similar sight. The Swede had improvised a pair of skates from a couple of knives and amazed the Lop men as he'd taken a spin around the ice. A frozen lake was a familiar sight to Stein, having grown up in Hungary, but for Naik Ram Singh, from steamy Punjab, it was almost beyond comprehension. Nothing impressed the carpenter more. He was so astounded by the frozen lake he did not think the people from his village would believe him if he were to describe it to them.

Other events of nature did impress Stein. On a rare rest day beside the frozen Tarim River, he was working at his table within his tent mid-morning when the sky suddenly darkened. At first he thought the yellow-brown cast to the sky forewarned a sandstorm was approaching. Yet the air was still and eerily silent. This was no sandstorm. Rather it was a total solar eclipse, and Stein was captivated by the play of light. Intense blues, yellows, and greens flitted across the landscape of riverine scrub, frozen river, and distant dunes. The silver corona was like a halo around the darkened sun. As the sunlight slowly returned so too did the sound of birdsong. Yet Stein was alone in his wonderment; his men seemed unmoved as they huddled around their fires.

So far, Stein had stuck to the plan he mapped out in India: Kashgar, mountains, and Loulan. Now he made a diversion. He wanted to see where Tokhta Akhun had found the scrap of paper with Tibetan writing. In late January Stein rode in darkness toward the light of a campfire near Miran. There he had arranged to meet a party of hired laborers from Abdal to help with fresh excavations. With them was Chiang. Stein had sorely missed his companion since their parting six weeks earlier. It was a joyful reunion and the pair sat talking beside the campfire until late into the night.

The logistics were easier at Miran than Loulan. A nearby stream provided plenty of ice for drinking and cooking, plus there was grazing for the camels amid roots and the dead foliage of toghrak trees, or wild poplars—curious trees whose leaves vary in shape from branch to branch. The solitary Stein always slept under canvas and pitched his tent away from his men. It meant he was at times even colder in his tent than his men were around their fires, so cold his moustache would freeze as he slept. (In contrast, Hedin camped out with his men, where he benefitted from an ingenious local method of keeping warm. Hedin's men dug a hole, filled it with glowing coals which they covered with sand, then slept soundly on top of their heated bed.)

During eighteen days at Miran, Stein made remarkable discoveries. Already his latest expedition was overshadowing the finds of his first as thoroughly as the moon had eclipsed the mid-winter sun. At Miran, he worked in almost unbearable conditions—and not merely because the daytime temperature dropped at times to minus five degrees Fahrenheit. In a ruined fort, he uncovered thousands of Tibetan documents. But they were buried in the most putrid ancient rubbish heaps Stein ever encountered—far worse than at Loulan. The stench in the Tibetan soldiers' quarters suggested they had been used for functions other than sleeping. There were "sweepings from the hearth, litter of straw, remnants of old clothing and implements, and leavings of a yet more unsavoury kind." In places the filth was nearly nine feet deep. Stein may have longed for helpers more interested in the work than the fleshpots, but few men anywhere have the dedication to tramp across a frozen wasteland for the privilege of digging in a filthy windswept midden.

Miran had been a vital garrison for the Tibetans in the eighth and ninth centuries, Stein concluded. It lay at the intersection of two routes across Tibet to the southern oases of the Silk Road. But when Tibetan power waned, Miran sank into insignificance and into the sand. He had a reminder of the ancient trade one evening when a caravan of about seventy camels laden with brick tea from Dunhuang passed his lonely camp. They were Kashgar traders who had seen no one else for twenty-three days. They were eager to find food and water and could not stop for more than a hasty greeting before they passed into the night and the echo of their camels' tinkling bells faded. Stein thought often of his patron saint Xuanzang who had probably passed Miran's ruined walls when he crossed the Lop Desert. "I sometimes wondered behind which of the Stupa mounds he might have sought shelter during a brief rest. In a region where all is dead and waste, spiritual emanations from those who have passed by long centuries ago seem to cling much longer to the few conspicuous landmarks than in parts where life is still bustling," Stein wrote.

Stein wasn't sure which was worse: watching over the digging from the fort's ramparts and being sandblasted by the icy wind, or descending into the dig where clouds of stinking dust covered him—and everyone else—and froze in his moustache. He risked frostbite each time he removed his gloves to inspect a document. Conditions were so atrocious his men could not work for more than half an hour at a stretch. After days in bitter winds, digging and inhaling putrid muck, many became ill. Only Chiang remained healthy. The surveyor Ram Singh was so immobilized with rheumatism that Stein sent him back to Abdal. It was clear the surveyor's health was failing, and he would have to be replaced. His handyman, Naik Ram Singh, suffered from fevers. Even Ramzan, Stein's troublesome but hardy cook, developed a skin disease and hibernated under his furs for the rest of the time at Miran. Meanwhile, his substitute cook showed not "the slightest capacity for turning out tolerably digestible food."

Conditions were hellish but the finds were divine. They were utterly unexpected and yet strangely familiar, and none more so than in a ruined Buddhist temple complex where about four feet above the floor Stein uncovered delicately painted images of winged angels. With their aquiline noses, pink cheeks, dimpled lips, and feathered wings, these were Western-looking cherubs.

[handwritten annotation: Angels in Buddhist sanctuary because it was on Silk Rd south. route — i.e. western]

"What had these graceful heads, recalling cherished scenes of Christian imagery, to do here on the walls of what beyond all doubt was a Buddhist sanctuary?" he wondered.

The answer was that long before Miran became a garrison town and the Tibetans arrived, it had been a cosmopolitan oasis. In its third- and fourth-century heyday, distant merchants and monks were drawn to the bustling trading place and Buddhist center along the Silk Road's southern route.

Other strange sights emerged from the debris—secular images of young men and women that would not have been out of place in ancient Rome. He could hardly believe his eyes. "In one chapel the cycle of feasting youths & girls looks as if meant originally for the dado of some Roman villa," he wrote. "In the other shrine I lighted to my surprise on a dado formed by exquisitely painted angels, better I should think than most of the early Christian art in the Catacombs."

The paintings used light and shade, or chiaroscuro, a technique well known in classical painting. But it had never before been seen in the early pictorial work of India or Central Asia. Stein wondered how such images and techniques had ended up in a Buddhist shrine on the edge of the Lop Desert. "I had longed for finds raising new problems, and here, indeed, I have got them. I know of no pictorial work in India or Central Asia which is so Western as this, on the very confines of the Seres [China]."

In the temple complex he also found colossal Buddha heads and the remains of seated Buddhas. And he found wall paintings reflecting Buddhist legends. One in particular intrigued him. It depicted a well-known legend in which a prince gives away a magical rain-making white elephant. The image showed the mustachioed prince, richly dressed in Indian clothes and jewels, leading the elephant by the trunk. Behind the elephant was a procession that included four horses wearing the saddlery of ancient Rome. A clue to this mystery was suggested in writing on the elephant's hind leg. The words told how much the artist had been paid for his work and, most importantly, gave his name: Tita, which Stein recognized as a variation of Titus. It was the most Roman of names. Stein concluded that in the first few centuries after the death of Christ, a Roman subject skilled in its artistic traditions had somehow made his way east to a remote Buddhist center on the edge of China. For Stein, fascinated by the ancient links between East and West, the images were spellbinding.

> For my eyes, which had so long beheld nothing but dreary wastes with traces of a dead past or the wretched settlements of the living, the sight of these paintings was more than an archaeological treat. I greeted it like a cheering assurance that there really was still a region where fair sights and enjoyments could be found undisturbed by icy gales and the cares and discomforts of desert labours.

Stein had little time to stand in wonder. He was determined to take away what he could and send it to Europe. The first hurdle was how to get the fragile murals safely out of the temples. Some had slipped from their original place and were leaning against the walls. The fragments, several feet wide and half an inch thick, were liable to crumble if touched.

He had to improvise a way to remove and pack the murals without destroying them in the process. And he had to do so using materials at hand. His men dragged trunks of dead poplars to camp, where they were sawn into boards and cases. Stein knew Naik Ram Singh could produce packing cases with his few tools and some precious iron nails and screws brought from India. Although he was still battling fevers, the carpenter helped devise a way to salvage the fallen wall paintings. He slipped tin, improvised from empty cases, behind the artwork and padded the front with cotton wool and tough paper from Khotan. The winged angels and other attached murals were sawn from the walls and placed on padded boards before being packed into made-to-measure wooden cases. Some of the filled cases weighed nearly 200 pounds each. Others, including Titus's elephant frieze, were too fragile or time-consuming to remove. Stein hoped to return to Miran after Dunhuang.

At the foot of a fallen mural he found the remains of a pigeon and its nest, apparently killed when the wall that held its nest had collapsed. The bird had landed just under a Buddha whose hand was raised in a gesture of protection. The irony was not lost on Stein. Perhaps he hoped divine protection would not be too late for the wall paintings. They had thousands of miles to travel and faced months of buffeting by camels, yaks, ponies, and men. The odds of them arriving safely seemed slender, but he had provided every protection he could muster. To protect those he could not remove, he ordered that they be reburied, as he had done at Rawak Stupa in 1901.

He could not remain at Miran much longer. Not if he wanted to cross to Dunhuang before the spring heat and sandstorms arrived. With the vivid murals re-entombed, Stein's thoughts turned to the bleak landscape around him. "Truly this part of the country is dying & its conditions a foretaste of what 'desiccation' will make of our little globe—if things run long enough that way," he wrote. As he returned to his Abdal depot, he noted how the Tarim River was dying. The arid desert was previously home to a rich, diverse civilization. What had happened? Why had oasis after oasis been abandoned? Lack of water might be the most obvious reason. Stein had seen evidence of this across the southern Tarim Basin. Mountain-fed rivers no longer reached the once-thriving settlements, now silent ruins. Yet natural causes—shrinking water supply and changing water courses—alone did not account for their abandonment, he suspected. Human factors may have played their part. Cultivation in these oases relied on complex and carefully tended irrigation and that needed a substantial workforce. When that was disrupted—through wars, disease or political unrest—the oases could no longer grow enough food to support their population. And soon the towns were abandoned. Sodom and Gomorrah stories of ancient settlements suddenly overwhelmed by sand were plentiful in the folklore across the desert region, but Stein had deduced they were just that. The evidence suggested the settlements had been abandoned slowly. Any jewels and valuables had gone with the departing population. Rumors of bewitched hoards of gold and silver lying within desert ruins were as fanciful as the local belief that anyone attempting to remove these would be driven mad until they threw away their treasure.

✑

Four frigid months in the desert yielded far more than Stein had hoped for, nearly triple the volume of his entire 1901 expedition. At Abdal, he watched his caravan of camels and ponies loaded with Miran's finest murals and other antiquities set out on the two-month journey to Kashgar. Stein had temporarily consigned most of his treasures into Macartney's safekeeping at Chini Bagh. Meanwhile, Macartney updated Stein on his rivals. The French, whom Stein had so feared he would find at Loulan, were far away to the north. So were the Germans. "This sounds hopeful for the next goal," he confided to Allen.

That goal was Dunhuang and it lay beyond Turkestan on the edge of Gansu province within China itself, 380 miles across the Lop Desert. China was unknown terrain to Stein and aside from Chiang, his men knew nothing of the country either. But they feared the worst. They were far more uneasy at the prospect of entering China than the desert waste they still had to cross to get there. Turkestan was "God's own land" to them. It was their home soil; they spoke its language and were part of its culture. Stein's Indian men had come to enjoy the easygoing, hospitable way of life in the Turkestan oases. Of China, they had heard only alarming rumors of strange customs.

Stein bid farewell to his Abdal guides, Old Mullah and Tokhta Akhun, whose scrap of paper had led to such spectacular finds. Stein admired how the hardy pair, like their fellow Lopliks, seemed impervious to the extreme climate in which they lived—the icy gales in winter, the mosquitoes and dust storms in summer. Such resilience had no doubt contributed to the long lifespan of so many of Abdal's inhabitants. Tokhta Akhun had an elderly mother to care for. Even Old Mullah—himself long past middle age—still had his elderly parents, which was why, to Stein's regret, Old Mullah could not accompany him along the route he had rediscovered. Instead, Stein's guides on his final leg to Dunhuang would be the voices from the past, including the pilgrim monk Xuanzang and Marco Polo. The Venetian traveler had described the route by which he crossed and estimated it took twenty-eight days. It was still reckoned to do so.

Having spent so long at Miran, as it yielded such rich rewards, once again Stein needed to hurry. But this time the rush was prompted by the seasons rather than the advance of his rivals. His chosen path was northeast following the old caravan route. Stein knew the route was passable for only a few weeks more. Soon the pure chunks of ice that could be hacked from the frozen salt springs would thaw. Spring would render the heat unbearable and the water undrinkable. With his winter diggings over and the laborers paid off, Stein was looking forward to the crossing since it afforded a rest from the burden of overseeing so many men and excavations. It is a mark of how difficult the winter dig had been—and of Stein's stamina—that he would approach a 350-mile trek across a frozen desert as a respite.

He set out for Dunhuang on a morning in late February. Relying on Marco Polo's estimate, he left with a month's supplies for his thirteen men, eleven ponies, eight camels, and nearly forty donkeys.

The extra donkeys he had hired to carry provisions would be dispatched back to their owners at intervals along the way when no longer needed. But within a couple of days of departing, three died. Soon six donkeys were dead. Stein feared the loss of more would make it hard to transport the supplies. The fates of men and beast were intertwined in the desert. As one after another died, Stein suspected foul play—that the donkey drivers were deliberately underfeeding their charges so their owners could get compensation. He put the entire donkey train under the command of one of his own men, Ibrahim Beg, and he promised the donkey drivers extra money for each animal that survived the journey. The strategy worked.

The first week passed in exhausting marches of up to twenty-six miles a day along the edge of dried-up salt marshes, clay terraces, and gravel slopes devoid of vegetation. They were "a drearier sight than any dunes," Stein told Allen.

Stein was cheered by Chiang's good humor and the pair chatted together, Stein in his halting Chinese. "My unmusical ear fails to remember or distinguish the varying tones of the identical syllable & I fear it will take long before others will be as clever as [Chiang] to catch the meaning of my conversation . . . Often we have talked of Marco Polo who had described this old route so truthfully," he wrote.

As they camped one night, Stein pulled from his bags Marco Polo's account of the route and read it to Chiang. It was hardly cheerful reading:

When travellers are on the move by night, and one of them chances to lag behind or to fall asleep or the like, when he tries to gain his company again he will hear spirits talking, and will suppose them to be his comrades. Sometimes the spirits will call him by name; and thus shall a traveller ofttimes be led astray so that he never finds his party. And in this way many have perished. Sometimes the stray travellers will hear, as it were, the tramp and hum of a great cavalcade of people away from the real line of road, and taking this to be their own

*company will follow the sound; and when day breaks they find that a
cheat has been put on them and that they are in an ill plight. Even in
the daytime one hears those spirits talking. And sometimes you shall
hear the sound of a variety of musical instruments, and still more com-
monly the sound of drums. Hence in making this journey 'tis common
for travellers to keep close together.*

The supernatural account evoked awe in Chiang. If the desert
could cast such a spell over the otherwise skeptical Chiang, a
scholarly, erudite man, its effect was felt even more keenly among
the more superstitious members of Stein's party. Little wonder
they were getting restive. So all were relieved when midway
through their journey they spotted five toghrak trees. It signaled
they had arrived at the place where they would rest for a day—
the only one on the entire crossing. The windswept trees, bravely
clinging to life in the desert, were rare enough in this wasteland
to give their name to the site, Besh-toghrak, meaning simply five
toghrak trees. Saddles were repaired and the camels and ponies
were watered at two nearby wells and treated for sore backs.
Stein planned to leave eight of the weakest donkeys no longer
needed at this lonely spot. A young Abdal donkey man was left to
care for them. The man was given a twenty-eight day supply of
rations and a box of matches. Until the caravan collected him on
the way back, he would "have to make the best of his solitude—or
the visits of goblins," Stein commented dryly.

A fierce cold wind was blowing a few days later when, through
the dust-filled haze, the party caught sight of an abandoned fort.
They made their way toward it in a thin line to shield against the
headwinds. Six times the height of the tallest man among them,
the fort was entered via an archway carved into walls fifteen feet
thick. Centuries ago, this would have seemed an impregnable
stronghold for a ruler's army. Now, nothing hinted at human habi-
tation, save for the debris of a recent caravan that had attempted
the perilous crossing.

77

Stein climbed a staircase hewn perhaps 2,000 years ago into a corner of the massive clay fortress. Thirty feet up, he held his ground as he was buffeted by the gale. He reached for his binoculars and surveyed the forbidding expanse: beyond the beds of reeds near the fort, tamarisk scrub and bare gravel stretched to the barren foothills of a distant mountain range. He turned into the wind and focused his gaze on four distant mounds that stood out against the hazy grey horizon: watchtowers. His excitement rose. These were more evidence of a long-forgotten military frontier. He had spotted traces of a ruined wall and other watchtowers in recent days. As he stood on the immense clay walls, he imagined an ancient military chief surveying the line of watchtowers under his command, eager for signals—fire by night, smoke by day—that passed along them. Beacons that once signaled the approach, or retreat, of armed enemies. Could this fort and the watchtowers be part of that forgotten frontier? In the empty isolation of the desert, such answers seemed unknowable. And yet he would soon find an answer.

Stein descended the fort's staircase and rejoined his party. This was not the time to explore further, no matter how much curiosity the watchtowers provoked. The food and water were almost gone. The animals were hungry and his men were irritable and exhausted. They had not seen another soul since leaving Abdal nearly three weeks ago. They had crossed quickly, in a week less than Marco Polo estimated. But all now needed rest. They must get to Dunhuang as quickly as possible.

✣

A distant line of bare trees and cultivated fields on the edge of Dunhuang were heartening sights for Aurel Stein and his caravan on March 12, 1907. While a persistent wind howled its numbing welcome as they approached the town, at least the weary men and beasts were not enduring its blasts in the desert. Warmth and shelter would soon be at hand. Not that Stein wanted to linger in Dunhuang; he was eager to return to the ruined wall, fort, and the string of watchtowers he had seen as he crossed from Abdal.

Dunhuang was the Silk Road's gateway between China and Central Asia, which was why he planned to use it as a base for six months of archaeological work and exploration in the surrounding desert and mountains. He planned a short halt, just long enough for his men and animals to rest and for him to visit the painted meditation grottoes—the Caves of the Thousand Buddhas—about fifteen miles to the southeast. He had longed to see these remote, sacred caves, and he was determined to realize this dream. But his real work lay elsewhere. Or so he thought.

His approach to his first oasis within China was unsettling after the hospitality he had enjoyed in Turkestan and where he felt at home. He knew its ways, its language and its daily rhythms, punctuated by the sound of the Muslim call to prayer. But now he was on foreign ground. In Turkestan, local headmen invariably rode out to meet his party as he approached an oasis. So too did the rapacious Hindu money-lenders, no doubt eager for business. But this time there was not so much as a single merchant to acknowledge his arrival. As always, Stein had attempted to smooth the path, sending word of his approach, his intended business and requesting accommodation. But unusually, no response had come. Was he being deliberately neglected? Was this how things were done on Chinese soil? What did it mean? Most immediately, it meant no quarters had been prepared for him or his party.

First impressions of Dunhuang, the once-vibrant oasis on the edge of the vast Gobi Desert, were hardly encouraging. Few people were outside on this bitterly cold and dust-filled day as he passed down the narrow main street. The few locals who could be found directed him to the caravanserai, the main stopping place for travelers needing accommodation, but it was so filthy and cramped he looked elsewhere for a more suitable camp. About a half a mile from the walled town's southern gate he found a large orchard with a dilapidated house. It was inhabited by a widow, her mother and several children, who agreed to house them in their unoccupied rooms.

Other differences from Turkestan soon became apparent. Stein was accustomed to—and approved of—the way Muslim women promptly removed themselves from the company of strangers. But purdah was not practiced in Dunhuang. Instead, Chinese women with bound feet teetered around as his dusty, travel-weary party settled in the unused rooms built around a courtyard. Stein erected his tent in the orchard, preferring its peace and relative comfort to the cavernous hall he had been offered as quarters.

Fuel, fodder, and food were his next concerns. But how to pay for them? Once again he was reminded that things were done differently in China, even in the far-flung western province of Gansu. As expected, no one would accept the coins of neighboring Turkestan, and the only silver bullion he had was in the form of horseshoes. Finding a blacksmith who could cut some silver into small change didn't occur to him the first day. Meanwhile, the daily market had closed and it took hours for supplies to arrive. The mood of his men darkened, frustrated by the delays in finding shelter and then food. Already apprehensive of venturing onto foreign soil, it seemed their worst fears of China's strange customs had been realized. All except Chiang, who instantly made friends with the widow's children, were on unfamiliar turf. Frustrating as his arrival in Dunhuang was, Stein later saw its absurdity, writing: "It amused me to think what our experiences would have been, had our caravan suddenly pitched camp in Hyde Park, and expected to raise supplies promptly in the neighbourhood without producing coin of the realm!" He quickly grew alert to the tricks of the money-exchange trade—silver pieces loaded with lead, and the way merchants used different scales depending on whether the customer was buying, selling or exchanging silver.

His men could at last rest the next day, fed and sheltered. Wrapped in their furs, they dozed in front of their fires. But, typically, Stein was not about to rest. He sent his last piece of yellow Liberty brocade to the local *yamen* as a gift for the magistrate. By midday he had swapped his travel-stained furs for his best European clothes—black coat, pith helmet, and patent leather boots—to pay his official visit. There the reason for the absence of a welcome became apparent. A new magistrate, Wang Ta-lao-ye, had himself only just arrived in Dunhuang—so recently that a fire had not been lit nor furniture installed in the bare reception hall. Stein felt the day's chill in his spiffy but all-too-thin clothes. The new magistrate had only just found his predecessor's documents about the impending arrival of this important visitor, and he was suitably impressed, even over-awed, by what he discovered in the papers. Whether through bureaucratic incompetence or clever mistranslation, Stein's travel document had elevated him to Prime Minister of Education of Great Britain.

Protocol required a return visit, and it came more quickly than Stein expected. No sooner had he arrived back at his tent and swapped his thin footwear for fur boots than the magistrate arrived. Seated on a thick felt rug and with a charcoal fire to warm them, Stein showed off some of the ancient Chinese records he had uncovered in recent months, and he found an appreciative audience in the learned man. "I instinctively felt that a kindly official providence had brought to Tun-huang [Dunhuang] just the right man to help me," Stein wrote. He soon called on the influential local military commander, the bluff and burly Lin Ta-jen, who provided a camp guard.

But it was a meeting with a group of Turkestan traders in the oasis that would prove most fortuitous. Unlike the magistrate, the traders knew the area well from living many years in the province. Among them was Zahid Beg, who, like many of the traders in town, was on the run from his Turkestan creditors. Zahid Beg told Stein of various half-buried ruins he claimed to have seen north of Dunhuang. His information was vague, rumors perhaps, but at least he was more forthcoming than the local Chinese, who greeted Stein's inquiries about ancient ruins in the area with steely silence. And Zahid Beg conveyed a tantalizing snippet, one that could not fail to ignite Stein's imagination. A huge cache of manuscripts was said to have been discovered a few years earlier, hidden in one of the painted grottoes at the Caves of the Thousand Buddhas. And, so the rumor went, the manuscripts were still there.

6

City of Sands

On the edge of the Gobi Desert near Dunhuang, a cliff about a mile long rises from a river valley. Beyond the cliff, sand dunes roll like ocean waves. In certain winds, these dunes were said to emit eerie music that inspired their name: the Ming Sha, or Singing Sands. But it was a vision, not a sound, that shaped history here, and it occurred more than 1,500 years before Stein's caravan arrived.

Legend has it that in AD 366, a wandering Buddhist monk named Lezun sat on the valley floor to rest from his travels across forests and plains. As he admired the sunset on Sanwei Mountain, he beheld a vision of a thousand Buddhas. Celestial nymphs danced in the rays of golden light, and Lezun watched the glorious scene until the dusk turned to dark. The monk, described as resolute, calm, and of pure conduct, was so inspired that the next day he set down his pilgrim's staff and abandoned plans to cross the Gobi. Instead, he chiseled a meditation cave into the cliff. The following day he mixed mud and smoothed the walls of his tiny shelter. And on his third day, he painted a mural on the wall to record the wondrous vision he had witnessed.

Lezun then visited Dunhuang to share his discovery, and the news quickly spread to the surrounding provinces, according to one folk tale. Similarly inspired, others joined him and honeycombed the conglomerate cliff with an estimated 1,000 hand-carved caves. The first caves were small, spartan cells, just big enough for a solitary monk. But as the religious community grew, elaborate grottoes were carved as chapels and shrines. Some were large enough for a hundred worshippers to gather. Murals in lapis, turquoise, and malachite covered the walls and ceilings in many of the caves. Nearly half a million square feet of magnificent murals were created. The wall paintings give an unparalleled picture of a thousand years of life along the Silk Road.

The location would eventually become known in China and beyond as a place of unrivalled beauty, sanctity, and knowledge. Although the monk Lezun is credited with founding the Caves of the Thousand Buddhas, or Mogao Caves as they are known today, he is but one of four men who have shaped their history through the centuries. The story of the Silk Road's most sacred site is inextricably bound with clandestine journeys, wandering monks, and intrepid travelers.

Why a sacred center flourished in such a remote place is simple. The reason is geography. Near Dunhuang, the Silk Road split in two to skirt the rim of the Taklamakan Desert. The roads met again 1,400 miles west at Kashgar. But between these two oases lay the Silk Road's most dangerous terrain. Among the threats were starvation, thirst, bandits, and ferocious sandstorms that were known to bury entire caravans. For those traveling west, Dunhuang was the last stop for caravans to rest and stock up before they faced the desert. For those heading east, it was the first oasis on Chinese soil. Any traveler would want to express gratitude for surviving such a journey or pray for safe deliverance before embarking, so it is little wonder that as long as the Silk Road thrived, the caves did too. Wealthy merchants and other patrons paid for the grottoes to be created and decorated as acts of thanksgiving. Dunhuang—the name means Blazing Beacon and refers to the nearby line of military watchtowers that guarded the area—might have begun as a dusty military garrison town, but it became a prosperous, cosmopolitan center, the Silk Road's great beacon of spiritual illumination.

The Silk Road, or roads really, was a network of trade routes that linked China with the West. From its eastern end in the ancient Chinese capital of Chang'an, now Xian, the route passed through Dunhuang before branching south to India, present-day Afghanistan and Pakistan, or west to Samarkand, Bokhara, Persia, and the eastern Mediterranean. For about a thousand years, caravans of camels loaded with silk, rubies, jade, amber, musk, and far more halted at Dunhuang.

But despite all its ancient connotations, the name Silk Road is relatively new, coined only in the nineteenth century by a German geographer and explorer, Baron Ferdinand von Richthofen. It conjures exotic images of heavily laden camels plodding through rolling dunes, bells tinkling. The name is far more romantic than if it had been named after another desirable commodity traded along the way, which might have seen it dubbed the Rhubarb Road.

Silk, which originated in China, was the best known and among the most prized of the route's merchandise. Few caravans traveled the entire route. Rather, the goods would change hands—as well as camels and donkeys—many times along the way, and inhabitants at one end of the Silk Road knew little about those at the other. Consequently, the Romans, who had an insatiable hunger for the exquisite fabric (despite a Senate ban on men wearing it), had only vague ideas about the land or people who produced it. But rumors abounded. Some talked of Seres, the Kingdom of Silk, as a land inhabited by giants with red hair and blue eyes. Others thought it home to people who lived for 200 years. For centuries, the Romans thought the gossamer thread grew on trees and was combed from leaves. This suited the middlemen through whose lands the goods passed and who lived off the profits. Even when a Greek traveler asserted that it came from insects—giant beetles, he claimed—the West lacked the means to make the luxurious fabric. But in the sixth century, two Nestorian monks returning from China are said to have reached the court of the Byzantine emperor Justinian with silkworm eggs concealed in their bamboo staffs.

⳨

Coveted as it was, silk was not the only treasure to travel the ancient trade route. Ideas, too, made their way along the Silk Road, the original information superhighway. The most influential of these was Buddhism, whose story began around 400 BC, when Prince Siddhartha was born into the ruling Shakya clan in the Himalayan foothills of present-day Nepal. He grew up in luxurious seclusion, sheltered from life's sufferings and harsh realities, according to Buddhist tales. At twenty-nine, he ventured beyond the palace and encountered the sufferings from which he had been shielded. He saw an old man, a sick man, a corpse, and an ascetic. Troubled by this confrontation with ageing, sickness, and death, he resolved to find a way to overcome suffering and mortality.

He rejected his privileged life and secretly slipped away from the palace to become an ascetic himself. He wandered for years, studying under various teachers but, unsatisfied, continually moved on. He sought answers through extremes of spiritual renunciation and physical deprivation, including near starvation. At the age of thirty-five, he sat beneath a fig tree near present-day Bodhgaya and vowed not to rise until he attained enlightenment. He realized what Buddhists call the Four Noble Truths: suffering exists; desires cause suffering; it is possible to end suffering; and a path exists to achieve this. Freed from the cycle of birth, death, and rebirth, he arose as Buddha Shakyamuni, the Awakened One and the sage of the Shakya clan. He spent the rest of his life—the next forty-five years—traveling around northern India and teaching what he had learned. His teachings were later written in the form of thousands of sutras. Buddha Shakyamuni is sometimes referred to as the historical Buddha. There are said to be countless Buddhas; many have existed in the past, others will appear in the future.

Buddha Shakyamuni delivered the teaching known as the Diamond Sutra in a garden near the ancient Indian city of Sravasti. According to Buddhist lore, a wealthy merchant named Sudatta, or Anathapindika, who was known for his generosity to orphans and the destitute, heard the Buddha teaching. The merchant was so impressed he invited the Buddha to Sravasti to teach. However, the only suitable place to build a temple to house the Buddha and his disciples was in a forest south of the city, and it belonged to the Crown Prince Jeta, who had no interest in selling his pristine real estate. "If you can cover the ground with gold pieces, I'll sell it," the prince allegedly joked. Undeterred, the philanthropic merchant went home, opened his treasury and brought back enough gold to carpet the 200-acre site. For twenty-five rainy seasons the Buddha gave some of his most important teachings in a park once covered in gold.

༃

More than 200 years after the Buddha Shakyamuni left his palace, another clandestine journey began, one that would ultimately result in the establishment of the Silk Road. It was a trip designed to prevent what China's Great Wall could not—raids by a marauding tribe of Central Asian horsemen called the Xiongnu. Some say the Xiongnu were related to the Huns who would later cut a swath through Europe. Whatever the case, the Han emperor Wudi wanted them stopped. The emperor knew his people were not the only ones being terrorized by these fierce fighters. A nomadic group had been driven from their lands on China's far western fringe, their king executed and his skull turned into a drinking cup. The Yuezhi, as the routed nomads were called, wanted revenge.

The emperor decided to seek an alliance with the Yuezhi— "the enemy of my enemy is my friend" is hardly a new diplomatic strategy. He dispatched an envoy from the ancient capital of Chang'an on a secret mission about a hundred years before the birth of Christ. The man who volunteered for the dangerous assignment was a court official called Zhang Qian. He was about thirty years old and considered bold and trustworthy. He was given an escort of a hundred men, a yak-hair tail atop a bamboo pole—a symbol of imperial power—and effectively told to "go west, young man" and forge the alliance. That was easier said than done. To travel west meant venturing into unknown lands and crossing enemy territory. There was also a fearsome desert along the way and no known route around or across it.

As a diplomatic mission it was a disaster. All but one of his men perished during the journey. Zhang Qian himself was captured and spent a decade as a prisoner of the Xiongnu. When the envoy eventually escaped, he tracked the Yuezhi to present-day Afghanistan but life had utterly changed for them. The Yuezhi had settled down to a peaceful, prosperous existence and weren't terribly interested in taking revenge on their one-time foe. The envoy turned around and trekked back to China. Although he returned from his thirteen-year journey without an alliance, he did not return home empty-handed. Aside from his remarkably resilient yak-hair tail, he brought something far more significant: knowledge. He had not only found a way around the Taklamakan Desert, he brought news of mysterious lands and great civilizations, places where dazzling goods and unknown foods such as grapes, carrots, walnuts, and alfalfa were traded. He also brought word of powerful blood-sweating horses from Ferghana, in present-day Uzbekistan, said to be descended from celestial steeds. (The blood is now thought to be the result of a parasite that causes lesions.) The strength of these horses made them ideal for battle, and the appeal of such superior steeds to the emperor was obvious. The Heavenly Horses have long inspired Chinese paintings, poems, and statues.

News of such horses and other desirable goods prompted moves to establish the trade routes that became the Silk Road and fostered exchanges between these distant lands. Over time, missions were sent and garrisons established, including at Dunhuang, to protect the growing commerce. Zhang Qian is pictured in a mural at the Mogao Caves taking leave of Emperor Wudi. His groundbreaking journey helped forge an overland route between China and the West—and laid the path for Buddhism's arrival from India. The path from the Himalayan foothills through Central Asia and into China was circuitous, but the vast mountain ranges between China and India posed formidable obstacles to a more direct route. As Buddhism meandered into China, a unique form of art developed as the religion bumped up against different cultures along the way. The art was a tangible expression of the Buddhist desire to be freed from the cycle of rebirth and suffering.

Buddhism split into two branches as it traveled. Theravada Buddhism, which emphasizes individual enlightenment, took hold in Thailand, Burma, and Sri Lanka. Mahayana Buddhism, which asserts everyone can become a Buddha and seeks to free all beings from suffering, became dominant in north Asia, including Tibet, Korea, Japan, and China. The Mahayana practitioner strives over many lifetimes to become first a bodhisattva, a wise, compassionate being who leads others to enlightenment, and ultimately a fully awakened Buddha.

Central to Buddhism is the idea of karma, a cosmic chain of cause and effect whereby everything a person thinks, says or does leaves a "seed" that will ripen in the future. Negative seeds ripen as suffering and virtuous seeds as happiness and, ultimately, enlightenment. Therefore performing virtuous, or meritorious, actions is imperative for a Buddhist. A virtuous act includes the making—or sponsoring the making—of holy images and objects. And the more that are created, the greater the merit. This is a key reason behind the creation of the Silk Road's numerous painted grottoes, of which the Caves of the Thousand Buddhas are the most splendid example.

⟩⊂⊙

For about 400 years, the Buddha's words were memorized and transmitted orally. They were not written down until the first century AD. But once they were, the Diamond Sutra and other teachings could propagate easily across the great trade routes, in particular the Silk Road. The written scriptures were exactly what a young Chinese monk was after when, in 629, he too embarked on a clandestine journey. His name was Xuanzang (Hsuan Tsang), and he was destined to become one of the world's greatest travelers. From beyond the grave he would play a pivotal role at the Caves of the Thousand Buddhas.

Xuanzang was on a quest for spiritual enlightenment rather than a sensitive diplomatic mission when, like the envoy with his yak tail, he traveled west along the Silk Road—by then a well-worn path— from Chang'an. He left behind the capital's floating pavilions and secluded gardens and slipped through the outer gates of the city's triple walls to embark on a sixteen-year journey that would take him across the desert and over the jagged Pamir Mountains to India and back to China. He would prove himself an intrepid traveler, a brilliant translator, and a remarkable eyewitness: one part Christopher Columbus, one part St. Jerome, one part Samuel Pepys.

His life has inspired numerous folk tales and legends, such as the classic Chinese novel known in English as *Monkey,* in which he is overshadowed by his companions, including a greedy pig and a trickster monkey. Japanese cartoons and a 1970s cult television series have also drawn on Xuanzang's adventures. The tale has even inspired an opera performed at London's Covent Garden in 2008, composed by Damon Albarn, the songwriter and vocalist for the rock band Gorillaz. Folk tales aside, the monk left a written account of the places he visited which has proved so accurate that geographers and archaeologists still consult it today. Like Stein, Xuanzang was fastidious, whether recording the distances between places and the heights of individual stupas or recording the myths, massacres, and monarchs he encountered along his way. But he reveals little of himself and his own life, leaving that for a devoted disciple, Huili, who wrote his biography. Xuanzang's account is written with philosophic detachment, his disciple's filled with vivid anecdotes. Together the two works give a unique account of a vanished world and one of the greatest journeys of all time.

Xuanzang began studying Buddhist scriptures when he was about thirteen and was ordained as a monk at twenty. After years spent immersed in Chinese translations, he found the teachings contradictory and incomplete. Likewise, he found the religion's various schools conflicting. What was true? He resolved to seek clarity from the great masters in distant India. More importantly, he wanted to bring back the original Buddhist texts for translation. Unfortunately, foreign travel was banned and as the young monk, then about twenty-six years old, did not have imperial permission to leave, he departed the capital in secret, traveling by night and hiding during the day. His journey was nearly a short one. His guide tried to murder him near the Jade Gate, the landmark near Dunhuang that marked the western edge of China, through which many Silk Road caravans passed. Amid the desert's demons and hot winds, he became lost and almost died of thirst. At Gaochang, near Turfan, the oasis city's king was so impressed by Xuanzang's knowledge that he forcibly detained him, prompting the monk to begin a hunger strike. The king relented, provided the monk with an escort, supplies, gold, and letters of introduction, and extracted a promise that Xuanzang would remain in Gaochang for three years on his return from India. The monk's chances of surviving such a trip may have seemed slim, but the gods were clearly on Xuanzang's side. He lived through a range of death-defying adventures which saw him attacked by bandits, captured by pirates and almost offered as a human sacrifice to the bloodthirsty Hindu goddess Durga.

Apocryphal as the stories sound, the descriptions of the terrain he covered have attracted the attention of explorers, historians, and archaeologists, not least Aurel Stein, who was the same age as Xuanzang when he, too, first departed for India. (Stein suggested there was some truth and wisdom in one of the odder, seemingly more fanciful stories in which the monk is persuaded to swap his good horse for a scrawny nag ahead of a hazardous desert crossing because the old horse had made the trip many times before. Stein knew all too well how horses and camels could not only detect water and food in the desert from a great distance but also remember their locations from previous visits.)

Xuanzang crossed the Pamir Mountains and journeyed through the Buddhist kingdom of Gandhara. Along the way he gave one of the first accounts of the then sparkling new Bamiyan Buddhas of central Afghanistan. They glinted in the sun with their gold paint and jeweled ornaments. They had been carved into a cliff about a hundred years before the monk arrived. The figures—one stood 180 feet tall, the other 125 feet—rose above a valley that was home to a flourishing Buddhist community with thousands of monks. And there they remained for 1,600 years— long after the Buddhist culture that created them had vanished

from the valley—until the Afghan Taliban blew them to pieces in
March 2001. Curiously, Xuanzang describes a third, much larger
Bamiyan Buddha, a sleeping figure 900 feet long said to be within
a monastery nearby. His description has prompted a search for its
elusive remains in recent years, although a smaller reclining Buddha was found in 2008.

Xuanzang made his way along the Himalayan foothills to the
Buddhist "holy land" in northeast India. He arrived at the great
center of Buddhist learning, Nalanda, one of the world's first universities. The center had about 10,000 students and was in its
heyday when Xuanzang first saw its pointed turrets, sparkling roof
tiles, lotus ponds, and flowering groves. It drew scholars from
other lands—Japan, China, Persia, and Tibet—to study not just
Buddhism but medicine, mathematics, and astronomy. Its three
libraries were so extensive that when they were razed by Muslim
invaders in the twelfth century—about the time the University
of Oxford was established—they were said to have burned for
months. The ruins of what was once an architectural masterpiece
remain today in Bihar state. A memorial hall to Xuanzang was
opened at Nalanda in 2007, with a statue of the pilgrim carrying
scrolls on his back.

At Nalanda, the great abbot Silabhadra was expecting him.
Years earlier, the abbot had a dream foretelling that a monk would
come from China and ensure the survival of Mahayana teachings abroad. Xuanzang became the abbot's disciple. As well as
studying, Xuanzang visited Buddhism's sacred sites in India and
present-day Nepal: Buddha's birthplace at Lumbini; Bodhgaya,
where he attained enlightenment; Sarnath, where he preached
his first sermon; and Kushinagar, where he died.

Xuanzang also visited Jetavana Vihara, the place where the
Buddha first delivered the Diamond Sutra teaching. A seven-
story temple was built and one of the first statues of the Buddha
was said to have been created there out of sandalwood. But the

park named after Prince Jeta was in ruins, and little remained other than a solitary brick building containing an image of the Buddha. The city of Sravasti, too, lay in ruins, although a stupa marked where the generous merchant who procured the site had lived. Pilgrims still visit the remains northeast of Lucknow today.

After years of study and travel—and having acquired hundreds of sacred texts to translate—the monk planned his return home. But it was a dangerous journey, as he knew all too well. Would he make it? How long would he live? And how would he get his sacred material safely back to China? He put his questions to a fortune teller, a naked Jain, who appeared in Xuanzang's cell at Nalanda one day. Yes, he would get home safely. He would live another ten years. (He lived another twenty-plus.) As well, the Jain said, Indian kings would help Xuanzang on his way. And indeed one king provided an enormous white elephant, the equivalent of supplying a private Learjet today. No one could remember a monk ever being given an elephant before. The animal could carry Xuanzang's baggage but his fuel costs were high, requiring forty bundles of hay a day. Thoughtfully, the monk's regal patron provided plenty of gold and silver to pay for the elephant's prodigious appetite and Xuanzang's caravan. The monk's heavy baggage included more than 200 sutras, six statues of the Buddha, and other relics. His return to China, though, was not without mishap. He lost some of his manuscripts while crossing a treacherous stretch of the Indus River. In the mountains on his way to Kashgar, he was attacked by robbers. In the ensuing panic, his normally placid elephant plunged into a river and drowned. When Stein read of this, he took the pilgrim's tale at face value. From the topographical description, Stein identified the likely gorge, a narrow spot particularly vulnerable to attack by robbers.

At the Buddhist kingdom of Khotan, Xuanzang awaited the delivery of more manuscripts to replace those lost in the Indus. The monk's description of Khotan evokes a Paris of the desert, where sophisticated and beautifully dressed inhabitants thrived on art, music, and literature. He also described a local legend about how the closely guarded secret of silk-making spread beyond China. According to his story, the king of Khotan, determined to learn the secret, sought the hand in marriage of a Chinese princess. He sent an envoy to collect the new bride and warn her that her new homeland was without silk. If she wanted robes of the precious material, she would need to bring the means to make the fabric herself. The princess discreetly acquired silkworm eggs and mulberry seeds and hid them in her headdress. She smuggled them across the Chinese frontier knowing the border guards would not dare search the headdress of a princess. Stein recognized the same legend depicted on an ancient painted panel he plucked from the desert.

Having slipped out of China without permission, Xuanzang decided it was prudent to let the Imperial Court know he would soon be returning but was presently stuck without transport across the desert since losing his elephant. The emperor sent officials from Dunhuang to meet him. Xuanzang rested at Dunhuang, where it is assumed he visited the nearby caves, before traveling to Chang'an and a hero's welcome. He did not return to Gaochang because its king had died during Xuanzang's long travels, thereby releasing him from his promise. Instead, he spent the rest of his life translating Buddhist scriptures, including the Diamond Sutra, and is still considered among China's greatest translator monks. He too is commemorated at the Caves of the Thousand Buddhas in a vivid Tang dynasty image, in which he is shown crossing the Pamir Mountains with his white elephant and caravan. As well as his translations, he wrote the account of his travels, *Records of the Western Regions,* a work Stein consulted like a seventh-century Lonely Planet guide.

Silk Rd
~1390

The Caves of the Thousand Buddhas had been left to the mercy of the encroaching sands and largely forgotten when, at the end of the nineteenth century, another wandering monk arrived. What brought Wang Yuanlu, or Abbot Wang as he is also called, no one knows. He came from Macheng in Hubei province. He was born in about 1850, probably into a farming family, and received only a basic education. Famine forced him to leave, and he joined the army as a foot soldier stationed in Suzhou, about 250 miles east of Dunhuang. After leaving the army, he became a Daoist monk in Suzhou. Like the visionary monk Lezun, the envoy Zhang Qian and the intrepid Xuanzang, Wang was a long way from home when he reached Dunhuang in the 1890s.

By then the Silk Road too had been abandoned for more than 500 years. Even before the fourteenth century, sea routes began to replace the dangerous overland route between China and the West. With its fate inextricably tied to the Silk Road, cosmopolitan Dunhuang became a dusty outpost, and the great monastic community that thrived there dispersed. The caves entered a sleep lasting centuries during which many filled with sand; others were destroyed by earthquakes. The wooden entrance pagodas, where temple bells and silk banners once hung, rotted or burned down.

Although Abbot Wang was a Daoist monk, not a Buddhist, what he saw when he arrived at the ruined, deserted caves changed his life. Perhaps the contrast between the desert beyond and the meditative art within the caves resonated with the contemplative monk like a teaching on the aridness of the outer world and the richness of the inner. He abandoned his wandering life, appointed himself guardian of the caves, and dedicated the rest of his life to their preservation and restoration. He planted poplar trees by the river bank and eventually built a guesthouse for pilgrims. Wang hired laborers to dig out centuries of wind-blown sand from the caves to expose the wonderful images within. He ordered new statues and arranged for the repainting of old ones. He commissioned paintings to depict legendary scenes from the life of his hero, the wandering monk Xuanzang. Wang was no scholar. What appealed to him were the folk tales of the great monk's daring deeds. Others might consider his statues and paintings gaudy, but not Wang. He was immensely proud of them. He sold Daoist spells and conducted begging tours among the wealthy landowners to pay for the work. The restoration and the fundraising were endless.

One hot summer's day in 1900, Abbot Wang was supervising restorations in a cave temple at the northern end of the cliff. It had taken more than two years of back-breaking toil to clear the boulders and drift sand that had blocked the cave's entrance. The pace of work was slow—he could afford to pay for only a few laborers at a time—but at last he was ready to install new statues he had commissioned for the chamber. As the work proceeded, Wang's laborers drew his attention to a crack in a mural along the narrow passage leading to the chamber. Just across the threshold, where the desert's dazzling sunlight gave way to flickering lamplight, the crack suggested the outline of an entrance. Plastered over and painted, it had been deliberately concealed. Wang ordered his workmen to break through the plaster. Behind it was a small, dark room. He peered inside. The space was little bigger than a walk-in pantry. Crammed from floor to ceiling were thousands upon thousands of scrolls.

At least, that is what Wang told Stein. But the history of the cave's discovery is muddied by conflicting versions. When the Frenchman Paul Pelliot subsequently arrived, Wang claimed that knowledge of the cave had arrived in a dream sent by the gods. A smile on the abbot's face, however, made it clear neither man put much stock in that version. A Chinese account speaks of a pipe-smoking scribe named Yang who set up a desk in the large adjoining cave to copy sutras. While taking a break, he tapped his pipe on the wall to empty it and heard a hollow sound, then noticed a hairline fracture in the plaster. The scribe alerted Wang and that night the pair broke through the hidden doorway to reveal the chamber and its treasure.

Whatever the truth, Wang sensed his discovery was significant and tried hard to interest authorities in the cave's contents. He informed officials in Dunhuang of the find, taking two yellowed scrolls with him, but the local magistrate dismissed the documents as useless scraps of old paper. About three years later, when a new, more learned magistrate arrived, Wang again presented evidence of the great find. This magistrate came to the caves and departed with a few manuscripts, but did nothing. Yet still Wang persisted. He took a donkey with two boxes of manuscripts to Suzhou, yet even there a scholar who inspected them was unimpressed. Finally, in 1904, the provincial government in Lanzhou ordered Dunhuang officials to protect the scrolls. But there was no money to transport up to seven pony loads of manuscripts to another location. Resigned by the years of inaction, a dismayed Wang did what he was told to do: he resealed the cave and consigned the cache of documents back to their dark, dry tomb.

In a place where there is something that can be distinguished by signs, in that place there is deception.

VERSE 5, THE DIAMOND SUTRA

7

Tricks and Trust

For years, Stein dreamed of seeing the sacred caves. He had learned about them from a friend, geographer Lajos Lóczy, who was with the first party of Europeans to reach the Caves of the Thousand Buddhas, in May 1879. Lóczy, a fellow Hungarian, had spoken in glowing terms of their magnificent art. To stand inside the caves was one reason why Stein had pressed to travel so far into China. But the rumor of a hidden cache of manuscripts made him even more eager. So his first days in Dunhuang must have seemed like torture. The caves were a mere fifteen miles away, but he was stuck at his desk tending to the necessary but most wearying part of his expedition. He brought his accounts and official correspondence up to date; he farewelled his donkey men with a generous tip; and he sent his camels off to graze.

He could barely contain his excitement when on a cold, bright March morning, four days after he had reached Dunhuang, he rode to the caves with Chiang and the Naik. He soon left behind the ploughed fields of the oasis and crossed a stretch of barren gravel. After nine dusty miles, he turned into a river valley where a cliff rose perpendicular on his right. At the gateway to the valley was a large ceremonial bell. Rusty and cracked, it was covered in Chinese characters from a Buddhist text. But what interested Stein most was that it contained a date, even if not a terribly old one. "It gave me the first assurance that the chronological precision so characteristic of Chinese ways was not ignored by Buddhist piety in these parts," he wrote. Indeed the Chinese inclination to date everything was a gift for an archaeologist. It removed the guess work—and would ultimately provide certainty about the expedition's greatest treasure, the Diamond Sutra.

From a distance, the honeycombed grottoes reminded him of troglodyte dwellings. Some of the dark cavities, layered in irregular tiers up the cliff face, seemed accessible only by rope. Others were connected by disintegrating steps or rickety ladders. As he drew closer and crossed the Daquan River in front of the cliff, he could see the painted walls inside the crumbling caves. "'The Caves of the Thousand Buddhas' were indeed tenanted, not by Buddhist recluses, however holy, but by images of the Enlightened One himself."

No one was around to guide or distract him as he wandered in awe from cave to cave. He marveled at Buddhas that looked Indian, Gandharan, Tibetan, Chinese. The changing face of the Buddha, as Buddhism wound its way from India along the Silk Road into China, evolving along the way, was literally on the walls. Many of the beautiful chapels appeared to date from the Tang dynasty, a time of peace and prosperity in Dunhuang and a high point of Chinese civilization from the seventh to the tenth century. The passageways that opened onto the temples were covered in processions of bodhisattvas. Many of the sculptures within the grottoes were damaged, either through decay, by iconoclasts or ham-fisted restorations. The fragile sculptures weren't made of stone—there was none to be quarried in the surrounding conglomerate cliffs—but of clay stucco over a skeleton of wood or bunches of tamarisk twigs. Some had modern heads and arms, but the original bodies survived and revealed exquisite color and drapery. Stein was relieved to find no many-headed, many-armed "monstrosities," as he disapprovingly described some Indian and Tibetan depictions. On his first visit he presumably did not see the examples that exist, including a pair of many-armed Tibetan Tantric deities wrapped in an intimate embrace, nor the thousand-eyed bodhisattva, Avalokitesvara.

As Stein walked from cave to cave, absorbed by the beauty of the murals and statues (and no doubt pondering how he might remove them), a young Buddhist monk approached. He appeared to have been left in charge of the small houses and chapels nearby. Stein seized the chance to sound him out about a concealed cave rumored to be full of manuscripts. Under Chiang's questioning, the young monk proved most forthcoming. Yes, a cave had been discovered. Yes, it was full of manuscripts. Enough to fill several carts. The cave had since been fitted with a locked door and only the temple guardian, Abbot Wang, had the key. But he was off on a begging tour and wouldn't be back for weeks.

Here was confirmation that the remarkable rumor Stein had heard when he first arrived in Dunhuang was true. But that was not all Stein gleaned from the monk. The young man's spiritual mentor, a Tibetan monk who lived among a small Buddhist community at the caves, had borrowed one of the manuscripts for his own use. He kept the document at a nearby chapel. The young monk agreed to fetch it. Stein waited anxiously near the locked door of the Library Cave for his first hint of what might be inside. The monk returned carrying a large paper roll. Stein and Chiang carefully unwound the forty-five-foot scroll. It was beautifully preserved, its paper smooth and strong, but there was no way to determine its age. It was written in Chinese and appeared to be Buddhist. But Chiang, unfamiliar with Buddhism, could make no sense of it. The intriguing scroll only increased Stein's determination to get into the Library Cave.

Stein quietly discussed with Chiang how best to get access to the cave and overcome any priestly objections. "I had told my devoted secretary what Indian experience had taught me of the diplomacy most likely to succeed with local priests usually as ignorant as they were greedy, and his ready comprehension had assured me that the methods suggested might be tried with advantage on Chinese soil too."

But Stein could see obstacles to his ambitions. Clearly, many caves were still used for worship, despite the neglect of centuries. This was not a problem he had confronted elsewhere in the desert, where he explored long-abandoned sites. Chipping off murals and statues from chapels that continued to attract pilgrims would hardly go unnoticed. "Systematic quarrying," as he put it to Allen, might even provoke outrage. Could the priest be persuaded to turn a blind eye to the removal of sacred objects? What about the locals? Stein didn't know.

But he did know the value of a well-placed offering. He was keen to reward the helpful young monk who had not only confirmed the cave's existence, but also shown a sample of its contents. "I always like to be liberal with those whom I may hope to secure as 'my own' local priests," he commented blithely. Chiang advised caution—too generous a tip would arouse suspicion about ulterior motives. So Stein offered a small piece of silver. "The gleam of satisfaction on the young Ho-shang's [monk's] face showed that the people of Tun-huang, whatever else their weaknesses, were not much given to spoiling poor monks," Stein wrote.

Having at last seen the painted grottoes and evidence the rumored cache of manuscripts did indeed exist, only the gathering dusk compelled him to leave the caves. He rode back to Dunhuang in darkness, his head swimming with the images he had seen and the prospect of realizing a scholar's dream—uncovering an ancient secret library. But he must wait until Abbot Wang returned.

ᔭᓇᕋ

Stein was not about to sit idle. He was eager to revisit the ruined walls and watchtowers he had glimpsed on his long, cold march to Dunhuang. However, he would need to start immediately if he hoped to complete his investigations before the arrival of summer's blistering heat made such work impossible. Before he could set out, though, he needed local laborers. Finding them would not be easy. Dunhuang's population, decimated by a Muslim rebellion forty years earlier, had still not recovered. The few laborers for hire did not relish swapping oasis life for hard, cold work in the feared Gobi. And another debilitating force held the town in its grip, which is why the team he eventually assembled seemed less than promising. They were "the craziest crew I ever led to digging—so torpid and enfeebled by opium were they; but I was glad to have even them."

Despite his drug-addled team, what he uncovered during a month in the desert while awaiting Wang's return would reveal as much about ancient secular and military life as the caves would about spiritual life. He returned to the ruined fort where he had halted en route to Dunhuang, on whose ramparts he had walked alone, pondering the rise and fall of empires. He soon realized this ruined fort was one of the very sites he had set out to find, and among the most important of the ancient world. It was the famed Jade Gate, the fort named after the precious stone from Khotan carried by caravans traveling east. Stein had uncovered what he described as the western extension of the Great Wall, built to keep out invaders, extend China's influence and safeguard the Silk Road trade. He marveled at the strength of the wall, built with bundled layers of tamarisk twigs, reeds, and stamped clay. "Across an extensive desert area, bare of all resources, and of water in particular, it must have been a difficult task to construct a wall so solid as this," he remarked.

At a watchtower near the Jade Gate he found a post bag lost in transit between China and Samarkand around 313. Within it was a unique collection of letters, written in Sogdian, a Persian language that was once the Silk Road's lingua franca. The Sogdians are remembered today as the Silk Road's great merchants—although in one of these letters a trader is recalled in far less flattering terms. The merchant's wife, abandoned with their daughter in Dunhuang, penned a letter cursing her fate. Her fury is evident 1,700 years on. Destitute and far from home she writes to him, "I would rather be a dog's or a pig's wife than yours!"

From the desert sand, Stein also pulled relics of China's ancient military might. There were mundane reminders, such as a "sorry we missed you" note, carved on a stick by three men and intended for their friend stationed at a garrison. Stein excavated a dungeon, like a deep well, whose grim horrors he preferred not to dwell on—horrors that seemed to be confirmed when he not only found a note about a man who had died after a beating but uncovered a stick used to inflict such punishment. He also unearthed shreds of the fabric intricately connected with the area: silk. Past and present seemed to merge as he found objects so well preserved they looked as if they had been abandoned the previous day. He was in his element. In a letter that seemed to reflect the Buddhist beliefs that surrounded him, he told Allen:

I feel at times as I ride along the wall to examine new towers, etc, as if I were going to inspect posts still held by the living. With the experience daily repeated of perishable things wonderfully preserved one risks gradually losing the true sense of time. Two thousand years seem so brief a span when the sweepings from the soldiers' huts still lie practically on the surface in front of the doors or when I see the huge stacks of reed bundles as used for repairing the wall still in situ near the posts, just like stacks of spare sleepers near a railway station. I love my prospecting rides in the evenings especially when the winds have cleared the sky . . . I feel strangely at home here along this desolate frontier—as if I had known it in a previous birth.

The ruined wall prompted a rare reflection on his "beloved father," who had followed the paths of old Roman walls in southern Hungary. "He had spent many a hot day in tracing their lines; but, alas, the day never came when he could show me what had puzzled & fascinated him." Perhaps Stein felt a twinge of sorrow that, as he too stood before an ancient wall, he was unable to share his own fascination with his late father, by then dead nearly two decades.

In a sheltered spot, he found evidence of a more recent visit: his footprints made a month earlier remained undisturbed by the desert winds. (He would be even more surprised when he returned seven years later to find an echo of 1907: not just his own footprints but also those of Dash the Great.) Amid the ruins of a recently abandoned homestead he left something for a future archaeologist who might visit in another two thousand years—a piece of dated newspaper.

Thrilled as he was by his discoveries, the weeks of marching from site to site were not without difficulties. Stein knew his opium-addled laborers, good-natured though they were, would far rather be elsewhere. "If they are people hard to keep at work, especially in the desert, they are yet jovial & wonderfully well-mannered. You ought to have seen the polite bearing, the pleasant smile of my laborers, though they were ever at the point of deserting," he wrote to Allen. Some of them did.

There were ructions too among his core crew. His camel man Hassan Akhun picked a fight with one of the Chinese laborers. This prompted retaliation from the entire group of laborers, who set aside their good manners and attacked the camel man. The rheumatic surveyor Ram Singh was full of complaints. There was too little rest and not enough comfort for his liking. He was dissatisfied with his pony and wanted a better one. He was unhappy about sharing a cook with the Naik and irritated by the latter's snoring. Stein's Kashmiri cook, Ramzan, went on strike before taking a pony and disappearing. Stein figured he would not get far. He knew the cook would go to Dunhuang, where his presence would soon be noticed. Sure enough, his arrival alone in the oasis aroused such suspicion he was arrested and locked up. And there he would have stayed until Stein returned from the desert had not the trader Zahid Beg, who had told Stein the rumors of the manuscripts, bailed him out and agreed to keep an eye on him. The cook, realizing he had no chance of escaping his contract, decided instead on a sulky apology. He pleaded "mental distemper brought on by the air of the desert." Even Stein's dog disappeared for a time. Dash took off in the desert with shepherd dogs only to return badly mauled.

ɔ҂ə

The change of seasons was swift and dramatic. Clouds of mosquitoes filled the air and Stein, who suffered from repeated bouts of malaria, attempted in vain to shield himself with a protective net. "So I have learned at last how the world looks through a veil. But I am glad that ladies always wearing it have something more pleasant to look at!" Soon desert digging would be impossible, and not just because of the baking heat. For spring, which elsewhere brings renewal and hope, in this desert unleashes its most destructive might: sandstorms, or burans.

Even witnessed from the safety of an oasis, a buran could terrify. Catherine Macartney described "a great black pillar advancing towards us through the clean air, with the sun shining on either side of the black mass. It grew bigger and bigger, while the sun became a ball of red before it disappeared entirely." The sky grew darker, and the distant wind shrieked before the storm burst upon Kashgar with a roar. "The trees bent as though they must break and it grew dark as night, while the dust in the air penetrated through the cracks and crevices covering everything, making it difficult even to breathe."

For those exposed in the desert, a buran could strike with deadly force. It obliterated all tracks and sense of direction, its fury impossible to withstand. The only defense for caravan men was to shield behind their kneeling camels or take cover under heavy felt blankets—no matter how hot the day—as rocks pelted down for hours. But that was no guarantee of survival. Many have perished in such sandstorms, including a sixty-man caravan en route to Turfan in 1905. "Like hell let loose" is how von Le Coq described a buran. Stein, less dramatic than von Le Coq, made a brief note in his diary shortly before concluding his desert dig: "Overtaken by violent sand storm driving before it even small pebbles."

Spring showed its more benign face when Stein returned to the Dunhuang oasis in mid-May. Fields of young green corn had sprung up in the weeks he had been away, and the wild blue irises growing beside the roadside reminded him of Kashmir. Elm trees that had looked like skeletons on his first arrival were now green, and peach and pear blossoms sprinkled his tent in the widow's garden. After so long in the desert, the sight soothed his "parched, dust-filled eyes." Although his thoughts had never been far from the Caves of the Thousand Buddhas, he soon learned he would have to contain his ever-growing impatience for a few more days. The good news was that Wang had returned from his begging tour. The bad was that the caves were swarming with visitors. An annual pilgrimage was under way and thousands of locals dressed in their bright holiday clothes were bumping their way in carts to worship at the shrines. Eager as he was to move his caravan to the site that drew him "with the strength of a hidden magnet," this was not the time to do so. What he had in mind could best be accomplished away from prying eyes. With the oasis in its spring dress, for once Stein welcomed a brief, peaceful interlude. He rarely seemed more contented or reflective as on the day spent beside Crescent Lake, Dunhuang's other magnificent sight.

ʕ୦ଡ

"The skill of man made the Caves of the Thousand Buddhas, but the Hand of God fashioned the Lake of the Crescent Moon." So said the Dunhuang locals, according to two hardy British missionaries, Mildred Cable and Francesca French, who stopped beside it in the early 1900s. Even today the perfect crescent in a hollow amid the towering dunes bewitches, reflecting clear blue sky amid golden sands.

At the lake, about three miles south of Dunhuang, Stein and Chiang spent a rare relaxing day. The pagoda and temples on the southern fringe of the lake, a quarter of a mile long, were filled with a mix of Buddhist and Daoist statues and murals. The offerings within were recent, but the annual pilgrimage to the caves meant the pious were elsewhere. No one was around to disturb their tranquil respite. The lake so enchanted Stein as he sat beside it writing to Allen that he volunteered he might choose it as the site of his own grave. "There could be no more appropriate place of rest for a desert wanderer than this charming little Tirtha [pilgrimage place] enclosed all round by sand ridges up to 300 ft in height."

If the sight prompted reflections on mortality in Stein, it prompted acts of levity in his assistant. Stein watched in amusement as Chiang slid down one of the dunes. It was, he told Stein, to test the local lore that the dunes could be made to produce miraculous music. In his dainty velvet boots, Chiang slowly ascended his chosen dune. With each step, the powdery sand gave way, but finally Chiang reached the summit, turned around and began his descent. As he skittered down the dune, both men heard a "sound like that of distant carts rumbling," satisfying them that the legend was based on fact. The Ming Sha dunes had earned their name: the Singing Sands. Chiang shared with Stein a local folk tale he had gleaned, that after the annual pilgrimage, the gods would send a violent dust storm to cleanse the sacred caves. Given that buran season was approaching, Stein felt the prediction of a "divine sweeping" was almost certain to come true.

After nearly a year in each other's company, a strong friendship had developed between the two men. Not only had Chiang adapted to the wandering life, he had developed a keen interest in the finds being uncovered, and he kept his ear to the ground for folk tales and far more besides. "My brave [Chiang] is an excellent diplomat and why I am even more grateful for an indefatigable worker," Stein told Allen. "It is great comfort to have a gentleman by one's side & one ever cheerful." As Stein sat by Crescent Lake on that idyllic spring day, penning lines to his dear friend in England, thanking good fortune for his Chinese comrade—and amused by his moment of sand-sliding whimsy—Stein could not know just how crucial a role Chiang was about to play.

꩜

The predicted sandstorm swept through the oasis the night before Stein moved his caravan out to the caves. He was up by 5:30 a.m. but delays conspired to keep him from getting underway until almost midday. The trip was slow in the storm's hazy aftermath, and a camel stumbled into a canal, soaking the Naik's baggage. But after five hours the men, camels, and baggage reached the silent valley in the late afternoon of May 21, 1907. The annual pilgrimage was over, and the caves had resumed their sleepy, decayed air and were deserted except for a fat jolly red-robed Tibetan lama.

Word had been sent ahead to Wang that Stein was arriving, and the abbot had been convinced to delay another begging tour planned for after the festival. But as Stein pitched his tent in the shade of some fruit trees away from the rest of his party, Wang was nowhere to be seen. Chiang found a room near the feet of a three-story Buddha, and the others took shelter in some tumbledown buildings. Soldiers from Dunhuang, sent to keep an eye on Stein, also found quarters nearby. The Naik set up a makeshift darkroom. Stein had abandoned any prospect of removing murals or statues. He quite simply could not get away with it. Photographing the artworks was the most he could hope for. But his real goal was to get access to the hidden manuscripts. He would need time and stealth to succeed. As he moved toward that goal like a hunter pursuing his quarry, photography and study provided the cover he needed to spend time at the caves.

When Wang eventually arrived to welcome his foreign visitor, Stein's first impression of the man on which everything depended was not reassuring: "He looked a very queer person, extremely shy and nervous, with an occasional expression of cunning which was far from encouraging. It was clear from the first that he would be a difficult person to handle," Stein wrote.

And so began a game of chess between the two, but one in which we know the strategy of only one player. Stein began work the next morning, conveniently photographing near the cave where the manuscripts were hidden. His spirits sank as he glanced in its direction. The cave niche, which had been locked with a rough wooden door when he first saw it in March, was now completely bricked up. Why? Was it to prevent his inquisitive eyes getting even a glimpse of the treasures inside? He didn't know, but feared the worst.

Stein's first objective was to see inside the cave. Only then could he assess what it contained and the possible age of the documents. He sent Chiang to the abbot's quarters in one of the restored cave temples to smooth a path. The ever-patient Chiang spent hours in delicate negotiations while inhaling the stifling air of the priest's smoke-filled cave-kitchen. Initially Chiang seemed to make progress. As he dropped hints about making a generous donation to the shrine, Wang in turn acknowledged why the cave had been bricked up. It was a precaution against the curiosity of the thousands of pilgrims who attended the festival. Clearly Wang took seriously his role of guardian. Chiang also learned that although authorities in the provincial capital of Lanzhou were aware of the cave's scrolls, no detailed inventory had been made.

But Wang was not about to let Stein into the cave. At best, he might allow Stein to see a few of its manuscripts, but only those he could easily lay his hands on. Chiang was encouraged by this glimmer of hope. So much so he then overstepped his mark and his mission. For Chiang cautiously suggested that Stein might want to acquire one or two manuscripts "for further study." It was a wrong move. Wang was so unsettled by the idea—overcome by religious scruples and a terror of being found out—that Chiang promptly dropped the topic. When Chiang left the smoky cave it was without the promise Stein so keenly wanted. Stein listened as Chiang recounted what had transpired and realized that achieving his goal would be even more difficult than anticipated. Clearly Wang would not easily be persuaded by a few pieces of silver. "To rely on the temptation of money alone as a means of overcoming his scruples was manifestly useless," Stein wrote.

He needed a different approach. He decided to pay Wang a visit that afternoon, taking Chiang along to interpret. Stein knew Wang's great joy was the large restored temple, so he asked if Wang might show him through it. Naturally, the abbot was delighted. Wang took him past the newly gilded and painted woodwork at the entrance and along a twenty-four-foot passage. On the right of the painted passageway was the antechamber where Wang had uncovered the hidden library. Stein shot a longing glance at the newly bricked-up wall that barred the way to the niche he longed to enter. "[But] this was not the time to ask questions of my pious guide as to what was being guarded in that mysterious recess," he acknowledged.

The passageway opened onto a large decorated chapel, fifty-four feet by forty-six feet, with a raised altar. Stein was appalled at the gaudy sight before him. "There rose on a horseshoe-shaped dais, ancient but replastered, a collection of brand-new clay images of colossal size, more hideous, I thought, than any I had seen in these caves." The workmanship looked all the more clumsy beside the original murals that covered the chapel's walls and ceiling. Repelled as Stein was by the new statues, he could not deny the abbot's sincerity and tenacity. Wang had overseen the removal of a ten-foot-high mound of drift sand and rubble from the cave's entrance, and he had commissioned new artworks as money from his endless begging tours permitted. "I could not help feeling something akin to respect for the queer little figure by my side," Stein wrote. "It was clear from the way in which he lived with his two humble acolytes, and from all that Chiang had heard about him at Tun-huang, that he spent next to nothing on his person or private interests."

Perhaps Stein sensed a kindred spirit, despite their vast differences in culture and learning. They were solitary wanderers, single-minded and determined about what they saw as their life's work. Both were indifferent to material comfort but struggled constantly for the money to undertake their work: Wang to restore and protect his caves, Stein to mount his expeditions in a quest to understand the past.

Stein wondered how to further gain Wang's confidence. The abbot was poorly educated. There was no point rattling on about lofty antiquarian interests or arguing about the value of first-hand study of ancient objects. Such topics might appeal to the erudite Chinese officials he met, but they would do little to persuade Wang. Maybe he should drop the name of his patron saint, Xuanzang, a much-loved figure among the Chinese he had met? As he stood before the gaudy Buddhist images, Stein told Wang of his devotion to the Chinese pilgrim. And he drew some not terribly subtle parallels. Like the saintly Buddhist pilgrim, Stein had made a difficult journey from India to China across rugged mountains and waterless deserts. He had followed in Xuanzang's footsteps, stopping at many of the very shrines and ruined places the pilgrim visited so long ago.

Stein could see from the glint in the shy abbot's eyes that his words made an instant impression. Although the Daoist abbot was poorly versed in Buddhism, he too was devoted to Xuanzang. So much so that he took Stein from the cave to look more closely at the loggia, or terrace, he had built just outside. On its walls were paintings Wang had commissioned of mythical scenes from Xuanzang's life. Wang proudly showed him the saintly pilgrim being snatched to the clouds by a demon, then restored to earth by the prayers of his animal-headed companions. In another painting, the pilgrim forced a dragon to surrender a horse it had swallowed. They were apocryphal images that in popular imagination had transformed the intrepid and scholarly pilgrim into a "saintly Munchausen," as Stein called him. Through Chiang, Wang excitedly related the stories behind the pictures as Stein listened attentively, knowing none of them had any basis in fact.

Before one scene in particular Stein displayed great interest—and not just because it was one that did have a basis in truth. It was an image Stein realized might help advance his own case. The painting showed Xuanzang on the bank of a raging river, his horse loaded with bundles of manuscripts. A large turtle swam toward the pilgrim to help carry the precious load across. It was a reference to the twenty pony-loads of books and relics Xuanzang brought back from India to China. "Would the pious guardian read this obvious lesson aright, and be willing to acquire spiritual merit by letting me take back to the old home of Buddhism some of the ancient manuscripts which chance had placed in his keeping?" Stein decided not to press the point just yet. Rather, he was content that a bond had been established between himself and the abbot.

He left Chiang behind with Wang to raise again the tricky question of borrowing some of the manuscripts the abbot had promised earlier in the day. But Wang would not commit to producing them. "There was nothing for me but to wait," Stein wrote.

8

Key to the Cave

Under cover of darkness, a figure quietly crept from the caves to Stein's tent beneath the fruit trees later that night. It was Chiang, and he was carrying a bundle of manuscripts. Wang, he whispered gleefully to Stein, had just paid him a secret visit. Hidden under the priest's flowing black robe had been the first of the promised scrolls. What they were, Chiang wasn't sure. But Stein could see that the paper they were made of was old, at least as old as the roll the helpful young monk had shown him on his first visit to the caves weeks earlier. The writing was Chinese and Chiang thought the documents might be Buddhist scriptures, but he needed time to study them. He returned to his quarters at the feet of the big Buddha and spent the night poring over them.

At daybreak, he was back at Stein's tent, barely able to contain his excitement. Colophons, or inscriptions, on the rolls showed they were Chinese versions of Buddhist texts brought from India. Moreover, they were copies from translations by the great Xuanzang himself. It was an astonishing coincidence. Even the usually skeptical Chiang suggested that this was a most auspicious omen.

Auspicious and convenient. Chiang hastened to Wang to plant the seeds of this "quasi-divine" event. Had not the spirit of Xuanzang revealed the manuscript hoard to Wang ahead of the arrival from distant India of the pilgrim's devoted "disciple"—Stein? The untutored Wang could not possibly have known the connection these manuscripts had with Xuanzang when he selected them from among the thousands of scrolls and delivered them to Chiang the previous night. Surely this was proof that opening the cave would have Xuanzang's blessing.

All morning, Stein kept away from Wang and the Library Cave, busying himself with photographing elsewhere. But when Chiang returned a few hours later with news that Wang had unbricked the cave's door, Stein could wait no longer. No one was about on that hot cloudless day. Even the soldiers who had tailed him all morning had disappeared for an opium-induced siesta as Stein made his way to the cave. There he found a nervous Wang. With Stein beside him, Wang opened the rough door that lay behind the dismantled wall. Stein looked on in wonder: "The sight of the small room disclosed was one to make my eyes open wide. Heaped up in layers, but without any order, there appeared in the dim light of the priest's little lamp a solid mass of manuscript bundles rising to a height of nearly ten feet."

He was looking at one of the great archaeological finds of all time.

ꙮ

There was barely room for two people to stand in the tiny room, about nine feet by nine feet, and certainly no space to unroll or examine the stacked bundles. Much as Stein wanted to remove every scroll from the cramped niche to a large painted temple where he could readily study them, he knew Wang would not agree. Wang feared the consequences if a foreigner was spied examining the contents of the cave he had been ordered to keep sealed. He could lose his position and patrons if rumors spread around the oasis. He was not going to jeopardize all he had worked for. Even in the quietest times, pilgrims occasionally visited the caves to light incense, ring a bell, and pay homage before the Buddha. But the abbot did agree to remove one or two bundles at a time and allow Stein a quick look. He also agreed to let Stein use a small restored cave chapel nearby that had been fitted with a door and paper windows. Screened from prying eyes, Stein set up what he called his "reading room."

As Wang busied himself inside the Library Cave, Stein looked for any hint of when it had been sealed and a clue therefore to the age of the manuscripts hidden within. Two features drew his attention: a slab of black marble and a mural of bodhisattvas. The three-foot-wide block was originally inside the cave, but Wang had moved it to the passageway outside. It was inscribed to the memory of a monk named Hong Bian with a date corresponding to the middle of the ninth century. This suggested the cave could not have been sealed before then. On the passageway wall were the remains of the mural—a row of saintly bodhisattvas carrying offerings of divine food—that helped conceal the entrance to the Library Cave. Fortunately Wang's restorations had not extended to these figures. To Stein, hungry for clues, they provided more earthly nourishment. Their style suggested they were painted no later than the thirteenth century. So somewhere between the ninth century and the thirteenth, the cave had been filled, then sealed. If his deduction was right, whatever was inside the cave would be very old indeed.

Bet. 800 – 1200 AD cave was sealed

☙

Stein at first believed the cave had been filled in great confusion, and from this he formed a theory about why it was concealed. "There can be little doubt that the fear of some destructive invasion had prompted the act," he wrote. But he also found evidence for a conflicting theory: that the cave was no more than a storehouse for sacred material. He noted bags carefully packed with fragments of sacred writings and paintings. "Such insignificant relics would certainly not have been collected and sewn up systematically in the commotion of a sudden emergency."

Scholars agree the cave was plastered shut around the beginning of the eleventh century, but the reasons why remain unclear. The cave's guardians may have feared Islamic invaders from the west. The sword of Islam had already conquered Dunhuang's ally, Khotan, in 1006. Invaders did come from the north, but these were Tanguts who, as Buddhists themselves, seem an unlikely threat to Buddhist scriptures.

But there is also support for Stein's other thesis, that the cave was a storeroom or tomb for material no longer needed by local monasteries. The printed Diamond Sutra, for example, showed signs of damage and repeated repair and may simply have been judged to have reached the end of its useful life. Buddhists did not simply throw away sacred material. They buried it reverentially. Even today Buddhism has rites surrounding the disposal of spiritual writings.

The cave does not appear to have been sealed ahead of an unrecorded exodus from the sacred complex. Nearby Dunhuang was still a bustling oasis when the cave was hidden. The area had a population of about 20,000, including about 1,000 monks and nuns in more than a dozen monasteries. The caves too were thriving, with some of their most beautiful chapels still to be created. Indeed the caves continued to thrive after the arrival of Genghis Khan in the thirteenth century. Although the Mongol chief ransacked Dunhuang, he not only left the caves undamaged, his rule saw new ones commissioned. The caves were still flourishing 300 years after the Library Cave was sealed. The last cave is believed to have been painted in 1357, just before the start of the Ming dynasty. Soon after, the Silk Road was abandoned, and the Caves of the Thousand Buddhas sank into a long decline.

Whatever the reason for its sealing, the Library Cave—or Cave 17 as it is prosaically known today—wasn't always used to house manuscripts. It was initially a memorial chapel for the monk whose name was on the marble slab, Hong Bian, who died around the time the Diamond Sutra was being printed. He was an important monk—so important he had the right to wear the highly prestigious color purple. A statue of him, seated in meditation posture, was initially installed in the cave. It was placed against a wall behind which was painted a decorative scene including two attendants—one holding a staff, the other holding a fan—and a pair of trees from which hang his pilgrim's bag and water bottle. The statue was removed when the cave was filled with scrolls and has since been found to contain traces of purple silk. When and why the cave changed from being a memorial chapel to housing the scrolls remains a mystery.

✂

As Wang brought the first of the bundles to Stein's "reading room," the explorer's excitement mounted. They were Chinese sutras, neatly rolled, about a foot high and some more than thirty feet long. The thick paper rolls, enclosed in protective cotton wrappers, even retained their yellow dye despite signs of having been much handled. The strong paper was astonishingly well preserved. Other scrolls had lost their wrappers and were fastened with rough cords, but even these were undamaged. The dry desert air, the darkness within the cave and even the insulating sand had all combined to provide a perfect tomb in which they had lain undisturbed for centuries.

"No place could have been better adapted for preserving such relics than a chamber carved in the live rock of these absolutely barren hills and completely shut off from any moisture that the atmosphere of this desert valley ever contained," Stein wrote. "Enclosed by thick rock everywhere, except for the narrow walled-up entrance, and that, too, covered up by drift-sand for centuries, the air within the small chapel could have undergone but slight changes of temperature. Not in the driest soil could the relics of a ruined site have been so completely protected from injury as they had been here."

With the documents finally in their hands, exactly what they were looking at was hard to say. Chiang had no understanding of Buddhist literature and Stein, to his immense frustration and regret, could not read Chinese. Not that they had time for more than a cursory look. Chiang's attempt to make a rough list of the findings was soon abandoned as Wang, having overcome his initial reluctance, began dragging out bundle after bundle from the cave. "It would have required a whole staff of learned scribes to deal properly with such a deluge," Stein wrote. As Wang clambered across the cave's mountain of documents to remove bundles, Stein feared the priest would be buried under an avalanche of tumbling manuscripts.

Each bundle contained about ten rolls, mostly Chinese scrolls. But there were also documents in Tibetan, Sanskrit, Uyghur, and Sogdian. Soon Wang began hauling not just paper scrolls but delicate paintings on silk and linen. He brought huge silk banners of graceful Buddhas and bodhisattvas that appeared to have once hung from temple entrances. To Stein's surprise, Wang apparently attached little value to the exquisite silks. The abbot had even used some of them as padding to level the floor of the cave. Wang kept bringing more and more bundles of the painted silks and other written material. Stein suspected they were a smokescreen to divert his attention from the sacred Chinese sutras.

By the end of the first day, Stein set aside the most promising manuscripts and paintings for what he euphemistically called "further study." These were the rolls he desperately wanted to acquire. Wang had already given away some manuscripts to curry favor with local officials. Stein feared the rest of the precious hoard would similarly dribble away and be lost to scholarship forever.

It was almost dark when Stein and Chiang emerged from the makeshift reading room with Wang. The three tired men stood on the loggia with its image of Xuanzang bringing sacred manuscripts from India. This was not the time to raise directly the question of selling the hoard, but there could be no more ideal backdrop for Stein to drop hints that would subtly reinforce the omens. He again invoked Xuanzang, whose guidance had surely led him to this magnificent hidden store of sacred relics—some of which may even have been the result of the ancient pilgrim's journey—within a temple tended by so devoted an admirer.

Chiang remained behind with Wang to press the point. Surely continued confinement in a sealed cave was not the reason the great Xuanzang had led the abbot—and Stein—to this precious Buddhist lore, Chiang argued. And given that Wang could not study the works himself, it would be an act of great religious merit to allow Stein, Xuanzang's great devotee, to make them available for the benefit of Buddhist scholars in that great "temple of learning in Ta-Ying-kuo"—England. And, Chiang hinted, it would be an act of merit that would be supported by a generous donation of silver to assist his restorations.

Chiang's powers of persuasion worked more quickly than he or Stein had dared hope. Around midnight, when Stein was about to retire to bed, he again heard footsteps outside his tent. Again it was Chiang, who had come to ensure the coast was clear. He returned a short time later carrying all the bundles Stein had set aside earlier in the day. Wang had agreed to allow the removal of the material—provided no one other than the three men knew. While Stein was on Chinese soil, he must not breathe a word about their dealings. This was hardly an onerous condition for a man such as Stein, who by nature kept his own counsel. And it was in his own interest; he might want to acquire more manuscripts.

The abbot could not risk being seen outside his quarters at night, so Chiang offered to fetch the material. For the next seven nights, Chiang's slight figure crept along the river bank to Stein's camp. He struggled under the weight of increasingly heavy loads made up of the most promising bundles set aside each day in the reading room. The days were spent hastily examining scrolls and silks. Stein was elated and oppressed by the volume of material that kept emerging from what he termed the "black hole," constantly anxious that Wang might change his mind.

Should we have time to eat our way through this mountain of ancient paper with any thoroughness? Would not the timorous priest, swayed by his worldly fears and possible spiritual scruples, be moved to close down his shell before I had been able to extract any of the pearls? There were reasons urging us to work with all possible energy and speed, and others rendering it advisable to display studied insouciance and calm assurance.

He could rarely do more than glimpse at what he called this "embarras des richesses." But somewhere among the cave's vast contents was a well-preserved scroll, fully intact with an elaborate image of a disciple kneeling before the Buddha. Unlike most of the other documents, this wasn't handwritten but had been printed with a block of wood. Unfurled, it spanned nearly sixteen and a half feet and contained a Chinese date equating to 868. It was the Diamond Sutra, the world's earliest dated printed book.

✺

Strolls at dusk up the valley with Dash trotting alongside were Stein's only relief from full days in the reading room that segued into long evenings writing up notes, letters, reports—and awaiting the late-night arrival of Chiang and the manuscripts. On his return from one such evening walk Stein was overjoyed to discover Turdi, the *dak* runner, had arrived with two huge bags of mail, having made another epic journey: 1,400 miles from Khotan in thirty-nine days. It was the first mail Stein had received since February. Although some of the letters from Europe were already five months old, he sat up until after midnight poring over 170 letters. He was quick to write back to Allen to tell him of his "harvest, rich beyond expectations," but urged him to keep the news to Stein's inner circle. Even amid what would be the greatest success of his life, he had pragmatic worries and was mindful that he lacked the money to ensure his continued explorations. Like Wang, he would have to continue to rattle the begging bowl. "Independence, the only protection against needless struggles & bureaucratic wisdom, is still far off; for I cannot claim a pension until 8 years hence (even allowing for furlough) and not until about the same date can I hope for my savings to increase sufficiently to assure to me that freedom for travel etc, which I am eager to enjoy still while life lasts."

Thrilling as the days were, the work was exhausting. The long hours, his anxieties about Abbot Wang and a recurrent bout of malaria were taking their toll. He confided to his diary: "Very tired with low fever."

ﯼ

A week later, Stein's heart sank when he arrived early one morning at his reading room. The scrolls had vanished. Just when he had finally convinced Wang to empty the Library Cave, the rolls, which had been carefully piled outside the cave, had disappeared overnight. Chiang had not carried them away in the night, so what had happened? The answer, he soon learned, was that Wang had shifted them back into their "gloomy prison of centuries."

Perhaps Stein should not have been surprised. Wang had appeared increasingly nervous during the previous couple of days, not least over the possible loss of the Chinese sutras. Relations had become strained, even as the tricky question of the size of the "donation" to the temple became more pressing. Wang had been allowed little opportunity to think as he had emptied the cave over the past week. "He had already been gradually led from one concession to another, and we took care not to leave him much time for reflection," Stein wrote.

To the explorer, it seemed Wang had been overcome by scruples and baulked. Stein described the abbot's mood as "sullen" when he encountered him that morning. All of this may well be true, but only Stein's version of the events survives. Given the timing of the priest's behavior, he might not have been as naive and credulous as Stein portrays him. Wang's action came at a crucial stage. A couple of days earlier, the priest had raised the issue of money and seemed keen to resolve the matter. But then Stein deliberately strung out the negotiations so he could see the entire contents of the emptied cave. It may be that Wang recognized Stein's delay for what it was and opted to force a resolution. If so, Wang was far more adept at negotiating than Stein realized. With the glittering prize seemingly within the explorer's grasp, he found it snatched away. It is easy to imagine the effect of such a move: it would increase the treasure's desirability, elevate anxiety about losing it forever and possibly raise the price. They are tactics familiar to any experienced negotiator. The natural response would be to close the deal as soon as possible.

Which appears to be exactly what happened. Within hours of Stein discovering the scrolls had been locked away, he and Wang agreed on a price and on what Stein could take. Wang felt sufficiently satisfied with the deal that he not only let Stein take all the material previously removed to his camp, but also agreed to part with further bundles of Chinese and Tibetan rolls. "Transaction settled by 11:30 a.m. to mutual satisfaction," Stein noted in his diary on May 29, 1907.

He would not give Wang time to change his mind. The extra rolls needed to be moved quickly and the job was too big for Chiang alone. Stein conscripted two of his most trusted men, Ibrahim Beg and pony man Tila Bai, to undertake the nightly trip to the caves. They transferred scrolls and silks by the sackful from the temple to Stein's camp.

The deal done, Wang was eager to resume the begging tour he had delayed when Stein arrived at the caves. Nervous, but relieved to have completed the difficult negotiation, Wang left for Dunhuang. He may have wanted to ensure that no word of their transaction had spread among his patrons in the oasis. He returned to the caves a week later sufficiently confident that their secret was safe, and sold Stein additional manuscripts.

For four horseshoes of silver, Stein acquired treasures beyond his dreams. He knew they were a bargain: "I secured as much as he possibly dared to give,—& for a sum which will make our friends at the [British Museum] chuckle," he wrote candidly to his friend Fred Andrews, whom he also urged to secrecy. "It would be a mistake to let the news get about, & I must ask you & all other friends who may see this, for discretion." A pittance it may have been to Stein, but perhaps Wang chuckled too. He had obtained money to restore his beloved caves and he now knew he had a valuable resource, one he would tap as other foreigners arrived in the months and years that followed.

Much as Stein might have wished to empty the Library Cave of all its scrolls and silks, he knew if he left Dunhuang with such a vast amount of material, it would not go undetected. Questions were being asked about what he was up to during his long visit at the Caves of the Thousand Buddhas. It is one reason why Stein commissioned a clay statue of Xuanzang for a cave temple. A Dunhuang sculptor produced what Stein regarded as an "artistic eyesore," but the statue helped allay suspicions. Wang, who saw the statue as evidence of a shared reverence for their mutual patron saint, was at pains to spread word of this commission during his trip into Dunhuang.

There were other reasons that would hasten Stein's departure. A diphtheria epidemic was rife in Dunhuang, and it came close enough to Stein and his men that a young local boy who kept a watch on his camp died of the illness. In addition, civil unrest over taxation was brewing in the oasis.

But his haul needed to be packed with great care and spirited away from Dunhuang without attracting attention. Stein knew that suddenly placing a large order for packing cases would cause alarm. Once again, he had thought ahead. Anticipating such a problem, he had bought some empty cases early on and secured others in discreet installments. He filled seven cases with manuscripts and a further five with paintings, embroideries, and other material. His camels were brought back from their grazing and five carts drawn by three horses each arrived from Dunhuang. On the morning of June 14 the caravan left the caves and he said farewell to Wang. "We parted in fullest amity," Stein wrote. It would not be his last dealing with the pious Abbot Wang.

You should know that all of the teachings I give to you are a raft.

VERSE 6, THE DIAMOND SUTRA

9

The Hidden Gem

Beneath a jeweled canopy in a leafy garden, the Buddha sits cross-legged on his lotus throne. Monks and bodhisattvas surround him. At his feet kneels an elderly barefoot disciple named Subhuti, his black slippers neatly beside him on a prayer mat. Subhuti's palms are together in supplication and he directs a reverential gaze toward the Enlightened One in a quest for answers to life's greatest questions. That image forms the frontispiece of the Diamond Sutra discovered in the Library Cave. At the opposite end of the scroll is the answer to a different question: how do we know the age of this singular document? There, a brief note reveals the answer: on the thirteenth day of the fourth moon of the ninth year of the Xiantong era. On the Chinese calendar, this corresponds to May 11, 868. It is this colophon which has established the Diamond Sutra's unique claim: that this complete scroll is the oldest dated printed book in the world. It was created 600 years before Gutenberg got ink on his fingers. And it was made of a material—paper—that in 868 was unknown in the West.

The scroll is sixteen feet five inches long and eleven inches high, and explicitly says it was produced to be given away for free. It is woodblock printed, so it is possible hundreds of copies were made, although this is the only one known to have survived. As well as the date, the colophon tells who commissioned the sutra and why. It reads: "Reverently made for universal distribution by Wang Jie on behalf of his two parents." Who this devoted son was, no one knows. He was probably wealthy to have commissioned the creation of a scroll with such an intricate frontispiece. But we do know he had it made as an act of merit, a good deed.

Between the ends of the famous scroll is one of Buddhism's most popular and revered teachings. It begins, as sutras typically do, with the phrase "thus I have heard." These are the words of the disciple Ananda, who is said to have memorized the Buddha's every teaching. The sutra then tells the circumstances in which the sermon was delivered. It relates how one morning, before noon, the Buddha put on his monk's robe, picked up his bowl and went into the nearby city of Sravasti to beg from house to house for his food.

The Buddha returned to the Jetavana Vihara where he lived with 1,250 monks. The Buddha ate the food he had been given, put away his bowl, washed his feet and sat down. A number of monks approached him and sat at his side. Among them was the Venerable Subhuti, and the sutra unfolds as a dialogue between the two. Subhuti is said to have been the nephew of Sudatta, the wealthy layman who covered Prince Jeta's park with gold to create the garden in which they sat. Although an intelligent young man, Subhuti had a temper so furious he was shunned by those who knew him. He cursed humans and animals alike. Even the Buddha is said to have told him that his short temper was written on his face. After hearing the Buddha's teachings, Subhuti was transformed; he developed a calm mind and became a prominent disciple.

In the sutra, Subhuti asks the Buddha questions about the practice of generosity, about enlightenment, and about how to be rid of attachment, the cause of all suffering. Subhuti wants to know whether, 500 years on, anyone will understand and practice the Buddha's teachings and is reassured they will. On contemplating the answers the Buddha gives him, Subhuti is moved to tears. Subhuti also asks what this teaching should be called. This is often translated as the Diamond Cutter or the Diamond That Cuts Through Illusion. The Buddha, too, asks questions of Subhuti that test how well his disciple has understood their conversation.

The Buddha is said to have first taught the Diamond Sutra toward the end of his life, and it is considered a distillation of earlier teachings. At its core, the sutra is about the nature of reality, how things actually exist. Nothing is what it seems, he says. When stripped of our illusions, we realize everything, including ourselves, is constantly changing and that nothing exists independently. When we look at a book, for example, we typically think it has never been anything else. But a book, even one as enduring as Stein's copy of the Diamond Sutra, was once just blank paper. Before then, it was a tree, a sapling, and a tiny seed that fell from another tree and so on. The implications of seeing the world in this way are far-reaching. The failure to do so leads ultimately to suffering.

The sutra concludes with a poetic verse that summarizes this.

Thus shall you think of this fleeting world:
A star at dawn, a bubble in a stream,
A flash of lightning in a summer cloud,
A flickering lamp, a phantom, and a dream.

ꫧ

It seems ironic that a work which deals with impermanence and life's fleeting illusions is the world's oldest known printed book. The Diamond Sutra is a puzzling and often paradoxical teaching.

Nonetheless, it is one of the most reproduced in the Buddhist canon. The illustrated scroll was not the only copy of the Diamond Sutra in the Library Cave. Aurel Stein removed more than 500. Of these, only twenty-one were complete and just thirteen were dated.

Devoted son Wang Jie commissioned his Diamond Sutra as a good deed, or act of merit, on behalf of his mother and father. Acts of merit were, and still are, central to Buddhism and help explain why the religion played such a vital role in the development of printing. The more merit one creates, the better one's rebirth and the swifter one's path to enlightenment. So Wang Jie's act, which harnessed the technology of printing to spread the Buddha's teaching, could accumulate merit for his parents at a rate previously inconceivable.

A clue to why Wang Jie may have chosen the Diamond Sutra from the thousands of possible scriptures lies in the text itself. The sutra says one of the best ways to create merit is by copying it. The spiritual reward for doing so, it advises, is far greater even than countless acts of self-sacrifice.

The Diamond Sutra, known in Sanskrit as the *Vajracchedika Prajnaparamita,* is not the only sutra to advocate its own reproduction. The Diamond Sutra belongs to the Perfection of Wisdom, or *Prajnaparamita,* genre of sutras. These are the cornerstone of Mahayana Buddhism. According to legend, these sutras were entrusted from the time of the Buddha to fearsome water snakes, the Nagas. They delivered them to Nagarjuna, the great Indian teacher and one-time abbot of Nalanda. All of the Perfection of Wisdom sutras advocate propagating Buddhist teachings and the books that contain them. (This is the antithesis of India's earlier sacred tradition, Hinduism. Long after the introduction of writing, it was forbidden to write down its ancient scriptures, the Vedas, and anyone who did so would be condemned to hell.) As one of the shortest Buddhist sutras,

Aurel Stein takes tea in Lahore in the 1890s. There, his eyes were opened to early Buddhist art in the city's "Wonder House."

Stein's desk at his summer camp Mohand Marg, in 1905, with Dash the Great, shortly before the explorer left Kashmir for his second Turkestan expedition.

The ever-watchful British consul and family in Chini Bagh's garden, Kashgar, circa 1913. Catherine Macartney, seated, with children Sylvia and Eric. George Macartney, rear, holds son Robin. © The British Library Board

Chiang, Stein's Chinese secretary, translator and friend on his desert travels. Hiring Chiang was one of the wisest decisions Stein made.

© The British Library Board

Stein and his core team in front of a tamarisk cone. From left: Ibrahim Beg, Chiang, Stein with Dash the Great, cook Jasvant Singh, surveyor Lal Singh and handyman Naik Ram Singh. © The British Library Board

Hassan Akhun, head camel man. His thirst for adventure made up for an explosive temper. © The British Library Board

Turdi, the *dak* runner, who made a perilous journey into the desert to deliver Stein's mail. © The British Library Board

Wall painting of a winged angel found at Miran. The Western appearance of the image inside a Buddhist sanctuary suggests travelers from afar visited the oasis.

© The British Library Board

Abbot Wang, custodian of the Caves of the Thousand Buddhas from whom Stein obtained the Diamond Sutra and other treasures. The Daoist monk is buried at the caves. © The British Library Board

Scrolls stacked outside the entrance to Cave 17, the hidden Library Cave in which they were discovered. (The scrolls were added by double exposure after Stein returned to London.)
© The British Library Board

Frontispiece of the Diamond Sutra, the world's oldest printed dated book, depicts the Buddha delivering his teaching to devotees. © The British Library Board

A detail from the Sutra of the Ten Kings, found in the Library Cave, depicts the Chinese Buddhist version of Judgment Day. © The British Library Board

Frenchman Paul Pelliot, Stein's rival, spent three weeks studying scrolls and other material that remained in Cave 17 in March 1908. Réunion des Musées Nationaux/Art Resource, NY

Stein's caravan crosses the Taklamakan Desert's ocean of sand in February 1908. © The British Library Board

Stein's laborers find the Keriya River after almost dying of thirst along the perilous Thieves' Road. © The British Library Board

The crumbling facades of the Caves of the Thousand Buddhas, near Dunhuang as Stein found them in 1907. The honeycombed grottoes reminded him of troglodyte dwellings.

Secret tunnel at the National Library of Wales in Aberystwyth where the Diamond Sutra and Stein's other valuable scrolls were hidden during World War II.

Entrance to the Caves of the Thousand Buddhas. Today more than 650,000 people arrive each year to see the once-deserted caves.

copying the Diamond Sutra had great appeal—as the number of copies in the Library Cave attests.

The creation of merit is a motivating force in Buddhism. Merit can be created in many ways, such as by not killing, stealing or lying. It can be generated through propagating the Buddha's image (as in the Caves of the Thousand Buddhas). It can also be generated by the transmission of the Buddha's words. Moreover, the Diamond Sutra promises that memorizing even just four lines of its text will produce "incalculable" benefit. But, most importantly for printing, it can also be achieved through copying a sutra.

The woodblock-printed Diamond Sutra may have belonged to one of more than a dozen monasteries in Dunhuang where it could be unrolled for study or recited by chanting monks. But it is unlikely to have been made in the oasis. Although Dunhuang was a place of spiritual knowledge and learning, it was not a center for printing. It is more probable that the scroll was made in faraway Sichuan, a cradle of the woodblock printing industry. But if this was the case, the circumstances of its 1,200-mile journey northwest to the Caves of the Thousand Buddhas remain unknown, although monasteries often acquired important scriptures for their libraries.

Skilled artists, calligraphers, and woodblock cutters, probably lay artisans rather than monks, created the scroll. It was made in seven sections, each sheet eleven inches tall by thirty inches wide (except for the narrower frontispiece). First, the text and illustration of the Buddha were painted with ink on pieces of thin paper. These were pasted face down on blocks of wood, then rubbed to transfer the image. The wood carver carefully cut away the uninked parts, leaving a mirror image in relief. The finished blocks were inked and sheets of paper were pressed against them. Finally, the sheets were pasted together to make a handscroll.

The scroll was printed on strong paper made from the bark of the paper mulberry tree. The paper was dyed yellow, a color sacred to Buddhism, but its purpose was more than simply auspicious or decorative; it contained an insecticide.

The Diamond Sutra's frontispiece is also the earliest known woodcut illustration in the world. The illustration is rich in detail and symbolism. The faces of the shaven-headed monks who surround the Buddha are drawn with such skill as to create individual portraits, some stern and mature with wrinkled brows, others youthful and open-faced. Two lions near the Buddha's feet look rather more benevolent than the two wrathful protectors who flank him. Above his head are two apsaras, or angels, carrying offerings of food. On the Buddha's chest is carved a swastika, a symbol which, long before it was appropriated by the Third Reich, was associated with good fortune. The lotus on which he sits is a Buddhist symbol of enlightenment—a plant that grows in mud but flowers into a magnificent blossom.

Aside from the benefits of merit, the printed book had practical advantages over hand copying. It was faster and cheaper to reproduce. A short handwritten scroll might take a scribe two days to complete. Woodblocks took longer to carve but, once completed, more than a thousand pages a day could be printed. They also avoided the errors a copyist might make, which was particularly important with sacred texts; great effort was made to ensure that texts were accurately copied. The blocks were carved from the close-grained hard wood of fruit trees, such as pear or apple.

The raw material was cheap. Blocks, which sometimes lasted hundreds of years, could be reused and woodblock carvers needed just a few simple tools. As printing advanced, color was introduced using multiple woodblocks. And here too a copy of the Diamond Sutra plays a starring role as the oldest surviving example of two-color paper printing. It was printed in black and red—with an illustration of a scribe at his desk—in the year 1341 at the Zifu Temple in Hubei province.

The Diamond Sutra of 868 was the product of a mature, sophisticated printing industry. Nothing like it existed in Europe. When the scroll was printed, the Vikings were raiding England, King Alfred was burning his mythical cakes and Emperor Charlemagne's reign had just ended. Although Celtic monks had by then created the magnificent Book of Kells, a high point of Western illuminated manuscripts, no one was printing from woodblocks. The technique did not develop in Europe until more than five centuries later. The earliest woodblock-printed European work is an image of St. Christopher dated 1423, now in the John Rylands Library in Manchester, England.

A century after Wang Jie commissioned his meritorious book, one of the most ambitious printing projects ever attempted was underway in China: the printing of the entire canon of Buddhist scriptures. The task took more than a decade, and while the Dunhuang Diamond Sutra required the carving of just seven woodblocks, this project required 130,000 blocks and a vast storehouse in which to keep them. By then, printing was widespread in China.

Although some of the documents Stein found at Dunhuang were written on palm leaves brought from India, most were on paper. China's invention of paper has been attributed to a court eunuch named Cai Lun in AD 105. All the paper documents in the cave were made when the material was still unknown in the West. Paper-making belatedly made its way to Europe a thousand years later, arriving in the twelfth century via Arabs who had learned the craft from the Chinese. Before then, European scribes used parchment and vellum.

In China, paper was in demand for the production of Buddhist manuscripts. Paper scrolls soon proved an advance on earlier forms of written communication. Until the third or fourth century, "books" were written on wooden and bamboo strips which were stitched together and rolled up. Paper was cheaper to make and easier to manipulate than bundles of wooden strips. By the year 500, paper scrolls were widely used in Central Asia. But they were not the only form of books found in the Library Cave. Concertina or accordion-shaped books were discovered too. These had advantages over scrolls which, though they looked beautiful, could be unwieldy to unroll. And in Dunhuang, the longest scroll was ninety-nine feet. There were also pothis, oblong sheets held together by a loose thread and sandwiched between protective wooden slats. The form originated in India. The presence of pothis in the cave suggests once again just how ideas, including about how to make books, spread and evolved.

ॐ

Although the colophon on the block-printed Diamond Sutra reveals little about Wang Jie, other handwritten copies of this sutra found in the Library Cave are more forthcoming about who created them and why. They reveal details that are at times intriguing, amusing, and poignant. Merit resulting from the good deed of copying a sutra could be transferred to others—and not only to other humans. One of the most touching copies tells how a farmer commissioned a Diamond Sutra on behalf of his late, lamented plowing ox. In doing so, the farmer prays that "this ox may personally receive the merit therefrom, and be reborn in the Pure Land, never again come to life in the body of a domestic animal. May this be clearly ordained by the officers dispensing justice in the underworld, so that there may be no further enmity or quarrel [between the ox and its owner]." Exactly what caused such ill-feeling between the remorseful farmer and his ox is not revealed.

Some who commissioned copies of the Diamond Sutra did so not just for benefit in future lives but also for aid with pressing problems in this one. An official with an eye on career advancement vowed to have a sutra copied each month if he received a promotion and two a month if he was further upgraded. He had been unable to keep his promise for some time because war had meant paper and ink were unavailable, but at last the materials were at hand.

One woman, homesick and fed up with living in far-flung provincial Dunhuang in the seventh century, made a copy of the Diamond Sutra in the hope that she could soon leave the desert frontier region and return to the imperial capital. Perhaps she missed its floating pavilions and secluded gardens.

But miracles could happen, especially, it seemed, when the Diamond Sutra was involved. Documents found at Dunhuang and elsewhere recount supernatural tales, such as one about a recently deceased woman who found herself in hell because she ate meat in a monastery and killed a clam. For her sins, her body was pierced with seven knives. From beyond the grave, she instructed her sister to commission copies of the Diamond Sutra, and as each copy was completed, a knife was withdrawn until all her suffering ceased.

Such tales are rooted in a belief that the Diamond Sutra and other Buddhist texts have sacred, even magical powers. Buddhist sutras came to be worshipped as sacred objects, rather like relics. Respect for the written word existed in China long before Buddhism arrived—it was an element of Confucian teaching. China has long respected books not just for their content but for their calligraphy too. But the Buddhist veneration of the book as a religious object—what today is termed the cult of the book—was a new development. Offerings of flowers and incense were at times made before sutras. Over time, the veneration extended to places containing the words of the Buddha, a behavior explained by the Diamond Sutra, which says that wherever it is kept is a sacred place.

Overwhelmingly documents in the Library Cave were handwritten in ink—Stein found only twenty examples of woodblock printing. But among the 500 Diamond Sutras he removed were two in which the Buddha's words were inscribed with an unusual additive. To demonstrate their dedication and self-sacrifice, and perhaps to increase their merit, devotees supplemented the ink with their own blood. Both copies were written by the same elderly man. The colophon of one explains how in 906 the eighty-three-year-old pricked the middle finger of his left hand. He mixed his blood with "fragrant" ink and copied the Diamond Sutra for people with a "believing heart." A few months later he made another, adding a simple prayer asking only that if he died while copying the sutra he would pass quickly from this world. The old man wasn't the only copyist using blood. One prominent Dunhuang monk was said to have drawn enough blood during his fifty-nine years to write 283 scrolls.

Blood writing wasn't confined to Dunhuang or the Diamond Sutra. Nor was it just elderly men or monks who engaged in the practice. Women, laymen, farmers and even a prince undertook this extreme form of merit-making. The pious pricking of bodily parts continued for centuries across China. Devotees found a scriptural basis for the bloody practice, but it did not meet universal approval. Some frowned on it as superstitious nonsense. In the case of the elderly man, his blood writing may well have been a token gesture. The amount of his blood mixed with the ink has so far proved too small for tests to detect.

Unlike the eighty-three-year-old man, not everyone who copied a sutra did so as an act of piety. Some did so for a living. A Dunhuang document relates how one grumpy scribe simultaneously used his hand to copy scriptures and his mouth to issue a stream of profanities directed at grandmothers and grandfathers.

꘠

Although the woodblock-printed Diamond Sutra is recognized as the oldest printed dated book, two earlier examples of printing are known. Both are from Asia and, significantly, given the nexus between Buddhism and printing, both are Buddhist texts. One is a scroll found in a Korean monastery in 1966 which is believed to date from the turn of the eighth century. It came to light by accident when thieves dynamited a twenty-seven-foot stone pagoda within the Bulguksa Temple in South Korea. The blast woke the sleeping monks before the thieves could make off with the treasures encased inside. As the pagoda was repaired, a relic casket was found containing the scroll, twenty feet long by two and a half inches high, printed with a passage from a Buddhist text. The undated scroll, believed to have been printed between 704 and 751, is now in the National Museum of Korea.

Around the same time, a Japanese empress commissioned a project known as the One Million Pagoda Charms. In gratitude for the end of a civil war, she ordered that a million charms be printed with Buddhist verses, which were rolled and inserted into miniature wooden pagodas. These were distributed to monasteries in the old capital of Nara, including the Horyuji Temple, the only temple that still possesses a collection of them. Examples of the pagodas, which resemble wooden chess pieces, are also in the collections of the British Library, the Library of Congress in Washington, D.C., and the Kyoto National Museum in Japan. Two of the pagodas sold at a Christie's auction in New York in September 2009, one for US$7,500 and the other for US$18,750.

The fact that the charms were inserted in mini pagodas suggests the text was never meant to be read or recited. The act of copying was itself beneficial. This is a longstanding and widespread Buddhist practice. Xuanzang witnessed it in India and described how verses from sutras were inserted into little paste stupas. The practice of creating text that will never be read continues today, where even a humble hand-held Tibetan Buddhist prayer wheel picked up from a tourist stall in Kathmandu contains a tiny rolled paper prayer.

In the West, the development of printing has been hailed as a great turning point for mankind, ushering in the modern age, contributing to the Renaissance, the spread of literacy and helping transform the role of the church and state. Philosopher Francis Bacon famously regarded printing as one of the three discoveries that changed the world, along with gunpowder and the compass. All three are Chinese inventions. Although much of the credit for the printing revolution has been attributed to Johannes Gutenberg and the development of moveable type, even that technology was known in China as early as the eleventh century, using characters made of baked clay. Pieces of moveable type, made of wood, were even found in the Mogao Caves in 1989. They were in an ancient Uyghur alphabet and dated between 960 and 1127. Four pieces are on display in the museum in Xinjiang's capital, Urumqi. But moveable type proved impractical for Chinese script with its tens of thousands of characters.

As it had in China, religion helped drive printing in the West. Gutenberg printed his first Bible in Germany in the 1450s. Fifty years later, about twenty million books had been printed, consisting of up to 15,000 different texts. These were mostly sacred works. It is a remarkable figure, considering Europe's population was far smaller then and few people could read. Printing meant that, for the first time, ideas and information could be shared widely and cheaply. For that reason it was a dangerous technology with the potential for political and social upheaval. Theologian Martin Luther was quick to use the medium to spread dissent. He opposed the Roman Catholic Church's sale of indulgences, the little paper certificates that remitted the punishment of sins. His printed objections soon spread around Europe and helped trigger the Reformation. The age of the book had arrived.

The key that unlocked the Library Cave for Stein was the translator monk Xuanzang. His versions of Buddhist texts were among the first batch of scrolls allowed (albeit furtively) out of the caves, a discovery that proved astonishing to Abbot Wang and convenient for Stein. However, the printed Diamond Sutra was not the work of Xuanzang but of an even earlier monk named Kumarajiva, who translated the sutra from Sanskrit into Chinese around 402. Although Xuanzang is revered for his sixteen-year trek to India and back, Kumarajiva is the most highly regarded of China's four great translator monks. His free-flowing translations remain the most popular even today, partly because they go beyond Xuanzang's literal versions.

The Diamond Sutra, usually divided into thirty-two verses, has been translated many times into many languages. Six Chinese translations alone made between 402 and 703 survive. There were also early translations into Tibetan, Khotanese and Mongolian. But centuries passed before the words of the Diamond Sutra became known in the West. The first significant English translation, penned by a German scholar named Max Müller, appeared only in the 1890s, little more than a decade before Stein arrived in Dunhuang. It took more than half a century for the next major translation to appear when scholar Edward Conze, a Marxist turned Buddhist, published his translation in 1957. In recent years, translations of the Diamond Sutra have gathered pace, including versions by prominent Vietnamese author and monk Thich Nhat Hanh, Western Tibetan Buddhist monk George Churinoff and American writer Red Pine (Bill Porter).

The Diamond Sutra is one of the most revered texts in Buddhism. It was among the most popular sutras in China during the Tang dynasty, the era when Wang Jie commissioned his scroll. Its enduring popularity is in part because of its brevity—it can be recited in forty minutes. It is shorter than the Lotus Sutra but longer than the Heart Sutra, two other popular and influential texts.

Some sutras can take hours, or even days, to recite. The Diamond Sutra has a special place among Zen Buddhists (known as Chan Buddhists in China) whose founding father, Huineng, is said to have achieved enlightenment when as a poor, illiterate youth he overheard a man reciting it.

꙳

In the Diamond Sutra, the Buddha acknowledges that those who study the text can expect to be disparaged and held in contempt. The Buddha encourages forbearance and persistence with the promise that such persecution will be beneficial. Perhaps devotees took heart in such words; the oldest known printed book was created against a backdrop of suppression of Buddhism in China. Just two decades before Wang Jie commissioned his sutra, attempts to eradicate Buddhism saw monasteries destroyed, bronze statues melted down for coins, land confiscated, monks and nuns defrocked, and foreign monks sent packing. Not until the Cultural Revolution of the 1960s would Buddhism experience a crackdown so extensive. The persecution reached its peak in 845 under the Emperor Wuzong, a Daoist who issued an imperial decree attacking the Buddhist faith. He condemned it as foreign and idolatrous. It had seduced people's hearts, corrupted their morals and robbed them of their gold and their strength to work. When men stopped farming and women stopped weaving, people went hungry and cold, yet the lavishly endowed monasteries rivaled palaces in their grandeur, according to the decree. In short, Buddhism was an evil that needed to be eradicated. Buddhists were not the only ones who felt the imperial wrath. Nestorians, Manicheans and Zoroastrians were also targeted as pernicious foreign imports, unlike home-grown Daoists and Confucians.

The emperor's actions were driven as much by economics as ideology. The monasteries were wealthy but paid no taxes. And the emperor needed money, especially after a war against the Uyghurs two years earlier had further emptied already depleted imperial coffers. The suppression of Buddhism was short. The emperor died in 846, possibly—and ironically—because of the long-life potions he consumed. But during his six-year rule many of China's estimated 4,600 temples and 40,000 shrines were destroyed, and more than a quarter of a million monks and nuns returned to lay and taxpaying life. Gold, silver, and jade were confiscated, and sacred images made of iron were turned into agricultural tools. Only images made of less valuable materials—clay, wood, and stone—were left alone.

Von Le Coq suspected he had found evidence of the suppression when he made a grisly find near Turfan in the winter of 1904–05. In a ruined Buddhist temple he uncovered the piled corpses of more than a hundred murdered monks. The dry desert air had preserved their robes, desiccated skin, hair, and signs of the fatal wounds. One skull had been slashed with a saber that split the victim's head down to the teeth.

Although the next emperor was more favorably disposed to the faith, Buddhism never fully recovered in China. Its golden age was over and its long decline began. Dunhuang and the Caves of the Thousand Buddhas escaped the extensive destruction. This was largely because the oasis was effectively cut off from China, having fallen under Tibetan control. Tibet, which had conquered a number of Silk Road towns, seized Dunhuang around 781. The caves thrived under Tibetan control. The Tibetans had only recently become Buddhist and brought the zeal of the newly converted and their own art forms, creating nearly fifty caves. Tibet continued to control the oasis for the next seventy years—providentially this coincided with the worst of the persecution. The locals resisted the Tibetans, but the invaders were not ousted from Dunhuang until 848, three years after the persecution ended. As a result, much of the Buddhist art destroyed throughout China survived intact at the caves. No one knows when the printed Diamond Sutra arrived at the Caves of the Thousand Buddhas, but it found refuge in a place that escaped the religious crackdown elsewhere.

10

The Thieves' Road

Storing his precious cargo was Stein's prime concern as the caravan of heavily laden camels left the caves. He intended further travels east and surveying over summer, but to do that he needed to leave behind all surplus baggage. The easiest option was to deposit his treasures at the *yamen* in Dunhuang. There the goods would be under the watchful eye of his learned friend and supporter, the magistrate Wang Ta-lao-ye.

But Stein changed his mind and decided to store everything at Anxi instead, seventy miles east of Dunhuang. Although a forlorn hamlet, it was a convenient crossroads. Anxi was little more than one rundown main street and had such an air of neglect that Dunhuang appeared a thriving city in comparison. Nonetheless, storing his haul in Anxi would prove a fortuitous decision.

The cases of manuscripts and textiles were hauled into the *yamen* of the Anxi magistrate, who gave Stein the use of a storeroom off his private courtyard. The room was well ventilated and could be easily watched. The cases were raised off the ground on timber beams laid over brick pillars. Although rain was rare, it fell while Stein was in Anxi—the first downpour he had seen in nearly a year. Ibrahim Beg remained behind to keep watch and ensure the cases were carried into the sun for a weekly airing. Ostensibly to prevent damp, the regular removal allowed him to discreetly check that the sealed cases remained intact.

Confident his cargo was secure, Stein again escaped the desert's summer heat and headed southeast to survey in the Nan Shan Mountains. As he did, civil unrest over taxation that had been simmering in Dunhuang finally boiled over. The town was gripped by riots during which more than a dozen people were killed. Amid the violence, the Dunhuang *yamen* of magistrate Wang Ta-lao-ye was looted and burned. The manuscripts that had been so perfectly preserved for a millennium narrowly escaped being reduced to ash within weeks of being released from the safety of the sealed cave.

Stein learned of the unrest during a week-long halt in Suzhou, where he was entertained by Chinese officials. On the eve of his departure, he wanted to repay their hospitality. But his Ladakhi servant, Aziz, whose enthusiasm outweighed his experience in such matters, insisted on serving the meal Chinese-style. In the resulting culinary confusion, the guests were expected to eat their custard with chopsticks. Many times Stein must have regretted that the expedition's sole capable cook, Jasvant Singh, could prepare food only for Stein's two Indian assistants, the handyman and the surveyor. For caste reasons, he could not cook for Stein.

The mountain trip was notable for one other bizarre event. At the eastern edge of Gansu province, the furthest they traveled, handyman Naik Ram Singh searched for a quiet camping area just outside a town. He ushered the party into the grounds of what he believed was an old temple. Although a local official tried to dissuade him from using the site, the Naik was insistent. These were just the kind of peaceful quarters his leader favored, he explained through an interpreter. Perhaps something got lost in translation.

The site was certainly as quiet as the grave. In daylight, Stein learned why. His tent had been pitched with a coffin tucked under the fly. The ramshackle building was not a temple but a mortuary, and it was filled with coffins, all occupied. The morgue was used by traders from distant provinces to store their deceased comrades until they could be returned to ancestral homes for burial.

Little wonder Stein was relieved to return to Anxi and his antiquities as autumn set in. He wrote a confidential report to his masters about the Library Cave. He told of his difficulty in getting access to the cave, the wealth of material it contained and how he had overcome the reservations of its guardian priest to obtain scrolls, silks, and other material. What he had acquired so far was potentially more significant than the murals in the Caves of the Thousand Buddhas themselves, he told them. As he had with his friends, Stein impressed on them the need to keep quiet about his finds.

Some weeks after he left the caves, Stein sent a message to see if Abbot Wang would sell more manuscripts. Emboldened by the knowledge that his previous transaction had remained a secret, the priest tentatively agreed. To avoid arousing local suspicions, Stein remained in Anxi, instead dispatching Chiang on a secret mission with Ibrahim Beg, Hassan Akhun, and four camels.

The trio duly arrived at the Caves of the Thousand Buddhas in late September, but the inopportune appearance of half a dozen Tibetan monks at the same time reignited Wang's nervousness. Chiang dodged the red-robed visitors and, once again, Wang relented. The manuscripts were hurriedly packed into sacks throughout the night and loaded onto the camels.

A week after setting out, traveling under cover of darkness and avoiding the high road, they returned to Stein. Chiang "trotted up gaily overflowing with glee at [the] success of his mission." He had secured a further 230 bundles, containing about 3,000 scrolls. Most were Chinese Buddhist sutras, but there were also twenty bundles of Tibetan Buddhist works and they filled twelve more boxes. The size of the second haul had exceeded Stein's hopes.

Just a few weeks after Chiang passed through Dunhuang, where he saw the results of the riots, another European, Baron Carl Gustav Mannerheim, also arrived. He was gathering intelligence for the Russians, as well as manuscripts and other artifacts for his Finnish homeland. He had traveled part of the way from Tashkent to Kashgar with Paul Pelliot and planned to visit the Mogao Caves. But when the time came, the aristocratic Mannerheim, who later became Finland's president, went off to shoot pheasant instead.

❧

Stein and Chiang had no more time to look closely at the scrolls and other documents while camped at Anxi than they had at the Caves of the Thousand Buddhas. The sheer volume of material made detailed documenting impossible. As a result, the printed Diamond Sutra wasn't properly numbered until it arrived in London, so it is not certain whether it was in the rolls Stein originally purchased from Abbott Wang or among the later bundles which Chiang secured. What is certain is that the acquisition of the world's oldest printed book was for Stein the happiest of accidents.

Of the material Stein did examine, it was not the Chinese sutras that most excited him but Indian manuscripts written on palm leaves. And he was delighted to have obtained so much material for so little money. The entire haul from the Caves of the Thousand Buddhas had cost just £130. "The single ancient Sanskrit MS [manuscript] on palm leaf might with a few other 'old things' be worth this," he told Allen. It was certainly a pittance compared with other book sales of the era. When the fifth Earl Spencer, Princess Diana's great-grandfather, sold his library at Althorp in 1891 the 40,000 volumes realized almost £250,000.

Just a few years later, a Gutenberg Bible sold in London for a record-breaking £4,000.

Stein had little time to reflect on the many pearls he had extracted. More mundane matters needed attention. He had a report to write and his Christmas mail to pen. Even in the desert Stein never forgot to send seasonal greetings or mark the birthdays of friends. He also had to replace his surveyor, Ram Singh, whom Stein had found increasingly problematic. Publicly, Stein acknowledged the work of his surveyor. But to Allen he was more candid: "Ram Singh's rheumatism has disappeared for the time being, but not his bad temper etc & I could not have expected from him effective assistance next winter. It has cost much firmness & constant care to get all needful work done by him so far & you can imagine that this means much additional strain," he wrote. With the arrival of a replacement surveyor, Lal Singh, Ram Singh was dispatched from Anxi on the long trip home to India, where he arrived safely three months later.

Stein was relieved to put sedentary work behind him and pull out of Anxi. Chiang had even greater reason to see the back of the dreary settlement. Until his gleeful recent arrival with the manuscripts, his only connection with the hamlet was a sorrowful one. About a decade earlier, he had set out with a friend on a rare journey home to Hunan when his companion suddenly fell ill and died. Chiang wrapped the corpse in felts and wrote and ceremoniously burned a prayer for his dead companion's soul, "asking him to keep his own body from becoming objectionable & to prevent a breakdown of the cart." For a week, Chiang traveled with the corpse on his cart. At Anxi he bought a coffin and accompanied the body, delivering it to his friend's relatives five months later. In his diary, Stein reflects on Chiang's loyal deed: "Not with a word he alluded to all the trouble arising from this pious performance. How many Europeans would be prepared for such sacrifices?"

ﮚ

Stein and his own cargo had much farther to travel. Anxi was a turning point. The summer excursion in the mountains, where he surveyed 24,000 square miles, took him as far east into China as he intended to go. When he came down from the mountains, he knew his journey back to India and Europe had begun. In early October 1907, he turned his caravan northwest and headed along the northern Silk Road, bound for the oases of Hami and Turfan.

The caravan skirted along the Turfan Depression, a region 500 feet below the level of the far-distant sea. Stein was happy to return to Turkestan, where he felt so at home. Although he had not traveled along the northern route before, with each step he felt he was on familiar terrain. He was again among Muslim people whose customs and culture he understood. Soon, there was milk to drink. He had been without it since arriving in Dunhuang seven months earlier. Despite the fine grazing land he had traversed in that time, the terrain had been devoid of cattle.

He noticed the women shared a fondness for the bright clothes of their Turkestan sisters farther west. Best of all, he no longer had to use silver weighed on scales—Stein considered them "instruments of torture"—to pay for everything. There were familiar sights from farther afield. The Turfan bazaars were so full of Russian goods—kerosene lamps, plate glass, and chintz—that he dubbed the area "Demi-Europe." And he saw signs of more ancient cultural exchange around the oasis. He realized a Christian minority had once lived peacefully alongside Turfan's Buddhists.

If Stein and his team were happy to return to Turkestan, perhaps only Chiang felt otherwise. For him it was a continuation of the long exile from the land of his birth. He did not expect to return to Hunan—and his wife and son—until his working life was over.

༄༅

Ancient sites were plentiful along the more populated northern Silk Road. Stein and his caravan passed through areas where farmers used temple ruins as manure for crops and manuscript fragments to paper over windows. It was evidence to Stein that antiquities could not safely remain where history had deposited them. Unlike the southern route, which Stein regarded as his own terrain, the more accessible northern route had attracted other foreign archaeological treasure hunters, from Japan, Russia, and Germany. Stein had little interest in digging where others had already been. With a certain one-upmanship he noted how less arduous it was for his rivals to excavate around Turfan, where laborers could return home each night. There was no need for complicated plans to transport water and food in preparation for weeks in the desert. It was "like excavating in one's own garden," he sniffed.

However, he was curious to see what the Germans had been up to. So in late November 1907, he stopped at the abandoned Buddhist grottoes of Bezeklik where Albert von Le Coq had cut out whole murals and sent them to Berlin's Ethnographic Museum. The German was convinced they would otherwise be destroyed by iconoclasts or by farmers for their fields. Nonetheless, above the door of the room where he'd stayed while removing Bezeklik's murals, von Le Coq had contributed a painting of his own, a message that said: "Robbers' Den."

It was while exploring in nearby Hami in mid-1905 that von Le Coq first heard the rumor of the manuscripts discovered at the Caves of the Thousand Buddhas—news that Stein would not learn for another year and a half. A merchant from Tashkent who had traveled through Dunhuang told von Le Coq about a walled-up cave that had been found nearby. The cave was full of manuscripts nobody could read. The temple guardian would surely be willing to part with them, the merchant told him. Von Le Coq was intrigued but wary. He had already been led on one excursion prompted by a rumor and returned empty-handed. Nonetheless, von Le Coq resolved to make the seventeen-day trip to Dunhuang—until a telegram arrived from Berlin. His boss, Professor Grünwedel, was headed to Turkestan and von Le Coq was to meet him in Kashgar in October. It was now late August. There was no way von Le Coq could get to Dunhuang and back in time to meet Grünwedel. Kashgar was 1,100 miles west and six weeks away, Dunhuang 250 miles southeast. Von Le Coq was in a quandary.

"Somewhat in despair, I left the decision to Fate by tossing a Chinese dollar," he wrote in an account of his travels. Heads he would go to Dunhuang, tails to Kashgar. He flipped the coin. It landed tails. Von Le Coq saddled his horse and left for Kashgar. And so, on the toss of a coin, he lost the chance to claim the Library Cave's treasures for Germany. Little wonder von Le Coq was not in the best of tempers when he reached Chini Bagh on October 17, 1905 and found no sign of Grünwedel, who did not arrive for another seven weeks. Stuck in Kashgar, von Le Coq knew he could easily have reached Dunhuang and investigated the merchant's rumor.

Stein, who long harbored fears about his competitors, had little idea just how close he came to being beaten to his greatest prize. By the time he learned of the Library Cave, von Le Coq was back in Berlin. As Stein stood in the abandoned Bezeklik caves and stared at the denuded walls, he was aware only that the grottoes there, unlike those at Dunhuang, were no longer places of worship. "How much greater would be the chance for the survival of these art remains *in situ* if only Turfan still held such a pious image-loving population as Tun-huang?" he wrote.

After his side trip to Bezeklik, Stein pushed west and soon marked his second Christmas of the expedition. A few days into 1908, boxes of chocolate reached him from the Allens in Britain. Stein immediately penned a gracious thank-you—one that illustrates his utilitarian approach to food. For Stein, even the rare luxury of chocolate was simply a means to stave off hunger pangs and supplement his diet. "How often I have thanked you at the late hours of the night when dinner was still far off & a headache approaching as a reminder of bodily needs, for your incomparable forethought! I shall need such nourishing & tasteful 'iron reserves' for the next few months too, for quick marches are needed to make up for time."

A couple of spills delayed his pace. Two cases and a camera fell into a canal and were soaked. A few days later, two rutting camels absconded and the rest of the day was spent tracking them. But these were minor hitches compared with the sorrowful tidings the new year brought for Chiang. Since he'd set out with Stein, Chiang had hoped for word of his elderly father. At Kucha he intercepted a letter to his uncle in Kashgar and learned the reason for the long silence. Chiang's father had died twenty months earlier. Grief-stricken, he lamented most that his sixty-four-year-old father had not seen him reach high office. Despite his usual skepticism about such rites, Chiang abandoned his customary bright silk clothes, dressed in dark cotton mourning, and arranged a funeral feast for his father's long-departed soul.

As Chiang grieved, Stein made preparations in Kucha for their return to Khotan on the far side of the Taklamakan Desert. In Khotan, he would pack all of his antiquities for their journey to India and London. To reach Khotan, he planned to cross the desert by a perilous shortcut he had learned about from a guide on his first expedition. The route was known as the old "Thieves'

Road" and was once favored by "robbers and others who had reason to avoid the highways." To some it might seem appropriate that the man who removed so many treasures would make his exit via a route so named.

The course was riskier than any he had ever attempted. No European had been known to cross the Taklamakan from north to south. Although Sven Hedin had traveled in the opposite direction in 1896, Stein's plan was far more dangerous. The reason is simple: Hedin followed the Keriya River until it disappeared into the Taklamakan's sands. Hedin knew that if he continued north, the west-to-east flowing Tarim River would cross his path. (Upon finding the Tarim River, Hedin sailed along it while dining on wild duck, pheasant, and rice pudding.)

But Stein's plan meant he had to leave the safety of the Tarim River and locate the very spot amid the dunes where the Keriya River trickled out. There were no maps other than Hedin's. Even if Hedin had mapped it perfectly, the river could have changed course by miles in the intervening twelve years, leaving Stein at risk of traveling parallel to—or even away from—the water. Why Stein undertook so dangerous a shortcut is unclear. He was determined, certainly, but never foolhardy. He was no longer racing the Germans or the French. And even if a rival expedition should suddenly emerge from the desert dunes, Stein had already secured his glittering prizes from the hidden library. Although he justified the journey by a desire to save time—and see some ruins—it was the pull of the desert itself that seemed irresistible. "I must confess that, even without this specific reason, I might have found the chance of once more crossing the very heart of the desert too great an attraction to resist."

His antiquities, his "precious but embarrassing impedimenta," could not come with him. Instead, he sent them under the care of Chiang and pony man Tila Bai along a safer and better known route that followed the Khotan River. For more than an hour on a cold winter day, all traffic in the narrow street of Kucha was blocked as the caravan of twenty-four heavily laden camels began their journey south to Khotan. If all went well, Stein would see Chiang and the antiquities again in two and a half months.

He needed a local guide before he could set out across the desert with his smaller party. But none of the potential guides knew anything about the alleged shortcut. They knew only the route his antiquities were taking. Even the most experienced guide in the area, a stooped hunter in his eighties named Khalil, denied any knowledge of such a route. Khalil walked with difficulty but could nonetheless ride, and he agreed to escort Stein to the Tarim River. It was better than nothing. From there, Stein would negotiate his way unaided through 200 miles of waterless towering dunes toward the river's end. Little wonder his conscripted laborers were reluctant, despite the promise of extra wages. First they argued they were unfit for such a journey or lacked ample clothing. Then they fell on their knees and prayed for release from dreaded sufferings and certain disaster. Who could blame them?

Eventually, led by Khalil, Stein's party of twenty men, fifteen camels (including eight to carry ice) and four ponies, carrying enough food for six weeks, headed toward the distant ocean of sand. After nearly two weeks of marching, they encountered a line of poplars tenaciously clinging to life on the edge of a dry river bed. But perhaps not for much longer. Water from the Tarim River that once ensured their survival no longer reached the trees, according to Khalil. It was hardly an auspicious sign as they were poised to enter the desert on January 31. Before turning back, old Khalil delivered a farewell blessing, one that might have unsettled, rather than comforted, the nervous assembly. "He gave it with more ceremony than I should have expected for the occasion, turning towards Mecca in a long prayer, and the men all joining loudly in the 'Aman'. From Khotan to Lop-nor I had made more than one start into desert quite as forbidding, without ever witnessing such a display of emotion."

The marches through the sand dunes were exhausting. Everyone walked on foot, some days covering fifteen miles. After eight days they reached a dried-up delta somewhere in which the Keriya River died away. But where? "Nowhere in the course of my desert travels had I met ground so confusing and dismal," Stein subsequently confessed. The view in all directions was bewilderingly uniform: endless dunes interspersed with stumps of dead trees and tamarisk cones—strange mounds that form as sand buries the tamarisk tree until only the top boughs are visible.

"My secret apprehension that our real trouble would begin on reaching this dead delta was about to be fully verified. It was as if, after navigating an open sea, we had reached the treacherous marsh-coast of a tropical delta without any lighthouses or landmarks to guide us into the right channel," Stein wrote.

His anxiety increased as each day passed without sight of the river. In the first days of the journey, wells dug into the sand had yielded only a little moisture, and Stein noted how the ears of the ponies would prick up at the sound of hoes striking mud. But as successive efforts to locate the source of the Keriya River proved futile and additional wells dug up to sixteen feet into the ground surrendered nothing, spirits sank. Water was rationed to one pint per man a day. It was a meager amount for hard marching across endless dunes. The camels received little food and no water. "How the camels held out so far is a wonder," Stein wrote in his diary eleven days after Khalil's ominous farewell.

By then the camels and ponies were being fed twigs for the moisture in the sap. Although Dash survived on saucers of Stein's tea, the ponies suffered badly. Stein knew they could not last much longer. On February 12, he counted the cartridges in the holster of his revolver to ensure he could end their suffering if necessary. The mood of the laborers was darkening and Stein feared they might steal what little ice was left. He assigned Lal Singh to guard the remaining supply. Twice in the night when Stein approached to check on its safety, he was challenged by his own surveyor. Stein had little sleep and was awake by 3 a.m.

By daybreak the laborers were on the verge of mutiny and refused to travel further. To turn around would have meant certain death. There was enough water for the men to last just a few days but nowhere near enough to retrace their steps to the Tarim River. They continued with Stein, but he knew time was running out. Lal Singh was ordered to halt the caravan and prepare what Stein termed a "starvation camp." Even the camels, without water for nearly two weeks, were reaching the limits of their endurance. Stein left his caravan behind and marched on until he reached a 300-foot dune. With Dash at his side he trudged to the summit. He scoured the distance through his binoculars. Four miles to the south, he could see four white streaks. Ice? Salt? Or the desert traveler's cruelest tormentor, a mirage?

News of Stein's sighting spurred his exhausted men. So too did the sight of footprints made by a bird that the laborers knew lived near fresh water. As they continued, a camel boy who had surged ahead rushed back toward them. He was too breathless to speak but carried a chunk of ice from the elusive river. When he recovered, he shared his life-saving news: the river was just half a mile ahead. The caravan crested one more dune and looked down on a glittering sheet of clear ice about 500 feet wide. The river had indeed changed course since Hedin's journey. The men rushed to the river bank and fell on their knees to drink the water. The camels and ponies swelled visibly as they slaked their thirst. After sixteen days of marching across the Taklamakan's dunes, they had at last found the end of the Keriya River.

A bodhisattva who still depends on notions to practice generosity is like someone walking in the dark.
VERSE 14, THE DIAMOND SUTRA

11

Affliction in the Orchard

Six weeks after Stein located the life-saving river, he reached
Khotan and was relieved to find his heavy caravan of antiquities had already arrived. They were stored at the house of Akhun
Beg. Stein was overjoyed to be reunited with his elderly friend,
who had returned from his own perilous journey, a pilgrimage
to Mecca. Stein set up his tent in Akhun Beg's garden, beneath
blossoming plum and apricot trees. But he had little time to enjoy
the brief Turkestan spring. Ever since he'd left the abandoned
sanctuary at Miran a year earlier, Stein was eager to return to
where he had found the exquisite winged angels—and endured
the most putrid ruins of his career. In his race to Dunhuang, he
had abandoned his labors in the freezing filth without extracting
all he knew lay buried there. Although Miran was 650 miles east
of Khotan, this was his last chance to document, photograph, and
remove the murals that remained. He could not go himself—he
had other work to do—so he dispatched his Indian handyman,
Naik Ram Singh. The young man, from a family of carpenters,
had proved a reliable, versatile worker. He was strong, stoic, and
quick to turn his hand to a range of tasks, including sketching,

surveying, and developing photographic negatives. Stein knew the resourceful Naik could work without direction and so had no reservations about sending him, with Ibrahim Beg for assistance, on the 1,300-mile round trip.

Meanwhile, Stein prepared to head in the opposite direction, west, for further explorations before the summer heat arrived. Just before he left Khotan, a parcel arrived from Fred Andrews. It contained a fountain pen, pince-nez spectacles, and a much-needed new pair of gloves. "I could not help smiling when I read how carefully you had considered the colour of the gloves," Stein wrote to Andrews. "You must think me quite a dandy in the desert, whereas in reality it is hard to look even respectable. You would make eyes if you would see me in my winter clothes, worn etc. almost beyond patching."

Stein traveled as far as the oasis of Yarkand, where he made the first of many partings. He needed to sell his team of hardy Bactrian camels, which would no longer be needed. Yarkand was a crossroads and, with the trading season about to start, he expected to get a better price for them there than in Khotan. As the weather warmed, camel man Hassan Akhun had shorn the double-humped beasts of their magnificent thick winter coats leaving them looking naked and gaunt. Nonetheless, their fame had spread along the desert oases as a result of their remarkable survival down the Thieves' Road. Eager buyers vied for the legendary animals, despite their high desert mileage after nearly two years of travel. The frugal Stein was delighted; he made a 70 percent profit on the deal. As a farewell gesture, he fed each camel a large loaf of bread before relinquishing the reins to their new owner, an Afghan trader.

Buran season arrived while Stein was in Yarkand and a violent two-day sandstorm brought down trees and destroyed ripening mulberries and apricots in the oasis. By the time Stein left, he had to contend with intense heat as well. He traveled by night but several times lost his way in the wind and darkness. "On one occasion when no light could be kept burning in the lantern there was nothing for it in the howling Buran but to lie down [...] & wait for the dawn," he wrote.

He was pleased to return to the shelter of Khotan in June, although he knew an enormous task awaited. He needed to pack everything he had gathered in the previous two years for the journey to India and, from there, to Europe. Akhun Beg's residence was too small to accommodate all of Stein's finds. He needed the space afforded by his favorite garden palace, Narbagh, with its pavilions, orchard, and beds of lilies. Since the previous year, when he had been guest of honor at a lavish feast, Narbagh's owner had died and the garden was divided between his heirs. The central pavilion, the most suitable place for summer quarters, had gone to the man's formidable dowager. She was reluctant to relocate a silkworm nursery, and it was only with the aid of an old Afghan friend that Stein managed to persuade her to house his large entourage.

Soon the many bags that had already arrived in Khotan under Chiang's care were joined by those Stein had sent for safekeeping to Macartney more than a year earlier, before Stein had crossed to Dunhuang. Macartney also sent sheets of tin—and drained Turkestan's supply of the commodity in the process—so Stein could safely pack his manuscripts and other treasures for their journey beyond Turkestan. Narbagh had once echoed to the gentle strains of flutes that serenaded Stein at the feast in his honor; now the garden clanged with hammering and sawing as up to forty local laborers constructed case after sturdy tin-lined case. Stein watched the work progress, but the careful packing of his fragile antiquities he trusted to no one but himself.

Stein thought hard about how best to get his huge cargo from Turkestan to Europe. He had two options: land or sea. He could take it west via Russia, or south via India and onto a boat from Bombay. The Russian route was shorter and familiar. He had taken his goods that way in 1901, traveling via Kashgar and across the border to Osh in Russian Turkestan and then by train to Europe. He had needed only eight ponies for his antiquities and baggage for his first expedition. This cargo was roughly eight times the size. He needed twenty-four ponies just to carry the manuscripts. But it would be impractical to take it all with him on a passenger train, and even if he could it would be prohibitively expensive. He also feared the loss of material conveyed on an unreliable train system—the same railway that had mislaid the luggage of the German Grünwedel and the Frenchman Pelliot.

India was a slower but safer option. He considered two routes via Kashmir. He ruled out one through Hunza and Gilgit, in present-day Pakistan, as impossible for heavily laden animals. The only solution was to take it all over the Karakoram Mountains via Ladakh and then to Kashmir. The hidden library's scrolls had survived entombed for a millennium because the dry desert atmosphere was devoid of humidity. They had reached Khotan unharmed. But ahead lay huge mountains, glacier-fed rivers, snow, and ice. It was potentially the most risky part of the journey for the Diamond Sutra and the rest of the manuscripts. One leaky case could ruin paper forever. The fragile murals from Miran needed extra protection. They were strengthened by gluing strips of cotton to them, then repacked between insulating layers of reeds.

Stein had much to occupy him. As he packed, the future of the finds and his own fate increasingly filled his thoughts. He cared little for London, where he would be hemmed in by arid deserts of bureaucracy and mountains of paperwork. He hoped he might at least find a quiet corner suited to the idiosyncrasies of a man whose preferred habitats were deserts and alpine meadows.

"I shall be more than ever bound to the collection & with it to London, and you can feel what that means for me," he wrote to Allen. "I dread in advance its turmoil, its 'cage' feeling etc, to say nothing of prospective incarceration in [the British Museum's] basements." If only he could have help with the huge task that would await him. Someone such as his friend Fred Andrews. Stein resolved to escape his British Museum "bondage" as quickly as possible.

Packing was tedious, with only a break at dusk to walk or ride through the dusty village roads with Dash for company. Returning to Europe would mean leaving behind his canine companion. The little dog had distinguished himself en route to Khotan when he detected a tiger near the camp. No one realized why Dash had barked constantly one night. The next morning the footprints of a huge beast were found nearby. It would be hard to part with brave Dash. But Stein didn't want to put him through a lengthy sea journey and quarantine in England. He had left behind Dash's predecessor in India in 1901, but the dog died the next year. Perhaps some friends in Punjab would take Dash II, Dash the Great. "It is sad to think that I shall have to leave Dash when I go to England," he told Allen. "How lucky those are who like Dash do not know of impending separation!"

But more immediate concerns demanded his attention. First he had to hose down a problem caused by his "worthless" Kashmiri cook. Ramzan, who had already absconded near Dunhuang, got into a scrap with a man in Khotan over a pony. The badly injured local was covered in bruises when he was conveyed to Stein on a litter. Stein paid compensation and hoped that might be the end of the problematic servant's trouble. But apparently a fight over a pony was not all Ramzan engaged in at Khotan. Chiang heard rumors the cook was also procuring young women. Wearied by his cook's bad behavior, Stein explained that he could not concern himself with the morals of his staff. Nonetheless, Ramzan's behavior appalled Stein. "Disgust at having to employ such a scoundrel keeps me awake half the night," he wrote in his diary. But Stein retained his services. A cook, it seemed, was harder to replace than a surveyor.

Chiang spent his days surrounded by bundles of scrolls attempting to make a rough list of the Dunhuang manuscripts. The results were thrilling, with Chiang turning up texts much older and more varied than Stein had expected when they began burrowing in the "treasure cave." It was time-consuming work. Chiang had looked at just a third of the manuscripts at Khotan. "You can imagine the trouble of unfolding rolls of thin paper, often 30 yards long & more, to search for colophons etc. Chiang is glued to his table from morning till late at night," Stein wrote to Allen.

Chiang's work came to a sudden halt when he suffered a serious case of food poisoning. A photograph taken at Narbagh shows a gaunt Chiang, almost unrecognizable from the round-faced figure photographed in Dunhuang fifteen months earlier. "He suffered awful pains for days & kept me busy as improvised doctor & superintendent of nursing. But at last he got over the attacks & is now slowly regaining strength & spirits. Faith in my medicines was the main cure," Stein told Allen. And he plied poor Chiang with doses of the salty yeast extract sent out from England. "Marmite turned to use at last," he noted with satisfaction in his diary.

Stein too endured ill-health at Khotan. His malarial fevers returned, he suffered from a toothache and he became temporarily deaf in his left ear. Yet both men's ailments paled beside the affliction suffered by Naik Ram Singh. Shortly after setting out for Miran, the Naik's neck and back grew stiff. Soon he was struck by headaches that grew more intense each day. After five days, while sitting in an orchard to escape the noon heat, he began to reel and lost sight in one eye. Nonetheless, the hardy Sikh insisted on continuing, hoping his condition would improve. It worsened. At Miran, while clearing a temple with Ibrahim Beg, the Naik lost the vision in his other eye also. Still he waited—and hoped—for nearly two weeks. Finally he agreed to turn back and let Ibrahim

Beg, a Muslim, guide him to Khotan. Although blind, Naik Ram Singh insisted on cooking his own food to avoid breaking caste rules, despite repeated campfire burns.

Stein was devastated to see the once-proud soldier so diminished. No event during the entire expedition affected Stein so deeply. In a heartfelt letter to Allen, his closest confidant, he shared his fears for the Naik.

You can imagine my feelings when I saw him arrive in this state of utter helplessness . . . [The Naik] luckily seems to bear his affliction with remarkable calmness & courage, perhaps a compensation of nature for a certain heaviness of mind & disposition. But whether this did not make him lose precious weeks on his return for the chance of proper treatment only the gods know. He himself seems confident of an early recovery & this is indeed fortunate. But alas I know only too well how delusive such hope may be & feel the full weight of his care.

Stein searched for some clue and cure for the handyman's blindness. Khotan's only surgeon was called and relieved some of the Naik's pain, but was unable to restore his sight. The best chance of medical help lay 200 miles away in Yarkand, where Stein had sold his camels and where the Swedish medical missionary, Dr. Gösta Raquette, was based. The Naik was transported by cart to Raquette, a friend of Stein.

Raquette diagnosed glaucoma. The headaches were a symptom of its onset. There was no hope of recovery. Only a timely operation could have saved Naik Ram Singh's eyesight. Raquette broke the terrible news to the Naik and reported back to Stein: "You have nothing to reproach yourself with. The disease might quite as well have come on if he had been at home & nobody can expect you to recognize a disease that very often in the beginning is overlooked even by medical men."

The letter was scant consolation. Stein knew that at home in India the Naik would have been among his own people and had the chance of prompt medical treatment. The soldier had paid a high price for his wish to better provide for his wife and son. He had been enticed from his regiment by the promise of pay five times his army salary. Although Stein warned him of the trip's hardships, this was a danger no one could have anticipated. Chiang was so distressed by the Naik's plight that he again set aside his religious skepticism and made offerings for the handyman's recovery at the shrine of a healing saint. Others, such as Stein's prosperous friend Akhun Beg, urged the use of local treatments. Stein dismissed as "truly mediaeval" remedies that involved the use of breast milk and baby's urine. The Naik, who had been so enchanted when he encountered a frozen lake, would never see such a sight—or any other—again.

Raquette advised that the Naik should head home as soon as possible. Arrangements were made for him to travel with a party of Hindu traders returning to India over the Karakorams to Ladakh. He rested in Leh, the capital of Ladakh, before being conveyed to Dr. Arthur Neve at the Srinagar Mission Hospital in Kashmir. He confirmed Raquette's diagnosis. From there, the Naik's brother escorted him to his family's village in Punjab.

The soldier's future weighed heavily on Stein. When Stein saw him in Punjab five months later, the explorer was shocked by the Naik's mental disintegration, exacerbated perhaps by hashish consumption. Stein argued for a special pension for his loyal handyman. The government of India granted it, but he did not benefit from it for long. Within a year of losing his sight, Naik Ram Singh was dead.

After four months in Khotan, punctuated by a few exploratory diversions, Stein was ready to move. The packing in Akhun Beg's orchard was complete. It had taken six arduous weeks, and the manuscripts alone filled thirty of the carefully made cases.

Although he made a brief note in Khotan about a well-printed Chinese roll, Stein did not grasp the significance of what is now recognized as the world's oldest printed dated book. It was simply one scroll among many. On August 1, more than fifty camels and a column of donkeys left Khotan under Tila Bai's care for the journey through the Kunlun Mountains via a well-known caravan route. Stein, determined as ever to take the road less traveled, planned a more difficult path. He would then unite with Tila Bai and the antiquities convoy in late September to cross the Karakorams together.

It was time for farewells: to Turkestan, where Stein the lifelong wanderer felt so at home, and to the desert that had yielded such treasures. And it was time to part from some of his loyal followers. Turdi, the courageous *dak* runner who had risked his life to find Stein in the desert on Christmas Eve in 1906, filled his saddle bags with Stein's mail for the last time. But no parting was harder than from Chiang. A deep friendship had developed during their two years together. The man hired as an interpreter had proved far more: an unlikely desert traveler, a trusted companion, teacher, witty raconteur, a skilled diplomat, and negotiator. Without him, Stein might never have secured Dunhuang's treasure from Abbot Wang.

While the journey together—and especially their three weeks at the caves—would create an enduring bond between Stein and Chiang, the explorer had been mindful they would eventually part. Before he left Dunhuang he wrote to Andrews to secure a special parting gift. In typical Stein style, he was precise not only about what he wanted but how much he was prepared to pay. He requested a good silver watch—then a rare and prestigious item in Turkestan. The cost was not to exceed £2 10 shillings, and it should be inscribed: "Presented by Dr M.A. Stein to Chiang-ssu-yeh as a token of sincere regard and in grateful remembrance of his devoted scholarly services during explorations in Chinese Turkestan, 1906–08."

Chiang dreamed of following Stein to London or India, but knew obtaining work in either country would be difficult. Stein, too, imagined spending summers with Chiang on Mohand Marg in Kashmir. But the bucolic idyll remained a dream. The reality was Chiang would remain in Turkestan, in exile from his home and family. Stein wanted to ensure Chiang had a good position and worked behind the scenes to secure one. In Khotan, Stein received welcome news from Kashgar that George Macartney had agreed to employ him as his secretary.

"Often as I look back on all we went through together, I have wondered to what merits (of a previous birth, perhaps?) I was indebted for this ideal Chinese comrade of my travels!" Stein later reflected.

Chiang accompanied Stein and his small party from Khotan for one last day's journey together. Appropriately, their parting would come not among the comforts of an oasis, but amid the solitude of a makeshift camp, an environment dear to them both. Chiang knew he was unlikely to experience such adventure ever again.

They crossed the flooded Yurungkash River by ferryboat before making camp on a gravel flat. Dash seemed to sense the impending separation, nestling up to Chiang for a final cuddle. The next morning, Stein, with his back to Turkestan, headed toward the mountains. "Then, as I rode on, the quivering glare and heat of the desert seemed to descend like a luminous curtain and to hide from me the most cherished aspects of my Turkestan life."

12

Frozen

Stein's high-altitude journey to India soon led him to the Kunlun Mountains, long rumored to be the site of great goldmines. Until he entered the Zailik Gorge on August 18, 1908, no European had ever seen the legendary gold pits, and what he encountered must have appeared like a scene from *King Solomon's Mines*. The cliffs were dotted with hundreds of diggings. In this deep, gloomy valley, generations of wretched souls—virtual slaves—had lived and died digging for flecks of gold. Their graves extended over every bit of flat ground around the twelve-mile gorge. Others were entombed in abandoned pits.

Most of the gold had long been extracted, but about fifty impoverished men still worked the mines in summer, when the 13,600-foot valley was accessible. The miners were astonished at the arrival of outsiders in their frigid valley. Eight or nine of the miners agreed to abandon their burrowing in the dark pits to work as porters for a couple of weeks through the mountainous terrain. They helped map the glacier-fed rivers that coursed through the mountains to Khotan and emptied far away in the Taklamakan's sands. On the movement of such life-giving rivers the fate of the ancient desert civilizations had depended. Even high in the mountains, Stein sensed a connection with the sand-buried sites. He suspected that long ago gold from these pits had been used to gild the temples of Khotan.

While he mapped the rivers, his murals from Miran and his manuscripts from Dunhuang, including the Diamond Sutra, were crossing the mountains via the main trading route between Turkestan and Ladakh. It was safer than his uncharted path. Nonetheless, the terrain that Stein's antiquities had to negotiate posed considerable difficulties, not least repeated river crossings, sometimes up to forty a day. The rivers were full of deep holes, and loose rocks could easily fell a horse. (Von Le Coq, on this route from Turkestan to Ladakh in 1906, watched in dismay as a leather case carried on horseback burst open during one such crossing. A collection of kettles and his supplies of sugar and condensed milk floated away on the swift current.)

Not knowing the fate of the treasures he had acquired over two years of hard toil must have added to Stein's worries when, having sent the porters back to their goldmines, he approached the most dangerous part of the mountainous journey. The going grew increasingly tough as he and his men were blasted with icy gales by day and endured temperatures that fell to fifteen degrees Fahrenheit at night. At the foot of a line of glaciers, 17,200 feet above sea level, Stein located the source of the Keriya River, the waterway he had found just in time on his hazardous shortcut across the desert eight months earlier. Once again fodder was running low and no grazing could be found. Several donkeys suffered in the cold and had to be shot.

Then Stein's pony, Badakhshi, became ill. For more than two years of rugged travel, he had conveyed Stein through the most inhospitable of mountainous and desert terrain. With little food or water, the hardy mount had crossed the Taklamakan without any apparent ill-effect. His implacable temperament had wavered only once, when a blast of horns had farewelled Stein's party from an oasis. What caused the animal's sudden illness, none of Stein's men knew, despite their knowledge of horses. Badakhshi was wrapped in extra felts and blankets for the cold night ahead. Stein gave him most of a bottle of port that he kept for emergencies. At daybreak, when Stein rose to check on him, the pony lay on the ground in convulsions.

"He recognized me when I stroked him, and on my holding some oats close to his mouth he struggled to get on his legs," Stein wrote. He had hoped Badakhshi would one day graze on Kashmir's lush grass. But just when the goal seemed near, the pony died in one of the most desolate places Stein had encountered.

"What he succumbed to I failed to make out. He was equal to the hardest of fares & would cheerfully chew even ancient dead wood. It was some consolation that he suffered but for a short time & had for his last night every comfort we could provide in that wilderness," he told Allen.

The dispirited party trudged on the next morning until they spotted two small stone mounds, or cairns, half buried under sand and gravel. It was what Stein had been looking for—the cairns that marked a disused route to Ladakh. The party rejoiced at having finally found a path where men had passed before. For two days, they followed the stone cairns that led down to a valley. Finally, the welcome remains of an old rock shelter offered refuge from the bitter wind. There were signs in the valley of more recent life—fresh tracks made by wild yaks and donkeys. The valley had just enough vegetation for the hungry animals. And not before time; the fodder had run out. Would those two days have made a difference for Badakhshi? Stein had no way of knowing. But as he watched the hungry ponies graze, he mourned the loss of his own mount, frozen stiff in the forbidding wastes higher up the mountain.

There was relief for men and animals when a team of Kirghiz guides arrived with yaks, camels, and much-needed supplies.

With them came word that Tila Bai and the heavy cargo of antiquities were waiting safely eighty miles ahead as arranged. After so
much long and hard travel, Stein must have thought his troubles
were behind him.

༄༅

Just one expeditionary challenge remained. Stein still wanted
to resolve inaccuracies in a map sketched by surveyor William
Johnson, who had crossed the Kunlun Mountains in 1865. Stein's
attempt to do this on his first expedition had failed. He had been
similarly thwarted two years earlier on his second expedition.
This was the determined Stein's third—and final—chance to
solve the mystery. The task would also allow him to locate the
watershed of the Kunlun Mountains. The side trip had to begin
the next day or not at all. There was not enough food for the animals to delay. On the night before his departure, a bout of colic
made for a fitful sleep, but the day dawned clear. Just after 5 a.m.
he set out with four Kirghiz guides and two of his own men—surveyor Lal Singh and the surveyor's assistant, Musa—all mounted
on yaks. After three hours of climbing, the terrain became too
difficult even for the yaks and they were abandoned for the final
ascent up a glacier.

As the sun rose higher, the snow softened and the men sank
up to their thighs. Roped together for safety, they struggled for
breath in the thinning air. Lal Singh especially felt the effects of
the altitude and had to be hauled along, stopping after every ten
steps to catch his breath. It took seven hours to climb four miles.

The panorama at 20,000 feet was awe-inspiring. They were
surrounded by majestic snow-covered crests that dazzled under
the intense light and cobalt sky. Some peaks appeared smooth,
almost benign, under a blanket of virgin snow, others harsh and
serrated. To the south were ranges whose rivers ended in the
mighty Indus. Far away to the north, Stein glimpsed the yellow

haze that hovered over the Taklamakan Desert. His mood was as elevated as the landscape.

"The world appeared to shrink strangely from a point where my eyes could, as it were, link the Taklamakan with the Indian Ocean," he wrote. The grandeur before him united his two beloved ancient worlds. To the south was India, where Buddhism had been born. To the north was where it had flourished before the great civilization sank under desert sands.

But Stein could afford little time for reflection that day. There was photographing and surveying to be done, and it was already mid-afternoon. From his vantage point, he corrected the miscalculations of Johnson's sketch. The temperature was down to sixteen degrees Fahrenheit at 4:30 p.m. when the guides insisted on starting the descent. They did not want to risk being stranded overnight on the glacier. Stein grabbed a few mouthfuls of food. In the rush, there was no time to change his boots, which had become wet during the ascent in the soft snow and then frozen as he worked. Nor did he have time to consider how fatigue, high altitude, and inadequate sleep might cloud his judgment.

It was already dark by the time the men rejoined the yaks and mounted the sure-footed beasts. At times the men dismounted as the yaks negotiated the rocky slopes. When they did, Stein struggled to find his footing, but attributed the difficulty to fatigue and slippery terrain. The six-hour descent seemed endless. When at last the camp came into view, he hobbled into his tent and removed his boots and two pairs of socks. The toes on both feet were frozen. He rubbed them vigorously with snow in an effort to restore circulation. A quick check of his medical manual had advised this as emergency treatment. It may have made matters worse. These days, friction is avoided so that injured tissue is not further damaged; immersing in warm water or wrapping in blankets is the preferred treatment. Nonetheless, the toes on Stein's left foot gradually warmed, though the skin was badly damaged. He had lost feeling in the toes on his right foot.

The pain in his feet immobilized him the next morning. He again consulted his medical manual: "The aid of an experienced surgeon should be sought at once." The advice was sound but hardly reassuring. He knew he was at risk of developing gangrene and must reach Ladakh and medical help quickly. But the town was two weeks' journey away—nearly 300 miles—through some of the most rugged and dangerous terrain on earth.

Walking was impossible. He needed to be carried, but his guides refused to convey him on a makeshift litter. So first he was put onto a yak and later strapped onto a camel. His pain was excruciating as he was bounced and jerked around. Eventually an improvised litter was made with a camp chair suspended from bamboo tent poles fastened between two ponies. Four days later, he was relieved to be reunited en route with his cargo. Despite encountering flooded gorges and the challenge of the 17,598-foot Sanju Pass, every case was safe. But there was still a long way to travel. The caravan had to negotiate two even higher passes: the 18,176-foot Karakoram Pass and the 17,753-foot Sasser Pass. Word of Stein's injury was sent ahead to the medical missionary in Leh as the explorer spent the next two days attending to vital tasks, issuing directives from his camp bed. The most important was to make onward arrangements for the cargo.

The Karakoram Pass, along the highest trade route in the world, was notoriously difficult. One nineteenth-century British traveler estimated he passed the skeletons of 5,000 horses, near which were vultures "so gorged they could hardly move." Men, too, perished on the deadly trail, their remains covered with piles of stones. Von Le Coq noted that if a caravan encountered misadventure, its cargo was left nearby in as sheltered a spot as possible until it could be rescued. A code of honor forbade any interference with these abandoned loads, according to the German, who reported seeing many, each with a tale of misfortune. Von Le Coq also witnessed the vestige of another misfortune along the route: a lonely memorial to the Scottish trader whose murder there in 1888 inadvertently sparked the manuscript race. It was a small marble pillar atop a cairn with a brief inscription: "Here fell Andrew Dalgleish, murdered by an Afghan." These days there are other attendant dangers. The route lies just east of the world's highest and most improbable battleground, the disputed Siachen Glacier, where nuclear neighbors India and Pakistan have fought intermittently since 1984. So far the greatest battle has been to survive the conditions; more soldiers have died in avalanches than armed conflict.

Stein put Lal Singh in charge of transferring the antiquities onto yaks since parts of the steep, icy terrain ahead were impassable by camel. Stein watched as the caravan left to continue on its mountainous route before its descent into the safety of Ladakh's fertile Nubra Valley. Meanwhile, the need for medical treatment was growing more urgent. Gangrene had set in to the toes on his right foot and he feared its further spread. The explorer shed most of his remaining party and baggage so he could be carried quickly along the same route as the antiquities. He crossed the Karakoram Pass on October 3, 1908, and the Sasser four days later. Like others before him, Stein witnessed how the skeletons of pack animals littered the route. It was a morbid sight at any time, but for a man with a life-threatening injury the sight must have appeared even more distressing. He had once dismissed the Karakoram route as a "tour for ladies"; now it was proving anything but.

To distract himself, Stein attempted to read. He turned to writings by Renaissance philosopher Erasmus—the subject of Percy Allen's years of scholarly study. Erasmus is credited with the adage, "In the country of the blind, the one-eyed man is king," but as Stein contemplated the philosopher's words, anxious questions about a different affliction must have preyed on him. Would his feet survive? Would he walk again? An explorer unable to walk was no explorer at all.

A week later, on the evening of October 8, he approached Panamik, the first village of Ladakh's Nubra Valley, where he was met by the head of the Moravian Mission Hospital. Alerted to Stein's plight, Dr. S. Schmitt had traveled up from Leh to meet him.

The missionary doctor examined Stein's feet. The toes on the left foot would survive, but those on his right foot were doomed. They would have to be removed to prevent the spread of gangrene. Schmitt dressed the wounds but was unwilling to operate on his exhausted patient until they reached Leh. Today trucks, buses, and military vehicles make the journey from Panamik to Leh in about ten hours along the world's highest motorable road. But for Stein, the town was still four days away. Once there, Schmitt amputated toes on Stein's right foot. He removed two middle toes completely and the top joint of the other three. As he recovered at the Mission hospital, Stein wrote Allen a lengthy, if dispassionate, account in which he glossed over the seriousness of his "unlucky incident."

> *Dr [Schmitt] assures me that the three toes left thus for the greater part intact will be ample to assure my full power of walking & climbing. The operations did not cause much pain [. . .] I am very sorry for the worry this unlucky incident at the very close of my explorations may cause you. But I have told you the details in all truth & hope you will join me in taking a philosophical view of the whole case.*

The version is at odds with his later accounts, in which he acknowledges the wounds from the amputation were both painful and slow to heal. No doubt he did not want to alarm his friend. But it was too late. News of Stein's injury reached Allen long before the explorer's nine-page letter. On the day Stein was penning his letter in Leh, *The Times* published a brief report.

The one-paragraph article, published on October 16, 1908, stated simply that Stein was being treated in Leh for frostbitten feet following his return from an expedition to Central Asia. The article added to Stein's distress. "I never thought of such a communication finding its way prematurely to London without any direct report on my part or else I should have sent you telegraphic news direct from Leh. Forgive the omission & all the worrying uncertainty which it must have caused you for weeks," he wrote soon after to Allen.

The inherently private Stein would hardly have been pleased that news of his injury had become public. Having worked so hard to keep confidential the details of his discoveries, this was news he could not control. The image of a crippled explorer—and the speculation such news would prompt—was not what he wanted just ahead of his return to Britain from an otherwise wildly successful expedition.

With a view to the help he would need in London, Stein asked Allen to nudge their mutual friend Fred Andrews to seek a role at either the India Office or the British Museum, where Andrews could use his expertise in Indian and Oriental art. "If you have a chance of talking to the Baron [Andrews] discreetly about the need of urging his own case at both places, kindly use it. He is far too modest & shy about seeing people & writing makes little impression."

Stein convalesced in the autumn sunshine on the mission's veranda, with its view of the majestic Leh Palace high on a barren ridge. The palace, like a smaller version of Lhasa's Potala Palace, dominates the town. Stein regretted not being able to explore this corner of what he called Western Tibet. But he glimpsed a fascinating world. Had he been able to walk the maze of narrow alleys that lead up to the palace, he would have seen a Buddhist culture very much alive. Ladakh's centuries-old monasteries, full of statues, sutras, and painted murals, continue to thrive.

Immobilized, he used the time to write letters and make arrangements for the transport of his antiquities. They had arrived safely in Leh under Lal Singh's care, and the surveyor was once again in charge as the convoy left for Srinagar in mid-October. The cases traveled in carts and then by rail south to Bombay. Stein knew that if he did not follow his antiquities soon, he would be stuck in Leh until spring. Winter was approaching and the first snows would close the pass between Ladakh and Kashmir. He maintained his optimistic tone in his letters to Allen, expressing a hope that he would be able to ride into Kashmir, walk soon after and be in Budapest for Christmas.

The reality was different. Unable to ride—or even sit up—when he departed on November 1, he had to be carried on his litter for the two-week journey to Srinagar. He was carried over the Zoji Pass that separates the barren high desert of Ladakh from Kashmir's fertile valleys. It was not how he had imagined his return to the area he so loved. He had to content himself with passing a night by the foot of Mohand Marg, his de facto home on whose meadows he had camped for years.

In Srinagar he was treated by Dr. Arthur Neve, head of the Church Mission Hospital and a keen mountaineer, who already knew the toll the expedition had taken on its members. The blind handyman Naik Ram Singh had been taken to Neve just months earlier. Although the surgeon could do little for the Naik, Neve had reassuring news for Stein: the explorer would be able to walk and, most importantly, climb again once the wounds had fully healed. The ball of the foot, so vital for balance, was unharmed. And enough of his toes, including the big toe, remained to ensure he could cope with hilly terrain. "Things might have fared a great deal worse—& you know what walking means for me & my work," he wrote to Andrews.

But the wounds would not heal overnight, and he had to remain in Srinagar until they did. He stayed at the elegant British

Residency near tranquil Dal Lake. In the summer, when British officials fled the heat of India's plains and headed for the hill stations, the Residency was one of the Raj era's most enchanting social hubs. At the height of the season its gardens were hung with Chinese lanterns for moonlight gatherings. The Resident's canopied barge glided by on the lake, rowed by liveried oarsmen. By late autumn, when Stein arrived, the glittering social set had long departed, no doubt to his relief. Nonetheless, he enjoyed what seemed to him luxurious trappings. After more than two and a half years of sleeping under canvas and writing his notes by candlelight, he had the novelty of a bed, furniture, and electric light. He took his meals in his old camp chair, and his two Turki servants, Muhammadju and Musa, remained with him. Although the Resident, Sir Francis Younghusband—Macartney's former superior at Kashgar—was absent, Stein was cared for by a young assistant as though he were a family member.

He rode in the Resident's carriage along the banks of Dal Lake, admiring the autumn colors and encircling mountains reflected in its calm waters. After a couple of weeks he began to hobble around on crutches. His injuries healed slowly, particularly the wound to his big toe, which reopened shortly before he left India. Despite the brave face Stein put on his injury, medical reports tell a different tale. The hardships of the expedition had caused "nervous overstrain, owing to his prolonged exertions and hardships; and of late owing to sleeplessness," according to Neve. Stein's health had been permanently damaged, in the opinion of another Indian-based doctor. He would need to rest aboard the ship to Europe to facilitate the healing, he was warned.

But before his departure, he wanted to ensure those who had served him so loyally were duly rewarded. As well as lobbying for Naik Ram Singh's pension, he sought recognition for his two surveyors, the rheumatic Ram Singh and his replacement, Lal Singh. For Chiang he arranged another watch—this time of gold—which was presented with much ceremony at an official dinner in Kashgar.

There was also his own future and that of his antiquities to consider. The two were intricately connected. Before he left India, he received news that the Viceroy, Lord Minto, who had taken an interest in his exploration, had granted him extended leave to work on his discoveries in England. Stein arranged to ship his ninety cases of manuscripts, silks and murals from Bombay to London aboard the P&O steamer *Oceana*. Stein's treasures set sail on December 19, 1908. "May kindly divinities protect them on their way," he wrote as the cases embarked on their two-and-a-half-week sea voyage via the Suez Canal and Gibraltar.

But what to do with Dash? Over two and a half years, the little fox terrier had trotted through deserts and mountains—dodging the feet of camels, horses, and yaks—and ridden on Stein's saddle. At night he had jealously guarded Stein's camp bed and snoozed under his master's blankets. He had chased gazelles and hares, detected a tiger, and survived a mauling by savage dogs. Since leaving Dunhuang, Stein had resigned himself to leaving his canine companion behind in India, as he had with Dash I, in 1901.

Then Stein had a change of heart. He could not face parting with his plucky companion who had traveled so far with him. Dash the Great would join him in England. It meant a temporary separation, for the dog was not allowed to accompany Stein from Bombay. Instead, Dash was put aboard the steamer *Circassia* to Liverpool and quarantined for four months in London. Quite how the peripatetic Stein would care for him in England he didn't know. He parted from Dash in Bombay on Boxing Day 1908 and later that day set sail for Europe.

The *Oceana*, with Stein's antiquities aboard, berthed in London on January 9, 1909. Forwarding agents Thomas Cook advised the British Museum three days later that it would deliver the ninety cases. Meanwhile, Andrews, who had secured a part-time role to help catalogue the mountain of treasures, was quick to telegram Stein, holidaying in mainland Europe en route to Britain, with the happy news of the *Oceana's* safe arrival. It could easily have been otherwise. The *Oceana* sank en route to Bombay just three years later when it collided with the German bark *Pisagua* in the English Channel. The P&O ship was carrying a £750,000 cargo of gold and silver ingots when it went down, just a month before the *Titanic* sank. Divers can still see the wreck of the *Oceana* off England's south coast today (although most of the ingots have been recovered).

After narrowly escaping incineration in the flames of civil unrest at Anxi, Stein's cargo of sacred relics—far more fragile than silver and gold ingots—had survived. Stein may well have had good reason to thank those kindly divinities.

Wherever this sutra is kept is a sacred site enshrining the presence of the Buddha or one of the Buddha's great disciples.

VERSE 12, THE DIAMOND SUTRA

13

Yesterday, Having Drunk Too Much . . .

In ancient China, the value of a domestic slave could be measured in silk. A petty official and his wife, having fallen on hard times in 991, relinquished their twenty-eight-year-old servant to settle a bill. She was worth three pieces of raw silk and two of spun. The deal was formalized on a single sheet of pale, coarse paper and signed with the brush marks of the slave and her owners. Once the pact had been witnessed by two Buddhist monks, her future was decided.

The contract to sell the young slave was among the thousands of documents sealed in the Library Cave. The material spans more than 600 years, and while not every manuscript is dated, many show not only the year of their creation, but also the month and day. Some fastidious scribes even recorded the time.

Although the cave was predominantly filled with religious texts, the secular documents are particularly revealing. They give poignant, amusing and remarkable detail about life along the

Silk Road over hundreds of years. The documents range from ways to entertain the living (such as hints for playing the board game Go) to funeral speeches for the dead (including a eulogy for a donkey). Stein's haul contains a list of ten reasons why children should be grateful to their mother, not least because she has endured the agony of childbirth and the stinky tedium of toilet training. Another manuscript sets out the punishment for disrupting proceedings at a women's club: the rabble-rouser had to provide wine-syrup for an entire feast. This hardly seems the ideal way to prevent such brawls—especially for a club probably comprised of nuns. And lest an offender try to abandon her membership, the penalty for leaving the club was three strokes with a bamboo stick.

Among the more frivolous manuscripts is a debate between Tea and Wine in which each beverage claims supremacy. Lionel Giles, who spent decades cataloguing Stein's collection, offered a translation in his book *Six Centuries at Tunhuang*. The debate begins with Tea introducing itself: "Chief of the hundred plants, flower of the myriad trees, esteemed for its buds that are picked, prized for its shoots that are culled, lauded as a famous shrub—its name is called Tea!" But Wine dismisses Tea's boasts as ridiculous. "From of old until now Wine has always ranked higher than Tea. What cannot Wine singly achieve? It will intoxicate a whole army; it is drunk by the sovereigns of the Earth, and is acclaimed by them as their god." Tea responds, Wine retorts. And the dispute continues as the two immodestly engage in self-promotion until Water finally intervenes, telling both Tea and Wine that their argument is pointless—without Water, neither could exist.

The cave also surrendered a series of model letters designed to resolve matters of etiquette. Some letters suggest a choice of words for offering condolences, others provide suggestions on inoffensive topics such as the weather. Among the trickier situations addressed is a pro forma apology for drunken behavior.

Giles translates: "Yesterday, having drunk too much, I was so intoxicated as to pass all bounds; but none of the rude and coarse language I used was uttered in a conscious state." The letter continues, explaining that the writer did not learn of his lack of decorum until others told him, at which point he wished "to sink into the earth for shame." The writer then promises to apologize in person, signing the letter: "Leaving much unsaid, I am yours respectfully."

If such letters are evidence of a pressing need, it must have been considerable, for another form letter offers the recommended reply: "Yesterday, Sir, while in your cups, you so far overstepped the observances of polite society as to forfeit the name of gentleman, and made me wish to have nothing more to do with you. But since you now express your shame and regret for what has occurred, I would suggest that we meet again for a friendly talk." Presumably *not* over a bottle of wine.

><del>๑

When sifting through the Library Cave manuscripts, a moment of time, seemingly lost among the centuries, can return to life. Sometimes all that survives is a fragment. One such scrap mentions Ming Sha—the Singing Sands—and confirms that the rumbling dunes were as entertaining for men and women in the tenth century as they were for Chiang and Stein in the twentieth century. Another telling fragment is a pledge signed by sixteen men who swear to care for the Caves of the Thousand Buddhas. "Even if Heaven and Earth collapse, this vow shall remain unshaken," the document says. Given the date of their promise—March 25, 970—it is unlikely any of the men lived to see the Library Cave sealed early in the next century, but they may have helped amass the documents placed inside.

Other material about Dunhuang includes ancient topographical records with details that Stein verified from his own travels.

One manuscript tells how a general drew his sword and stabbed a mountain to create a waterfall and quench the thirst of his men. Based on the precisely recorded distances in the ancient manuscript, Stein was convinced he knew the waterfall referred to. The same document also tells of a Dunhuang dragon that required regular sacrifices of local livestock. The dragon—Giles likened it to a local Loch Ness monster—was said to live in a spot known as the Spring of the Jade Maiden. Again, Stein matched the topographic details in the manuscript with his own surveys of the region and concluded he once camped beside the spring-fed lagoon considered to be the dragon's lair.

Most of the manuscripts in the Library Cave were written in Chinese, but some were in Sanskrit and others in Tibetan, including what is believed to be the world's oldest known collection of Tibetan sutras. Others contained the angular characters of Runic Turki (an early Turkish script), Syriac (a branch of Aramaic) and the vertical writing of Uyghur. The cave even held a fragment in Hebrew acquired by Paul Pelliot—all evidence of Dunhuang's rich monastic libraries and the cosmopolitan nature of the oasis.

For Stein and Pelliot, the presence of each language exposed an aspect of the region's past. The abundance of Tibetan Buddhist documents attested to Tibet's dominance two centuries before the cave was sealed. Others scrolls raised questions about the spread of religious beliefs, including Manichaeism. Once among the world's most widespread religions, Manichaeism became a rival to Buddhism and Christianity. "What had this neat, almost calligraphic manuscript to do in the Buddhist chapel?" Stein mused. The Library Cave held several Manichean documents, including two hymns titled "In Praise of Jesus." A translation, published in 1943, includes numerous references to "Jesus the Buddha"—evidence of the Manichean belief that Jesus and Buddha were different incarnations of the same person.

The Library Cave also yielded a painted portrait on silk, rendered at half life-size but with some unexpected features. In Stein's five-volume *Serindia*, the male figure with a halo around his head was listed as a bodhisattva, but this face was like no other in the cave. The nose was decidedly Western, as were the mouth and lips. And there were other strange features: the saintly figure, with a cross on his headdress, had a red moustache and beard, and the painting's only surviving eye was blue. After *Serindia* was published in 1921, Stein wrote to his one-time rival Albert von Le Coq to say he thought the figure was a Buddhist image that "Nestorian Christians could safely address their prayers to." How the Christian image found its way into the cave remains as unanswered as Stein's musings about the Manichean documents.

ﻼﻮ

Overwhelmingly the material in the Library Cave was religious, and some dealt with life beyond the grave. An illustrated copy of *The Sutra of the Ten Kings*, sixteen feet long, depicts the Chinese Buddhist version of Judgment Day, when the deceased pass through ten courts, and the kings of the underworld decide whether the dead will be reborn into a higher or lower realm. Colored paintings on the scroll depict a hell where sinners carry wooden stocks fastened around their necks, whippings are commonplace and limbs are gouged with spears.

Another Library Cave manuscript offers even more graphic descriptions through the story of one of literature's most devoted sons, Maudgalyayana. After her death, Maudgalyayana's greedy, deceitful mother is sent to the underworld. The son approaches the Buddha for help and learns his mother is suffering in the Avici realm—the worst of hell's eight levels. The young monk attempts a rescue. He arrives in a world as terrifying as anything Hieronymus Bosch imagined. A translation of the tale, by American professor Victor H. Mair, describes the horrific scene:

Iron snakes belched fire, their scales bristling on all sides. Copper dogs breathed smoke, barking impetuously in every direction. Metal thorns descended chaotically from mid-air, piercing the chests of men. Awls and augers flew by every which way, gouging the backs of the women. Iron rakes flailed at their eyes, causing red blood to flow to the west. Copper pitchforks jabbed at their loins until white fat oozed to the east . . . There were more than several ten thousands of jailers and all were ox-headed and horse-faced.

When Maudgalyayana locates his mother, her agonies are abundant. "At every step, metal thorns out of space entered her body; she clanked and clattered like the sound of five hundred broken-down chariots."

Through the Buddha's intervention she is released, only to be sent to the realm of the Hungry Ghosts where wants cannot be satiated. When she spots a stream of cool water, it transforms into pus. Her throat constricts until she is incapable of swallowing even a drop of moisture. Once more the Buddha tells Maudgalyayana how his mother can be saved, but her greed ensures she is reincarnated as a black dog that eats excrement from latrines before the diligent son finally helps her attain a human rebirth.

꙳

One of the richest themes to emerge from Abbot Wang's cave is science, although the scrolls that fall within this broad heading range from the practical to the perplexing. A first-aid manual, "Single Ingredient Empirical Remedies to Prepare for Emergencies," offered prescriptions for cholera, vomiting, gastric reflux, sores, ulcers, and more. In a preface, the unknown author wrote of his intention to have the medical manual's advice carved into rock so that its wisdom would be available for all.

It is possible that goal was achieved about 1,000 miles southeast of Dunhuang. In the Longmen Grottoes in Henan province is a cave with a stone stele engraved with 140 treatments known as the Longmen prescriptions. Wang Shumin, a Beijing scholar of traditional Chinese medicines, has pointed out that many similarities exist between the early first-aid manual written in ink on the Dunhuang scroll and the advice set in stone at the Longmen Grottoes.

Mere snippets remain of what was once part of a fifty-volume encyclopedia of medical knowledge. The Dunhuang copy survives as five scraps that discuss herbal uses for garlic, calabash (an edible gourd), various grains and fruits. The full text, compiled in 649, was so revered that the Tang dynasty's rulers distributed copies of the encyclopedia across the country, and it remained the definitive source of medical knowledge for 400 years. As China's first official medical handbook, it predates the earliest European counterpart, the Nuremberg Pharmacopoeia, by 800 years.

What constitutes medicine among the Dunhuang texts sometimes extends to what would now be considered cosmetics and domestic products. One torn scrap includes formulas for skin creams, a breath freshener, a fabric deodorizer, and even a hair tonic made from the leaves of a watermelon vine. Another medical manuscript attempts to divine the future based on where moles appear on the body. In auspicious locations, they predict that a woman will respect her husband and bear good sons. Elsewhere, they bode ill, such as one mole said to foretell that a wife will kill each of three husbands.

In the Dunhuang scrolls, medical science sometimes merges with the metaphysical. An intact text titled "Wondrous Instructions on the Skill of Quiescent Breathing" includes Daoist spells. Among these are an invocation to the crane spirit and "secret instructions conferring invisibility." A separate text promises to enable a person to fly. The levitation recipe is simple enough, but the ingredients could be hard to procure: the potion requires the seeds and root of a lotus plant that has been stored for a thousand years.

∽

The dating of the Dunhuang manuscripts is a mix of science and art. Some documents contain elaborate colophons that pinpoint their creation. In other instances, scholars look for changes in how Chinese characters are written. One trusted method of determining a document's age involves checking whether certain characters appear at all. As each new dynasty came to power, some characters became taboo and were banned from use. This was done out of respect for an important person, typically the emperor, but the effect was to leave a means of dating documents as leaders rose to power and fell from grace. Even the absence of a single stroke on a character can help date a manuscript.

China's preoccupation with documenting and dating events shows up elsewhere: in almanacs and calendars found in the Library Cave. Almanacs could only be printed with the emperor's approval, although the cave's treasures prove there was some bending of these rules. In the West, almanacs with their voluminous facts may seem like statements of the obvious, but China placed great importance on them. Their use in predicting cosmic events—eclipses, the alignment of planets and the like—was viewed as evidence of an emperor's perfection. If, through his diviners, the emperor could distinguish auspicious days from catastrophic days, it was proof of his divine entitlement to rule. But there was a downside to what was known as "heaven's mandate." Fail to predict the arrival of a celestial event such as a comet or even sun spots and the masses didn't merely grumble. They felt entitled to rebel against a leader who they believed had been abandoned by the gods.

The Library Cave contained a handful of black-market almanacs, including a complete copy for the year 877. Produced nine years after the Diamond Sutra was printed, it shows entrepreneurs willingly muscled in on the emperor's monopoly, even though the punishment for printing or possessing banned documents was harsh. Merely owning books on astronomy or prognostication could incur two years' forced labor. The rewards for printers, though, were abundant. For sellers, the books were in high demand but cheap to make, courtesy of the same woodblock-printing techniques that produced the Diamond Sutra. For buyers, an almanac could divine the opportune days for marriage or moving into a new house, even the best time to trim one's fingernails. In short, they provided the recipe for a better life.

The need for almanacs and calendars was acute, in part because China employed a complex method of calculating dates using the moon as well as the sun. Much as we now add a leap day to a modern calendar, the emperor occasionally added an entire month to reconcile solar and lunar time. While the superstitious modern man can easily work out the next Friday the thirteenth, his counterpart in ancient China was helpless without consulting the works of the emperor's astronomers.

Of course, to make such predictions required great precision in reading the heavenly omens. Chief among those were the stars and planets, and here, too, the mountain of documents inside the Library Cave contained vital material, including a seventh-century star chart. The 11-foot-wide chart is the oldest known map of the stars from any civilization. In China's world view, the heavens were part of the human realm, not distinct from it. The role of astronomers and astrologers was to monitor the celestial and terrestrial to ensure the two were in harmony.

The great Sinologist Joseph Needham is believed to be the first to recognize the significance of the Dunhuang star chart. In the late 1950s, he estimated the chart was created in 940. More recently, French scholars Jean-Marc Bonnet-Bidaud and Françoise Praderie, together with the British Library's Dr. Susan Whitfield, concluded it is centuries older. Chinese taboo characters were one factor, but the other involved a crudely drawn illustration on the far left of the scroll. The image depicts an archer, believed to be the god of lightning. Just as the fashion-conscious today can date a dress by its hemline or shoulder pads, the hats of ancient China can be assessed by the ear flaps. Those on the archer's hat are flat; later fashion saw men starch the flaps so they stuck out. The result of this detective work into language and millinery has been to push back the date of the star chart's creation to between 649 and 684.

Aside from the fact that it survived at all—the chart is the thickness of cigarette paper—the chart's accuracy and comprehensiveness are remarkable. Where Greek mathematician and astronomer Ptolemy catalogued 1,022 stars, Chinese astronomers recorded 1,339 stars. The celestial scroll begins with drawings and interpretations of clouds and vapors—one in the shape of a prancing wolf portends a son becoming a general or high official. It unrolls to reveal twelve panels showing the positions of the stars in black, white, and red, corresponding to three schools of Chinese astrology. The star chart is also notable for solving the challenge of how to render the three dimensions of a spherical world onto the two dimensions of paper. The West wrestled with the problem until the sixteenth century, when the Flemish cartographer Gerardus Mercator produced the solution still used today.

A comparison of the ancient map and the charts of modern astronomers reveals that the Chinese rendered the sky with startling accuracy. But there is one significant omission: the North Star. As with the prohibition of certain Chinese characters, the polar star is absent because it symbolized the emperor.

꙰

Apart from manuscripts on paper, the other great finds in the cave were splendid paintings on silk. At one point when Abbot

Wang was fetching items from the Library Cave in 1907, Stein rescued some cloth Wang used to level the floor on which the Library Cave's scrolls were stacked. Today, that fabric is among the most prized pieces of Chinese silk embroidery in the British Museum. The eighth-century piece, "Shakyamuni preaching on the Vulture Peak," is nearly eight feet long and more than five feet wide. The British Museum considers the split-stitch embroidery to be "one of the most magnificent of all the compositions found in the hidden library at Dunhuang." At its center is the Buddha, who stands on a lotus pedestal, flanked on each side by a crouching lion. From his indigo hair to each toenail on his bare feet, he has been rendered with exquisite Tang dynasty care. His right shoulder is bare and he preaches the Lotus Sutra. On each side he is accompanied by a bodhisattva and a disciple, and the cheek of the bodhisattva on the left is rendered in a whorl of tight stitching.

Of China's four great inventions—paper, printing, gunpowder, and the compass—the first three feature in the Library Cave. Paper and printing are obvious, but gunpowder figures as well. A painted silk banner, obtained by Pelliot and now in the Musée Guimet in Paris, contains the world's earliest known depiction of firearms. The banner shows the Buddha Shakyamuni withstanding an assault by the demon Mara and his fellow tormentors who are trying to prevent the Buddha's enlightenment. As the Buddha sits impervious in lotus position, the demons deploy a firelance—an early flamethrower—and a hand grenade against their serene target.

Another textile, one that speaks of human yearning, is an altar valance with colored strips of silk that dangle like a row of men's ties. Stein noted small knotted tassels hung from some of the streamers—indicating they were offerings by devotees praying for children. Stencils, too, were tucked among the piled manuscripts. Just as woodblock printing enabled mass production, stencils could render multiple images of the Buddha and hasten the accumulation of merit. Examples of stenciled art abound on the walls of the Mogao Caves.

Other uses of paper that emerged from the Library Cave include Buddhist paper flowers. Spanning four inches, the six hand-cut votive flowers probably once decorated the caves of Mogao. Glued to the walls, such flowers adorned the caves in lieu of real flowers that would have struggled in the extremes of the Taklamakan Desert. Stein even found a brush inside the Library Cave that was used to apply glue.

The Library Cave was a source of knowledge about ancient music, too, and Pelliot collected some of China's oldest surviving musical scores—works from the Tang dynasty (AD 618–907). Some of the music is for the pipa, a pear-shaped stringed instrument that features in the murals of numerous grottoes. The music is still played today. In 1987, twenty-five of the Dunhuang songs were recorded by Beijing's Central Folk Orchestra and released on compact disc.

Study of the scrolls, silks, and other items in recent decades has resembled piecing together a global jigsaw puzzle as fragments held in different countries are matched up. Some material, even more minute than the scattered fragments, has occupied the attention of scholars. Debris from Stein's packing crates that once held Library Cave material—stored for a century in two jars—has been the object of recent investigations. "Stein dust," as the British Library calls it, has undergone chemical analysis for what it might reveal about conditions inside the Library Cave in 1907. But it is the preoccupations of people, rich and poor, that have proved most illuminating. Across the centuries, some aspects of the human condition are unchanging, whether they concern a fascination with the heavens, questions about an afterlife or just the search for the right words after a drunken night on the town.

14

Stormy Debut

After the excitement and freedom of the expedition, Stein, now in London with his cargo, faced a period of what he considered drudgery and servitude. His desert finds needed to be unpacked, sorted, listed, photographed, and published. The task was immense but necessary if scholars were to benefit from the discoveries, and he wanted that work undertaken while the collection was still together, before London and Calcutta divided the spoils.

Stein was relieved when his friend Fred Andrews, whose case Stein had been pushing, was able to work with him on the sorting. The pair previously worked together on the finds from Stein's first expedition, and the General—as Stein's friends dubbed him—knew Andrews was the ideal loyal lieutenant. An artist, teacher and, by 1909, head of Battersea Polytechnic's art school, Andrews was reliable and attentive to detail. While Stein was in the desert, Andrews had dutifully filled every request: for candles, a fountain pen, pince-nez, and far more. "I am afraid you will find that distance is no protection from me," Stein had once warned Andrews. The requests were undiminished by Stein's return to

Europe, although now they turned more domestic as the explorer asked that his spats be mailed to him and his Khotan rugs be dry-cleaned.

Stein's antiquities were initially housed at the Natural History Museum in South Kensington, then part of the British Museum. They were not destined to stay there long. Instead, space was being made available at the British Museum in Bloomsbury. However, when Stein saw the rooms he had been allocated, he was furious. He and his antiquities—obtained at so high a human cost—were to be consigned to a basement. The space, previously used to store newspaper files, was dark and cramped. In short, it was a cave. The usually measured Stein protested bitterly.

"Neither during my official career in India nor in the course of my explorations have I been called upon to work in what without exaggeration may be designated a sort of cellar," he wrote.

In the course of my explorations I have been obliged to expose myself to a good deal of physical hardship and I believe that the strain incurred in the interest of my scientific tasks has not failed to affect my constitution to a certain extent. But I may safely assert that I could face these hardships more willingly than daily imprisonment for prolonged hours in a confined room partially below ground and devoid of adequate light and air. I believe that after the sacrifices I have made in the interest of the scientific tasks entrusted to me by Government, I ought not in fairness be called upon to work in conditions which apart from direct physical discomfort would make my tasks during my Deputation here unnecessarily irksome and trying.

He toyed with shifting the collection elsewhere, even out of London. He considered the Ashmolean Museum in Oxford. His plea to remain in the Natural History Museum was rejected, as was his attempt to relocate to its neighbor, the Victoria and Albert Museum. So seven months after arriving in London, the much-traveled collection was on the move again, across to Bloomsbury and into the British Museum's basement. Andrews reassured Stein: "The cellar has been made as habitable as such a place can be, with large writing tables, armchairs, writing materials, mats, hand basins, soap & towels, dusters etc. The lock . . . has now been altered so that only our key and the master keys will open it."

Stein kept a tight rein on who could access the rooms. Although the scrolls and other finds were based at the British Museum, they were not yet part of its collection. This couldn't occur until his backers agreed on a division—and that would take many acrimonious years. In any case, Stein didn't spend a great deal of time in the basement cave poring over his finds. With Andrews left to the grinding work of sorting, Stein traveled in Europe, lectured and, in 1910, accepted an offer of rooms at Oxford's Merton College, where Percy Allen was a research fellow. Stein was happy to do so. He disliked cities in general, London in particular, and the enclave of Bloomsbury most of all. His bay window at Merton College looked out on a meadow that was far different from his alpine vista at Mohand Marg, but his second-floor rooms provided the peace and solitude he needed to write an account of his expedition.

They also afforded him the companionship of Percy and Helen Allen, not to mention Dash, who would spend the rest of his life in their care. Dash's arrival in England had even been reported in the press. The little fox terrier had covered the 10,000 miles of the expedition mostly on foot, during which he survived on scraps from the camp larder, according to the Daily Mail. Dash was described as a useful watch-dog whose chief recreation was chasing wild donkeys and yaks and hunting hares. The report concluded on a patriotic note: "He has true British terrier blood in his veins, although India was his birthplace."

Stein lived amid Oxford's dreaming spires as though still camped in the desert. He kept his camp chair, which had accidentally been dropped on his perilous crossing of the

Taklamakan Desert. Incredibly, a Chinese official recovered the seat and posted it to Macartney in Kashgar, who ensured it eventually reached Stein. No one could accuse Stein of living extravagantly. He inquired about getting a cheap wooden writing-table made similar to his folding camp table. He even retained his well-traveled Jaeger wool blanket—although he did have it cleaned of bloodstains from his amputation.

Once settled, he turned to writing an account of his second expedition, *Ruins of Desert Cathay*. At the same time, he kept a close eye on the progress of his collection in Bloomsbury and everyone associated with it, right down to clerical assistants. He was impressed by a young Scottish woman, Florence Lorimer, a bright Oxford graduate who had been recommended by Helen Allen. Lorimer, then aged twenty-five and with a background in classics, was capable, intelligent and seemed able to take on some of the cataloguing. Lorimer began work in October 1909, leaving behind Oxford's Bodleian Library, where she was one of its first female employees. This was the beginning of a thirteen-year association with Stein. It is a mark of how much Stein valued Lorimer that she soon acquired a nickname, for such monikers were confined to his inner circle. She was dubbed the Recording Angel.

❧

With manuscripts in so many languages, including Chinese, Tibetan, Sanskrit, Uyghur, and Sogdian, Stein drew on the expertise of scholars across Europe. For the Chinese manuscripts, he turned to his one-time rival Paul Pelliot. In September 1910, Stein proposed that the French scholar make an inventory of the Chinese manuscripts. Pelliot, eager to see what Stein had acquired, agreed, and two crates containing more than four hundred manuscripts were sent to him in Paris—a not uncommon practice at the time. It is probable the Diamond Sutra was among the precious scrolls sent across the English Channel. Stein seemed happy with Pelliot's initial progress, noting the Frenchman made many interesting discoveries among the Chinese manuscripts.

A small private viewing of Stein's finds was held at the British Museum in 1910, and the first public exhibition was at London's Crystal Palace in 1911. The latter event was part of the Festival of Empire to mark the coronation of the new king, George V. The objects selected from Stein's material consisted mostly of silk paintings of Chinese and Tibetan deities but also included a manuscript wrapper, a fragment of damask, an embroidered miniature Buddha, and an embroidered cushion cover. Stein's disapproval of exuberant Tibetan Buddhist imagery was reflected in the small catalogue accompanying the exhibition. He noted with relief that none of the figures showed the "extravagant multiplication of limbs nor the other monstrosities in which the imagery of Tibetan Buddhism delights . . . there are found but very few figures which are of a form not altogether human; it is evidence of the sober sense and good taste of the Chinese donors, and of the monks under whose direction these votive pictures were prepared." *The Times* described the collection as of "epoch-making importance" for the study of Chinese religious art. But the Diamond Sutra—still to make its first public appearance—was not among the sixty-eight items displayed.

As work continued on the finds, Stein was busy in Oxford completing *Ruins of Desert Cathay*. The published "populist" account of his journey to Turkestan ran to two volumes, each a door-stopping 500 pages. Stein was reserved in his manner but prolix in his writing. He finished the huge work on July 5, 1911, and by the end of the year, with his three years of special leave almost over, he sailed again for India and planned another foray into Turkestan.

His book, published in 1912, contains the first brief description and photograph of the Diamond Sutra. He calls it simply a roll.

With what passes for scholarly exuberance, Stein wrote: "Greatly delighted was I when I found that an excellently preserved roll with a well-designed block-printed picture as frontispiece, had its text printed throughout." And the usually meticulous Stein gets its date wrong—twice. The scroll dates neither from 864 nor 860, as the text and a caption state, but 868. Such uncharacteristic errors suggest he was yet to grasp the printed scroll's full significance.

〜

In June 1912, within months of returning to India, Stein received unexpected news at his alpine camp on Mohand Marg. He had been awarded a knighthood. He wrote to Allen:

Late last night a heavy Dak bag arrived & to my utter astonishment brought a letter from the Viceroy's hand announcing the K.C.I.E. [Knight Commander of the Indian Empire], with a bundle of congratulatory telegrams from Simla. I scarcely believed my eyes, for how could I as a simple man of research foresee this more than generous recognition . . . It seems in some ways an overwhelming attention.

Later in the same letter, he sought Allen's advice on a tricky matter of protocol: would it be acceptable, he wondered, to call himself Sir Aurel, rather than, say, Sir Marc—his unused first name—or the more awkward Sir Marc Aurel? He was known as Sir Aurel Stein from then on. It is an indication of his acceptance by the establishment that, Hungarian-born and Jewish, Stein was accorded such a rare honor.

Stein was swamped with congratulations, the most amusing of which was penned by Allen on behalf of Dash II, who had just been replaced in Kashmir by a puppy, Dash III.

Many congratulations, dear Master. Am wearing my collar of achievement. If I had known this was coming, I should not have cried on the Wakhjir. Whip the young one & keep him in order. Bow wow. (Have assumed this title) SIR DASH, K.C.I.E.

The other notable tribute came from Chiang, still employed in Kashgar by George Macartney as his secretary at Chini Bagh. Stein had been eager for news from his devoted assistant, to whom he sent a copy of *Ruins of Desert Cathay*.

> *I cannot express on paper how glad I was to hear the grant of the title of K.C.I.E. on you. An honour well merited and bestowed on a deserving servant of the Govt . . . I received your book too in two volumes. The company of this book is to me as if I was in your company and marching in your train in the great plain-like Taklamakan . . . Please accept my best thanks for the kind thought of remembering by the gift of this book.*

By then, Stein knew Chiang had suffered a serious illness that had left him profoundly deaf. But Chiang was quick to reassure him. "Mr. Macartney has been kind to me and is patiently putting up with the inconvenience of shouting at the top of his voice occasionally and trying to make me hear what he wants me to write for him."

Macartney updated Stein on his secretary's health. Stein arranged for an expensive ear trumpet to be sent from London. Despite his hearing loss, Chiang still proved invaluable to Macartney. "Deaf as he is, poor old Chiang-ssu-yeh manages somehow to hear what is going on in the Yamens and keeps me well posted," Macartney wrote. Chiang's deafness was not the only change in Kashgar that Macartney reported. Revolutionary fervor swept across China in 1911 and 1912 and led to the collapse of the Qing dynasty, the abdication of Emperor Puyi, the last emperor, and the establishment of the Republic of China. Eventually the revolutionary zeal reached the Turkestan oases.

"Chiang-ssu-yeh can't quite make up his mind as to the respective merits of the old, and of the new, regime and his indecision is reflected in his head-dress. His queue [pigtail] has certainly gone; but now and then when a reactionary wave sweeps over the Chinese in Kashgar with murder in the air, he wishes he still had his appendage.

One day he puts on an English cap and another a Chinese hat, just according to how he is influenced by the political weather. Today the English cap is in favour with him," Macartney wrote.

Although Macartney made light of Chiang's response to the political change, the violence would reach Chini Bagh's gates. Across the Turkestan oases, Chinese officials had been murdered and their *yamens* looted. In Kashgar, officials had been beheaded and their bodies left in the streets as a warning. The Macartneys provided shelter within Chini Bagh's garden for terrified refugees fleeing the slaughter. "Massacres of Chinese officials by Chinamen in the old & new cities of Kashgar started," Macartney wrote. "You know old Yuen Taotai, well he was set upon at night by 15 assassins and cut to pieces."

᳴

Back in London, work was underway at the British Museum for the first major exhibition of Stein's great discoveries from Turkestan. Paul Pelliot, who had been examining the Chinese scrolls for two years, was helping to select material for the show. If there was a eureka moment as the Diamond Sutra was slowly unwound and the realization dawned that here was the world's oldest printed and dated book, Stein makes no reference to it. But by late 1912, the work had been identified. That was when Pelliot wrote to the museum about the items to be included in the forthcoming exhibition, saying: "Finally there is the substantial printed roll that Stein has already put aside, the Diamond Sutra of 868." Although Stein won the race through the desert, it may have been his greatest rival, Pelliot, who first recognized the significance of Stein's most celebrated find.

The exhibition was planned for spring 1914 to celebrate the opening of the British Museum's new wing. After nearly a thousand years in a cave and a perilous journey across continents, the Diamond Sutra was at last to be revealed to the public.

Neither Stein nor Andrews would see this event. Soon after returning to India, Stein started lobbying his friend to leave the Battersea Polytechnic "mill" and join him. Stein helped sow the seeds of discontent in a letter—by turns disparaging of London and flattering of his friend—that reveals much about his attitude to life: "The more I see of this glorious land the more I pity those who live & work in London whatever their pay, etc. For a pleasant existence in England one must have independence, plenty of money—or else tastes not too artistic or intellectual. Yours are!" Stein's persuasion worked. Andrews accepted a role as head of a new art institute in Srinagar and, with his wife Alice, readied to leave London for Kashmir. Stein's friend from his youthful Mayo Lodge days in Lahore would soon be back with him on Indian soil.

Stein's regret at missing the forthcoming exhibition was fleeting. His interest was exploring, not working behind the scenes to prepare a show. "In a way I am sorry that neither of us will see the exhibition, on the other hand we shall both be saved from spending time over what is scarcely to be regarded as altogether productive work. Our experience at the 'Empire Exhibition' was enough for a long time," he wrote to Andrews. Lorimer was left to oversee the details, sending weekly updates to Stein from the museum "cave."

The museum's new wing, due to be opened by King George V, was much anticipated. *The Times* of May 2, 1914, noted Stein's antiquities would be on show and singled out a star attraction. "[The collection] contains some of the most remarkable curiosities of literature hitherto discovered. Among them is a complete printed roll of Chinese workmanship. It is 16 ft long and was printed in 868 by Wang Chieh [Wang Jie]. This is the oldest specimen of printing known to exist."

The same day as *The Times* published its report about the Diamond Sutra, a death threatened to derail the public unveiling.

The ninth Duke of Argyll, a former governor-general of Canada, died at Kensington Palace. The long-awaited opening planned for five days later might be delayed, Lorimer wrote.

✼

Late on a spring morning, two open landaus, each pulled by four horses, left Buckingham Palace. The royal party, King George V and Queen Mary and their daughter Princess Mary, made the short journey along Pall Mall, Regent Street, Shaftesbury Avenue and Charing Cross Road before arriving at the museum, where they were met by a guard of honor provided by the Artists Rifles, a volunteer regiment initially raised among painters, musicians, and actors.

Although the royal visitors wore mourning dress to mark their bereavement, the official opening went ahead on May 7 as planned. The Queen's outfit was somber, but nonetheless impressed *The Times* correspondent, who noted approvingly that "the Queen wore a hat covered with black jet and a string of magnificent pearls." In another newspaper, the *Daily Sketch*, the entire event was overshadowed by the appearance of the teenage princess and the sign of her growing maturity. Its headline the next day read: "Princess Mary makes her first public appearance since she put her hair up."

The Archbishop of Canterbury, the museum's principal trustee, was waiting on the steps. No doubt security was tight. Just a few weeks earlier, a suffragette had taken a meat cleaver to Velazquez's *The Toilet of Venus (The Rokeby Venus)* in the nearby National Gallery, and the British Museum itself had been warned to expect similar attacks. The Prime Minister, Henry Herbert Asquith, politicians, ambassadors, and the building's architect, John James Burnet, were among those gathered to hear the Archbishop's opening address— "needlessly long," according to *The Manchester Guardian*.

After unveiling a bust of the late King Edward VII, the royal party toured the new galleries.

"The King and Queen showed especial interest in the astonishing collection of finds brought home by Sir Aurel Stein from Chinese Turkestan. These pictures and manuscripts—vestiges of civilisations hardly known to the experts in these matters—are arranged with strange effect in the wide bleak spaces of the great ground floor gallery," the same paper noted.

The Times also singled out Stein's collection, calling it the most exciting part of the opening exhibitions of museum treasures, which also included works by William Hogarth and Leonardo da Vinci. "His two greatest finds were, first, the remains of a very ancient Chinese frontier wall, with towers and guard-houses, the whole of which was absolutely unknown; and secondly, in a region that is still inhabited, the marvellous contents of a certain walled-up cell in the caves known as the 'Caves of the Thousand Buddhas.'"

After the morning's pomp and ceremony, a private viewing was held in the afternoon. It took place in an elementally charged atmosphere. Clouds blackened the sky making it hard for visitors to see the Diamond Sutra or any of the other material in the thirty-two cases. Lorimer updated Stein: "There was a succession of heavy thundershowers and it became extremely dark. After a time they put on the big lights in the gallery but the lights at the top of the cases themselves were not yet finished, so that one could not see anything at all well."

Among those peering into the cases was Stein's one-time rival Albert von Le Coq. The German had arrived back in Europe two months earlier after another eight-month trip to Turkestan with his assistant, Bartus. Von Le Coq had returned with more than 150 cases of antiquities, but few of these matched the treasures he saw before him.

There was no sign of Paul Pelliot. Long before the exhibition opened, disquiet had been brewing over what came to be dubbed the "Affaire Pelliot." Pelliot was a dazzling scholar, but the dawdling pace at which he was working on the cataloguing ignited fears the task might never be completed. Lionel Barnett, the British Museum's keeper of Oriental Printed Books and Manuscripts, wrote a pointed letter to Pelliot. What progress was he making? When did he expect to finish? Barnett alluded to the possibility of appointing a replacement.

Stein was quick to defend the Frenchman. "He is better qualified than any scholar living to deal with the hundreds of local documents comprised in the collection. His readiness to prepare the inventory therefore represents an advantage such as is not likely ever to be offer [sic] again," Stein wrote to the British Museum's director, Sir Frederic Kenyon.

Pelliot insisted he would complete the work, yet soon a replacement was being discussed despite the Frenchman's assurances. Lionel Giles, then assistant keeper of Oriental Printed Books and Manuscripts, could take on the role, Barnett suggested to the museum's director:

> *If you should prefer to break off the bargain [with Pelliot], I should think that Giles might do the work sandwiched in with his other cataloguing. He is not by any means a specialist in this subject; but he has a really good knowledge of the literary language, and could make a useful hand list. The work would probably not proceed very rapidly, but it would go on regularly.*

The director concurred, and the huge task fell to Giles, among others. And it took years. Giles's catalogue of Chinese manuscripts—the largest category—was not published until 1957. Stein did not live to see it.

〜❀

How to divide Stein's huge haul of manuscripts, murals, and other antiquities was a thorny question. With two backers, the British

Museum and the government of India, the intention was the larger share of the treasures would return to India. Under the agreement reached before Stein left for Turkestan, India would get three-fifths of the treasures, having contributed £3,000 of the £5,000 allocated to the expedition, the British Museum two-fifths. The deal was agreed to long before anyone knew the nature of what Stein would uncover.

Most of the antiquities Stein brought back were fragile, and the contents of the Library Cave especially so, consisting mainly of paper scrolls and silk banners. A damp, unstable atmosphere could quickly destroy what had been preserved for a thousand years in the dry desert. Stein wrote to Kenyon setting out his views:

> *It is from every point of view desirable to keep those objects which are specially liable to injury through atmospheric and other influences in a place where every care can be given to their preservation. In the second place there can be no doubt that among such objects must be reckoned all paintings on silk and other fabrics; the tempera paintings on friable mud plaster; the wood carvings; the embroideries and figured textiles; and all written records on wood and paper. All these have during long centuries of burial become impregnated with fine disintegrated particles of salt from the desert and thus particularly liable to attract atmospheric moisture, etc.*

Stein feared that even if the objects survived a return journey to India, no museum there would be able to care for them adequately. The tropical hothouse environment of Calcutta's Imperial Museum—"a vast marshy delta"—was particularly unsuitable. The delicate material should remain in Britain, he argued. This effectively meant most of the finds—as well as the most valuable—should stay. There was another reason too: imperial pride. It would be difficult to compete with the great collections of Eastern art being built up by institutions in Berlin, St. Petersburg,

Paris, and elsewhere unless most of the collection was retained by Britain.

But when the India Office learned of Stein's views on the inadequacy of their museums, its officials were furious:

> *The museums in this country have the first claim to such articles of archaeological interest as may be collected at the expense of Indian revenues . . . To the view that our Indian museums are, for climatic reasons, unsuitable for the preservation of articles of a perishable nature, we are unable to assent. On the contrary, we have reason to believe that, with proper precautions, antiquities can be quite as well preserved in Calcutta, Lahore or Delhi as in London.*

Anyway, the intention was not to house the Indian share in Calcutta but in a new museum proposed for Delhi. In the meantime, India's share of the manuscripts and documents still needed for study could remain for up to five years at the British Museum.

The tussle between Britain and India over the antiquities continued behind the scenes during the early years of World War I. There was agreement on one matter: it was too risky to remove anything until after the war ended. Barnett protested vehemently at what he called the proposal to assign "rotting lumps" to the British Museum. The acrimony escalated when Fred Andrews, then in Srinagar, weighed in on the Indian side. Andrews objected to some of the swaps suggested by Laurence Binyon, the museum's deputy keeper of Oriental Prints and Drawing.

Binyon was also a poet and is best remembered for penning *For the Fallen*, with its lines still repeated at annual commemorations for the war dead in Britain and Australia: "Age shall not weary them, nor the years condemn . . ." But over Andrews's proposed division of some silk paintings, Binyon penned fighting words: "Mr Andrews's disadvantages in the matter are apparent from the inaccuracies in his report, and from his own admissions."

Eventually an agreement was reached, and today the manuscripts are in the British Library; silk paintings, sculptures, and coins in the British Museum; textiles in the Victoria and Albert Museum; and murals and silk paintings in the National Museum in New Delhi.

When he had heard this much and penetrated deeply into its significance, the Venerable Subhuti was moved to tears.
VERSE 14, THE DIAMOND SUTRA

15

Treasure Hunters

Stein was the first, but by no means the last, foreigner to arrive on Abbot Wang's doorstep eager to relieve him of treasures. As Stein's caravan desperately searched for the end of the Keriya River in the Taklamakan Desert and he counted cartridges ready to relieve the suffering of his ponies, his arch rival, Frenchman Paul Pelliot, arrived at Dunhuang on February 12, 1908. Pelliot was unaware that Stein had seized the Silk Road's greatest prize.

Pelliot, too, had heard the rumor of a hidden cache of manuscripts, when passing through the Turkestan capital Urumqi, 600 miles from Dunhuang. Clearly word had spread along the northern Silk Road, which is where Albert von Le Coq heard the tale.

Pelliot, on the cusp of his thirtieth birthday, was joined on his first and, as it turned out, only Turkestan expedition by a photographer, Charles Nouette, and a doctor, Louis Vaillant. Like Stein, Pelliot found no sign of Wang on his initial visit to the site and discovered the Library Cave was locked. The Frenchman found Wang in Dunhuang and the pair agreed to meet at the caves. But when they did, a frustrated Pelliot learned that the key had been left behind in Dunhuang. He also learned that Stein had preceded him. But, Wang assured Pelliot, Stein had spent only three days at the caves. In fact, Stein stayed twenty-four days.

It was March 3 before the cave was unlocked and Pelliot was allowed inside. When he entered the holy of holies, as he called it, he was dumbfounded. The cave was still crammed with between 15,000 and 20,000 scrolls. Pelliot spent three feverish weeks going through them. He estimated it would take six months to examine every scroll properly. But he was determined to look briefly at each and raced through a thousand a day. Dust in the cramped cave caught in Pelliot's throat and the fragrance of ancient incense still lingered in some of the scrolls. A photograph from the time shows him in a heavy dark coat, hunched over a scroll just inside the Library Cave. The mural of the two trees, before which Hong Bian's statue once stood, is just visible on the rear wall. Pelliot is surrounded by tightly packed bundles. In front of him, the naked flame of his candle is perched alarmingly close to the priceless paper scrolls.

Although beaten to the cave by Stein, Pelliot had one clear advantage. He knew exactly what he was looking at, for he spoke and read Chinese. The Professor of Chinese at the École française d'Extrême-Orient in Hanoi had no need to rely on an assistant's scant knowledge of Buddhism. He could cherry-pick the best—and did. He set aside two piles of scrolls: those that he wanted at any cost, and a second pile that he would take if he could. As well as the Chinese scrolls, he picked his way through a range of other documents in Tibetan, Uyghur, Khotanese, Sogdian, even Hebrew, and a Nestorian Gospel of St. John. He also examined the silk banners. Among the best were a silk depicting an ancient pilgrim carrying scrolls on his back—an image that evokes Xuanzang—and the painting of demons attempting to distract the Buddha with a fire-lance.

Pelliot learned Stein had paid Wang for manuscripts and resolved to do likewise, and his negotiations with the abbot appear to have been less fraught than Stein's. By the time Pelliot arrived, Wang had already successfully sold scrolls and other material to a foreigner and was reassured to realize that no one had discovered his secret deal. Stein had laid the groundwork, and Wang had begun spending the money on restorations to his caves. But emboldened as he was to enter into a deal with Pelliot, Wang was not prepared to sell all the cave's remaining contents. Pelliot paid Wang about £90 for his haul, which included more than 4,000 scrolls in Tibetan, 3,000 in Chinese, thousands of fragments in Sanskrit, and about 230 paintings on silk, cotton, and hemp. The scrolls and manuscripts are now in Paris's Bibliothèque nationale de France and the textiles, including the silk banner of the ancient pilgrim, are in the Musée Guimet.

As the antiquities safely steamed to France, Pelliot headed to Beijing. There he showed Chinese scholars some of what he had purchased. The reaction was immediate. Word went back to Dunhuang: everything left in the cave was to be sent to Beijing. Compensation would be paid to Wang.

Wang had seen the last of Pelliot, but not the last of the foreign devils. A Japanese aristocrat, Count Otani Kozui, head of the Pure Land School of Buddhism, was behind an expedition that arrived late in 1911. He was a mysterious figure—Britain suspected he was a spy—who sent two assistants to Dunhuang. Over eight weeks, the pair bought manuscripts from Wang and left behind their names in two of the caves.

༻❀༺

Seven years after Stein first arrived at Dunhuang—and just as the Diamond Sutra was being readied for its first exhibition in London—he returned. Zahid Beg, the trader who first told Stein about the manuscripts, rode out to meet the explorer as he arrived at the oasis on March 24, 1914. His caravan included his new fox terrier—Dash III—and some of his old retainers, although not Chiang, who was still ensconced as Macartney's secretary in Kashgar. Chiang's hearing had improved, but he was no longer fit for harsh desert travel. Stein was less than impressed with the "listless" replacement and dearly missed Chiang's companionship.

Much had changed at Dunhuang in the intervening years. Gone was the magistrate Wang Ta-lao-ye in whose *yamen* Stein had nearly frozen while wearing his thin European clothes, and the influential military chief Lin Ta-jen had died. But Wang was still the guardian of the caves, and the priest welcomed back his former patron. Wang was "as jovial & benign as ever," Stein told Allen. "He had suffered in no way from the indulgence he showed me in a certain transaction and only regrets now that fear prevented him from letting me have the whole hoard in 1907."

It was an opinion shared by Wang's Dunhuang patrons, Stein claimed—with more than a touch of self-interest—so impressed were they on seeing how the money from Stein and Pelliot had been spent. Outside the caves Wang had planted an orchard, built stables and a large guesthouse. He had also been busy within the caves. Drift sand had been removed and gaudy new statues installed. But Stein's heart must have sunk when he saw the fate of the murals. Fresh plaster had been applied over some, others Wang had demolished to allow access through the rock walls to about fifty hard-to-reach grottoes. Stein could see for himself how the money had been used. Nonetheless Wang insisted Stein inspect a big red book that accounted for each horseshoe of silver.

Wang complained bitterly that money promised as compensation for the removal of the manuscripts to Beijing never arrived. It had been skimmed off at the various *yamens* along the way. Some of the manuscripts bound for Beijing also disappeared. Wang described how the scrolls had been carelessly bundled onto six carts. The carts were delayed in Dunhuang, during which time some of the manuscripts were filched by locals. The pilfering continued during the journey, Stein later wrote. He was convinced many of the manuscripts he bought in Gansu and in neighboring Turkestan during this third expedition came from the Library Cave. Although Beijing had ordered the cave be emptied, Wang, the former soldier, had not exactly followed orders. "Honest Wang, the priest, has been acute enough to keep back abundant souvenirs of the great hoard," Stein confided to Allen.

Wang's former quarters were now a storeroom, and from them he produced boxes crammed with manuscripts. Stein knew Pelliot had since selected the best of the scrolls and so did not realistically hope for important finds among Wang's secret cache. Nonetheless, he filled four cases with nearly 600 rolls. The manuscripts Wang apparently squirreled away after the cave was emptied raise questions for scholars today. Were they really from the Library Cave? If not, where have they come from? Could some be forgeries? The jury is still out.

◇─∽

Four months after Stein's caravan pulled out of Dunhuang in April 1914, a Russian expedition arrived. Its leader, Sergei Oldenburg, also bought manuscripts. Then, for a decade, the foreign explorers vanished from Dunhuang. Even so, Stein's thoughts at least were never far from the City of Sands. He worked on a five-volume scholarly account of his second expedition, *Serindia*. On the evening he finished it on Mohand Marg in 1918, he celebrated by lighting a bonfire, signaling the event to the Kashmiri mountains and to Andrews, who could see it fifteen miles down the valley in Srinagar. It was a fitting way to signpost a work that included his discovery of the beacon watchtowers from which ancient Chinese soldiers lit fires to signal to their comrades far across the desert.

The last of the foreign explorers to arrive in Dunhuang was American Langdon Warner in 1924. Warner knew the cave had been emptied, but his interest was in murals not manuscripts, in the visual image rather than the written word. In spite of that, he too claimed to have bought manuscripts that had "strayed," as he put it, from the Library Cave to nearby oases. Warner—purportedly a model for Steven Spielberg's Indiana Jones—was an art historian with Boston's Fogg Museum. Like those who preceded him, Warner was overwhelmed by what he saw: "There was nothing to do but gasp," he wrote.

But he did far more than gasp. Warner stripped murals from the walls with the conviction that, like Stein before him, he was "rescuing" the artworks. In the years between Stein's departure and Warner's arrival, other foreigners had reached the caves. In the early 1920s, about 400 Russian soldiers fleeing the revolution across the border were interned at the Caves of the Thousand Buddhas. Camped there for six months, the White Russians left their marks. Magnificent murals were blackened by soot from their fires. Others were deliberately defaced. Warner was appalled: "Across some of these lovely faces are scribbled the numbers of a Russian regiment, and from the mouth of the Buddha where he sits to deliver the Lotus Law flows some Slav obscenity."

Damage by other visitors was accidental and thoughtless, but no less destructive. Warner recorded how worshippers put greasy palms on delicate murals or leaned against them. And he saw how sheepskin-clad visitors had brushed so often against a row of saintly figures in a narrow entrance that part of the painting had rubbed away. "My job is to break my neck to rescue and preserve anything and everything I can from this quick ruin. It has been stable enough for centuries, but the end is in sight now." He had no reservations about his actions. "As for the morals of such vandalism I would strip the place bare without a flicker. Who knows when Chinese troops may be quartered here as the Russians were? And worse still, how long before the Mohameddan rebellion that everyone expects? In twenty years this place won't be worth a visit."

By the time of Warner's arrival, Wang's secret stash of manuscripts had been depleted. What Stein, Pelliot, and others failed to take had been souvenired by visiting magistrates, Warner believed. "Each one visits the caves at the end of his term and carries off as many of the precious rolls as the priest admits are remaining. These rolls avert fire and flood and bring luck. They make splendid gifts to higher officials and sell for several hundreds of *taels* each."

Warner's determination to strip the wall paintings was no snap decision. He arrived at the caves equipped to remove murals. Despite the January cold that froze the chemical fixative, he nonetheless removed about a dozen murals as well as a three-foot-tall kneeling Tang dynasty figure which he broke from its pedestal, wrapped in his woolen underwear and sent back to Harvard. "No vandal hand but mine had disturbed it for eleven hundred years," he wrote.

Within a year, Warner returned for more. But by then the mood had changed. His party arrived just as news swept China that a British police officer had shot dead a dozen protesting Chinese students in Shanghai in May 1925, sparking antiforeigner campaigns across the country. Anger at events in Shanghai was not all that turned the tide against Warner. Foreign explorers who were once welcomed were now shunned. The backlash focused on Stein and Pelliot, "neither of whom could ever come back and live," Warner wrote.

Warner's men were forbidden to camp at the caves and were threatened by angry locals who gathered nightly outside their Dunhuang inn. Warner had been so demonized that he was accused of blasting entire hillsides to remove chapels. He had even been blamed for causing a local drought and famine, he told

Stein in a letter. Nor did Abbot Wang escape the shift in local public opinion. The modest amount of money Warner had paid Wang on his first visit had ballooned to a vast sum around the oasis rumor mill. There were demands that Wang share his non-existent fortune. When he failed to produce it, he was threatened with death. He saved himself by feigning madness.

Despite Warner's cautionary letter, and well aware of the changed political climate, Stein decided to mount a fourth expedition, funded by Harvard. Stein was sixty-seven years old and retired from the Indian civil service. If he hoped for a final victory lap of Turkestan, those dreams could not have been more misplaced. The expedition ended in a humiliating retreat.

The signs were ominous. Just as he was about to set off, he learned his good friend Thomas "the Saint" Arnold had died. Arnold's one-word telegram—"Rejoice"—had elated Stein in 1905. Now the loss of the friend he had known since his Lahore days left him grief-stricken. Still, he departed from Kashmir in August 1930. Even before reaching Turkestan, one of his surveyors fell ill and abandoned the journey. And soon after Stein arrived in Kashgar, his dog Dash V died.

China's attitude toward his work had changed dramatically. Its National Commission for the Preservation of Antiquities strenuously opposed his expedition. The commission regarded Stein's stated aim—to explore ancient trade routes and the path taken by Xuanzang—as cover for his true purposes: to excavate archaeological sites in Chinese Turkestan and to export artworks. The commission made its views clear in a 1,000-word document that reached the British Museum in early 1931.

The commission argued that the export of archaeological objects could be justified only when the objects were obtained legally, their removal caused no damage and if no one in the country of origin was sufficiently competent or interested in studying them or in their safekeeping. "Otherwise it is no longer scientific archaeology, but commercial vandalism. Sir Aurel Stein's conduct during his previous journeys in Chinese Turkistan verges dangerously on the latter." The commission was scathing of Stein's treatment of Abbot Wang:

> *Sir Aurel Stein, taking advantage of the ignorance and cupidity of the priest in charge, persuaded the latter to sell to him at a pittance what he considered the pick of the collection which, needless to say, did not in any way belong to the seller. It would be the same if some Chinese traveller pretending to be merely a student of religious history goes to Canterbury and buys up the valuable relics from the cathedral care-taker.*

The document, signed by nineteen scholars and the heads of Chinese cultural institutions, lamented that the collection lay scattered and unstudied between London, Paris, and Tokyo, while "their rightful owners, the Chinese, who are the most competent scholars for their study, are deprived of their opportunity as well as their ownership."

The Times weighed in, spirited in its defense of Stein and withering in its attitude to China, where people were "still in the stage of grinding down fossils in the belief that these are dragon bones with special medicinal properties." By the middle of 1931, Stein's passport had been cancelled and he had retreated to Kashmir. He would never see Turkestan again.

16

Hangman's Hill

On a January morning in 1934, high above the quiet Welsh seaside town of Aberystwyth, a letter arrived on the desk of William
Llewellyn Davies, head of the National Library of Wales. The
imposing granite and stone building, with its sweeping view to
the west over tranquil Cardigan Bay, faced away from the political
storm clouds gathering over mainland Europe.

In Germany, Adolf Hitler had come to power a year earlier.
Meanwhile, in London, thoughts turned to protecting the nation's
cultural treasures in the event of another war. The chiefs of the
nation's museums, libraries, and art galleries had met a few weeks
earlier to discuss finding safe havens for their valuable works. The
letter to Davies touched on that very question. It was from the
British Museum and wanted to know if the National Library of
Wales could offer shelter for some of the museum's treasures,
including books, manuscripts, prints, and drawings. It would not
be the first time the library had done so.

The library, which opened in 1916, was the realization of
the dream of a young Welshman, a politician named Thomas
Edward Ellis who, like Stein, had been inspired since boyhood

by ancient civilizations. As a result, he looked for a way to preserve his own culture and envisioned a repository of Welsh treasures. His vision became reality with the aid of local quarrymen and coalminers, who chipped in part of their meager wages to help pay for it.

By early 1918, the library, built on a humpbacked hill known locally as Grogythan, or Hangman's Hill, was housing more than Welsh treasures. In the closing months of World War I, the British Museum sent prized items for temporary shelter. Although only a small number went from London to Wales—most objects were protected on site, including in vaults in the Bloomsbury basement—it was a dress rehearsal for what was to come.

Tensions across Europe escalated throughout the 1930s. As the Nazi regime became increasingly aggressive, war seemed inevitable, especially after the major European powers signed the Munich Agreement of September 1938. It was an act of appeasement that allowed Germany to annex the Sudetenland on its border with Czechoslovakia. British Prime Minister Neville Chamberlain returned from Munich to reassure a nation and deliver his famous "peace for our time" speech. Many rightly believed Chamberlain's agreement with Hitler would deliver no such thing. However, it did deliver breathing space to prepare— as much as possible—for another conflict. A new war with Germany would be vastly different from the Great War. This time the conflict would be fought not in trenches but in the air above cities, and inevitably London would be targeted.

Air attack was rare in World War I. Nonetheless, the damage inflicted was high. London was bombed twenty-five times between May 1915, when the first German Zeppelin airship attacked, and May 1918. Almost 600 people were killed and 174 buildings destroyed. The British Museum escaped unscathed— the nearest bomb exploded about 450 feet away—but a new war might have vastly different consequences.

Within the British Museum, lists were drawn up of portable treasures to be evacuated, based on existing inventories of what to rescue in case of a fire. The twelfth-century Lewis Chessmen carved from walrus tusks and the Sutton Hoo treasures from a medieval Anglo-Saxon ship burial were among the top priorities. A month after the Munich Agreement was signed, the Oriental Department of the British Museum had its list ready. Stein's manuscripts were among those singled out for rescue. From the King's Library, six Oriental treasures on exhibition were earmarked for evacuation. Among them was the Diamond Sutra.

༄

In March 1939, Hitler invaded Czechoslovakia. In May, the Nazis forged an alliance with Italy. With each passing month, Germany's aggressive intentions toward Poland became more apparent. On August 23, 1939—a week before World War II began—late-night calls went out to staff at the British Museum. Others received telegrams. Some were told to prepare for an early start next morning; others were ordered to pack a suitcase. Behind the scenes, word had come from the Home Office: war was inevitable. It was time to move the nation's treasures.

Long before normal opening hours on August 24, vans drew into the museum's forecourt and people began arriving at the building. Thousands of folding plywood cases the museum had amassed in its basement over the previous year were brought out of storage and packing began soon after 7 a.m. Members of the public arriving to use the Reading Room—it remained open that day—may have been puzzled to see box after box being carried out of the building and into waiting vans. However, anyone who had read *The Times* that morning knew Germany and the Soviet Union had just signed a non-aggression pact, paving the way for the invasion of Poland, and may have guessed what was happening.

The destination of each box was initialed in chalk on the side. An initial "T" meant the tube. Many large sculptures and objects that would be unharmed by damp made the short trip to a disused section of the Aldwych tunnel, part of London's Underground. The advantage of the tube—where the Elgin Marbles were stored—was its proximity to the museum. But there was a risk: if an airstrike hit one of the tunnels beneath the nearby River Thames, the entire network could be flooded.

Most material went to safe areas outside London. "Safe" meant at least two miles from towns, factories, and aerodromes. Coins, medals, and small, portable antiquities were bound for more salubrious surrounds than the tube. They went to two stately homes, Boughton House and Drayton House, about seventy miles away in Northamptonshire. Books, manuscripts, prints, and drawings were destined for a 250-mile journey to Aberystwyth.

For months, museum staff had been preparing for wartime, refining the lists to determine which among the hundreds of thousands of objects were most precious and practicing fire drills in case of an air raid. Now museum personnel were positioned at seven loading points around the building: one for material bound for the nearby Aldwych tunnel, and six for material destined for the railways. At the front of the museum's colonnaded building, they filled vans with books, manuscripts, prints, and drawings to be loaded onto trains and transported to the National Library of Wales.

Late that day, a Great Western Railway train left London's Paddington Station for Aberystwyth. The railway was dubbed the holiday line and since the mid-nineteenth century trains had brought vacationers to the seaside town to spend a week promenading along Cardigan Bay. But some of the passengers who alighted with their suitcases at Aberystwyth station were not embarking on a late summer break, and at least one would spend most of the war years there. They were part of a team of

British Museum staff sent to receive the first of the irreplace-able cargo. For the next twelve days, consignments arrived, each accompanied by a museum escort and a railway inspector. They arrived by the ton. By the time Britain declared war on September 3, 1939, about a hundred tons had already arrived in Aberystwyth, including 12,000 books and the same number of manuscripts, and three-quarters of the museum's most prized prints and drawings.

The volume of the works was breathtaking. So was their rar-ity. The gems of the collection went to Wales. These included the Magna Carta, quartos and folios of Shakespeare, Milton's *Paradise Lost,* early books printed by William Caxton, and two Gutenberg Bibles. There were letters and documents written by England's kings and queens, by Oliver Cromwell, Sir Walter Raleigh and Sir Francis Drake. There were prints and drawings by Leonardo da Vinci, Michelangelo, and Raphael as well as by British artists J.M.W. Turner and William Blake. The jewels of Western culture were not all that went. So did 171 cases containing 6,000 Oriental books and manuscripts in more than fifty languages, including illuminated manuscripts in Persian and Hebrew as well as the Dunhuang scrolls.

꒰ꍑꆚ꒱

Even today, Aberystwyth on the mid-Wales coast is remote—if not by Gobi Desert standards then at least by British standards. In 1939 it was considered an unlikely target for military attack, which is why its library was chosen for safe storage. Many other institutions also sought refuge within it for their treasures. Some of the National Gallery's smaller paintings went to Aberystwyth. Its larger ones—too big to pass through the doors or windows of the library—went elsewhere. Jan van Eyck's *The Arnolfini Portrait* and John Constable's *The Hay Wain* were among those sent to Penrhyn Castle in north Wales. (That was not without problems; there were fears its habitually drunken owner might topple into the master-pieces.) Pictures in the Royal Collection arrived at Aberystwyth as did works from St. Paul's Cathedral, the Ashmolean Museum in Oxford, Corpus Christi College Cambridge and, curiously, from the New South Wales Government in Australia.

Cardigan Bay along the Welsh coast had little to attract enemy bombers. But the National Library of Wales, prominent and almost impossible to camouflage, could serve as a landmark for aircraft en route to attack British cities, including the key port city of Liverpool, just 100 miles northeast. The main fear in Aberyst-wyth during the early days of the war was of a stray bomb rather than deliberate attack.

Air raid precautions were established at the Welsh library. Buckets of water and sand were placed throughout the building, along with stirrup pumps, hoes, shovels, and other fire-fighting equipment. Scholars whose pre-war days were spent scrutinizing ancient Hebrew script or early European printed books became familiar instead with steel helmets, respirators, and asbestos cloths. Twenty-four-hour rosters were organized so the collec-tions were never unattended. Each night two armed constables patrolled the premises.

Room had to be found for the massive influx of books, manu-scripts, prints, paintings, and people. Carpenters erected shelves, and rooms were assigned for the collections and staff. Every bit of space was needed. Even ancient papyri found a temporary home in a disused elevator shaft.

Overseeing Stein's Chinese scrolls and other non-European treasures was Jacob Leveen, the British Museum's deputy keeper of the Department of Oriental Printed Books and Manuscripts. He was a Hebrew scholar who spent much of the war in Wales. Air-attack aside, his biggest worry was theft, and he feared the Orien-tal collection was the most vulnerable. Unlike the material of other departments that went to Aberystwyth, the Oriental manuscripts were not isolated from the public but were housed in the Readers' Room. Locks on the fifty-five latticed manuscript cases were flimsy. He wanted chains and padlocks. The most secure option of all, however, was being secretly constructed only a few minutes' walk from the library. When finished, it would create a place in which Stein's collection would be strangely familiar. For tucked into Hangman's Hill, just 200 yards below the National Library of Wales, a manmade tunnel was being carved. During the war years, it was surrounded with every bit as much secrecy as Abbott Wang's grotto, and guarded far more closely.

Even before World War II began, thought had been given to creating underground storage for Welsh cultural treasures. A tunnel was first suggested in late 1937. Work began in August 1938, by which time the British Museum had agreed to pay half the cost of the bomb-proof cave in return for half of the space. The horseshoe-shaped tunnel—six-and-a-half feet wide, ten feet high, and eighty feet long—was dug into the grey slate hillside. The tunnel hit geological snags and was still being built when war broke out and the first trains carrying the British Museum treasures arrived in Aberystwyth.

The site was referred to as the Air Raid Precaution tunnel—a name even more prosaic than Dunhuang's Cave 17—and construction of the £7,000 secret project was finished by October 1939. But before any of the fragile works on vellum, papyri, and paper could be placed inside, atmospheric testing was undertaken. This damp cave in the Welsh hillside lacked the natural climatic advantages of Abbot Wang's grotto in the arid desert. But it did benefit from cutting-edge technology. It was the United Kingdom's first experiment in air-conditioned underground storage. Electricity, heating, and ventilation were installed. In case the local power station failed, a hand-operated ventilation system was fitted. After several months of tests, the tunnel was ready to serve its secret purpose.

Printed books and manuscripts were packed into millboard boxes and on August 2, 1940, the first treasures were discreetly carried down Hangman's Hill and into the tunnel. For nearly three weeks through the long summer days and short nights of that month, material was taken down what is now a track between fields where sheep graze. After nearly a millennium hidden in the Gobi Desert, Stein's precious manuscripts were once again in a manmade cave.

✼

German troops marched down the Champs Elysees, Hitler stood before the Eiffel Tower and France fell by June 1940. The Nazis had reached Britain's doorstep and the threat of invasion loomed. Nowhere was considered safe, at least nowhere above ground. Not even the library at Aberystwyth. The tunnel was considered bomb-proof, but anything that could not be housed underground needed to be moved.

The British Museum looked at alternatives. It needed something bigger than the little Welsh tunnel. Eventually a disused stone quarry in Wiltshire (then being used to grow mushrooms) was selected. Boxes and boxes of material were sent from Aberystwyth and elsewhere to Westwood Quarry in 1942. The National Gallery sent its paintings to a former slate mine, Manod Quarry, on a mountain above the town of Blaenau Ffestiniog in North Wales. There, a road under a railway bridge was lowered to allow Anthony van Dyck's large *Equestrian Portrait of Charles I* to pass underneath without the monarch losing his head—as he did in life. Meanwhile, the space freed up in the Aberystwyth tunnel was quickly filled with additional material from the British Museum. Leveen updated his boss in June 1942 about what had gone to Westwood Quarry and what was still to be removed. He also listed some documents that were to remain in Aberystwyth. These included Hebrew and Arabic scrolls, mostly illuminated manuscripts, that Leveen planned to work on. But also listed to stay in Wales were Aurel Stein's scrolls.

Back in London, the British Museum's galleries had been emptied of their greatest treasures. But when the air raids that had been anticipated failed to materialize, a small show was mounted in August 1940 comprising duplicate antiquities, casts, and models that had been left behind. Staff dubbed it the "suicide exhibition." But within a month, the intense bombing of London—the Blitz—began. The British capital was targeted for nearly sixty consecutive nights. More than 43,000 people died across Britain in the Luftwaffe air strikes. The Houses of Parliament, St. Paul's Cathedral, and Westminster Abbey all took hits. So, too, did the British Museum.

The museum's first direct hit, on September 18, 1940, pierced the roof and went through four concrete floors before lodging in a sub-floor. The 2,200-pound bomb was enough to destroy the entire building. Fortunately, it did not explode. Four days later, a smaller bomb hit with uncanny precision; it plummeted through the same hole—again, incredibly, without exploding.

Then devastation arrived. On September 23, at 5:38 a.m., a bomb passed through the roof and floor of the Ethnographic Gallery and exploded in the King's Library, the room where the Diamond Sutra had been on display. The King's Library bomb destroyed thirty feet of bookcases and set fire to others. More than 400 volumes were destroyed or damaged beyond repair.

Just a month later, on October 16, an oil bomb hit the building's magnificent domed Reading Room. Once again the museum was fortunate. Most of the burning oil spilled across the roof's copper sheeting. Of all the attacks, though, none was more destructive than that on the night of May 10, 1941, when dozens of incendiaries struck the building. Fire spread through many rooms, and more than 200,000 volumes were lost, either destroyed in the flames or damaged by water from fire hoses. By then, the wisdom of removing not just the Diamond Sutra but all the treasures was apparent.

Bombing in World War II, of course, was not one-sided. Berlin alone was subjected to hundreds of air raids. The city's Ethnological Museum—which held many of the Silk Road objects Albert von Le Coq returned with—was among the buildings damaged in bombing runs launched by the Allies. Some of the largest of Bezeklik's magnificent murals, which had been permanently attached to the museum's walls, were reduced to rubble.

Not all the wall paintings the Germans brought from the Silk Road were destroyed. After Berlin fell in 1945, the Russians carried off some of what survived. The fate of the paintings was little known until 2008 when the Hermitage in St. Petersburg displayed a number of them as part of a Silk Road exhibition. The exhibition catalogue obliquely acknowledged that part of the German collection "found itself in the Soviet Union" after World War II.

In the UK, when the war ended, the treasures that had been stored in the Hangman's Hill tunnel returned to the British Museum and elsewhere. The last load left the tunnel on May 23, 1945, and power was switched off the next day. Today vines tumble over the tunnel's brick entranceway. Behind its locked metal door, damp has seeped through the arched brick ceiling from which disconnected electrical wires dangle. Long abandoned, the tunnel has been largely forgotten.

꙳

Soon after the scrolls he had removed from a manmade cave in the Gobi Desert found refuge in a manmade tunnel in the Welsh hillside, Stein was back in India. Retired from the civil service, he continued to camp in his tent on Mohand Marg during the warm Kashmiri summers. There he enjoyed the solitude to write and walk amid the alpine scenery with the latest Dash by his side. He left, reluctantly, when duty called or the autumn chill arrived.

He never ceased his intrepid travels and explorations, including through Swat Valley, coastal Baluchistan, and the Middle East. In his later years, on a tour through the mountainous North-West Frontier region of present-day Pakistan, he was accompanied by a hardy young Pashtun soldier. At the end of the trip, the exhausted man reported on his experience to his military superior: "Stein Sahib is some kind of supernatural being, not human; he walked me off my legs on the mountains; I could not keep up with him. Please do not send me to him again, Sir." Even in his sixties Stein could tire men half his age. He ventured into Iran four times and, in his mid-seventies, took to the air to survey Iraq.

In the summer of 1943 as war raged in Europe, eighty-year-old Stein was about to fulfill a boyhood dream: to visit Afghanistan. His desire to see the land where Gandharan civilization once flourished and Alexander the Great left his mark had shaped Stein's life. It was why he took up Oriental studies, why he went to England and why he then went to India. In 1906, he briefly stepped on Afghan soil as he crossed its slender northeast finger on his way to Dunhuang, but repeated attempts to return had been thwarted by bureaucracy and politics over four decades, until an unexpected invitation arrived.

In late September 1943, he left Mohand Marg and stayed a few days in Srinagar with his friend Dr. Ernest Neve, whose late brother had treated Stein's injured foot decades earlier. On his last evening with Dr. and Mrs. Neve, Stein fainted but had sufficiently recovered by the next morning to leave by truck for Peshawar, near the Afghan border. In Peshawar, once a center of Buddhist learning, he visited a longstanding friend. Without a trace of irony Stein confided to his diary that his friend appeared alert "but his age of 60 shows." Stein traveled by car from Peshawar to the Afghan capital, Kabul, arriving on Tuesday, October 19. He stayed at the US Legation, hosted by another friend, Cornelius Engert, America's representative in Kabul. Stein wanted to spend the winter in

Helmand Valley, where Alexander the Great had passed, but within days of arriving in Kabul, he caught a chill. He cancelled a trip to the cinema to watch *Desert Victory*—not about the Taklamakan, but World War II and the battle for North Africa. His condition worsened by Sunday evening and he had a stroke. He knew he would not recover and requested a Church of England funeral.

He approached his death without regret. "I have had a wonderful life, and it could not have been concluded more happily than in Afghanistan, which I had wanted to visit for sixty years," he told Engert. Stein died on the afternoon of October 26, a week after he arrived in Kabul and exactly a month short of his eighty-first birthday.

He was buried in the Christian graveyard in Kabul. Within the mud walls and wooden gate of the cemetery, his grave and those of other foreigners—nineteenth-century soldiers, sixties-era hippies, aid workers and other victims of more recent conflict—have so far survived the ravages of the past decades. His gravestone reads: "A man greatly beloved." Above it is engraved: "He enlarged the bounds of knowledge."

His death prompted effusive tributes. One obiturist compared Stein to his great Venetian hero: "As Marco Polo is regarded as the greatest traveller of medieval times, so Marc Aurel Stein is likely to be considered . . . the greatest traveller and explorer of modern times." Another described him as "the last of the great student-explorers who have written *Finis* on the exploration of the world." The same writer noted that the discovery closest to Stein's heart was not the hidden Library Cave but a fortress associated with Alexander the Great in Swat Valley, the once-Buddhist valley where more recently the Taliban have battled for control. Said *The Times*:

He brought to light a vast realm of buried and forgotten history. His excavations in the arid and deserted spaces of Central Asia drew aside the veil from conditions which existed hundreds and even thousands of years ago . . . He had a genius for unearthing ancient remains and for

reconstructing from them a picture of the past, piling up detail on detail
with cumulative effect. He was a little man, but sturdy and hard as nails.

The most eloquent tribute came not in death, but in life. Following Stein's return from his second Turkestan expedition, his friend at the British Museum Lionel Barnett compared him to ancient Greece's great traveler. "Like Odysseus, Dr Stein has travelled wisely and well, and has seen the cities of many men, and learned their thoughts, and like Odysseus, he has also gone below the face of the Earth and questioned the mighty dead."

Indestructible as Stein appeared in life, in death his name has not been so enduring. He has sunk from memory as quietly and almost as thoroughly as one of his sand-buried cities. Many factors have contributed to this. At the time of his death, the world's attention was focused elsewhere, convulsed by the Second World War. His death was hardly a dramatic, untimely explorer's demise, even if he was poised to embark on a journey few octogenarians would contemplate today. He was not murdered on a Hawaiian beach like Captain James Cook or frozen in the Antarctic like Robert Scott. He remained a reserved, conservative, scholarly man and his writings reflect that. Even his "popular" accounts are largely devoid of the colorful adventures and anecdotes of Albert von Le Coq or Sven Hedin. There is no image of Stein posing in "exotic" local costume, resplendent in turban and flowing robe, as there are of other explorers of the era.

Stein worked in the twilight years of the great age of exploration and archaeological discovery. Even then, the public was far more dazzled by the discoveries of others than by what Stein found. Agamemnon's mask has immortalized Heinrich Schliemann's name; Tutankhamen's tomb Howard Carter's. Stein did not return with gold, jewels or richly decorated sarcophagi. His greatest finds were scrolls. He died just as the sun set on colonialism, imperialism, and the British Empire, which left their own troublesome legacy. The Great Game ended, India became independent, China and Russia locked their doors and Central Asia was off-limits to the West. Stein died barely a decade before the space race dawned, bringing a new field for scientific exploration. And for the popular imagination, the prospect of life on Mars was bound to seem more enticing than the nature of life long ago in a little-known desert.

In the British Museum, a key beneficiary of his travels, hardly any of the objects from Stein's expeditions are on show. In that sense, little has changed since author Peter Hopkirk lamented in 1980: "One cannot help feeling that he merely dug them up in China only to see them buried again in Bloomsbury." Still, no large museum or gallery can display its entire collection, and the material from Stein's expeditions could easily fill a museum of its own. His finds, once the centerpiece of the British Museum's new wing, now occupy only a few glass cases in the museum's Joseph E. Hotung Gallery of Oriental Antiquities, sharing the long gallery with other objects from China, India, and South Asia. In 1914, when thunderstorms darkened the gallery for the King's visit, Stein's objects filled the room. Today, visitors can see little more than a carved wooden balustrade from Loulan, leather armor from Miran, a handful of coins, and a few stucco busts of the Buddha as proof of Stein's arduous journeys through the unforgiving deserts of Central Asia.

*The happiness of one who writes this sutra down, receives,
recites, and explains it to others cannot be compared.*
VERSE 15, THE DIAMOND SUTRA

17

Facets of a Jewel

Stein's name barely registers today and the treasures he found are rarely on view, but the philosophy his work drew attention to has captured popular imagination. Once the preserve of specialist bookstores, today even mass-market chains are likely to stock works on Buddhism. In music, the Buddha's name and image have been appropriated by the popular Buddha Bar series of chill-out CDs. Arthouse directors such as Werner Herzog and Bernardo Bertolucci have made films on the subject, while Buddhism's impact on such Hollywood films as *I Heart Huckabees* and *The Matrix* has been widely discussed in popular reviews and the blogosphere. The religion's leap from the rarefied scholarly world to mainstream Western culture has come in just over a century. Oddly, it began with a poem.

The Light of Asia, an epic in blank verse published in 1879, recounted the life of the Buddha. It was a best seller. More than a million copies were snapped up, and it was read aloud in Victorian parlors across Britain as well as in America. Perhaps the time was right. The publication of Charles Darwin's *Origin of Species* in 1859 questioned long-held religious beliefs. Across the Atlantic, in an America still reeling from the Civil War of the 1860s, it is not hard to imagine why a popular account of a non-violent philosophy may have found fertile ground.

The poem's author was English journalist Edwin Arnold, the editor of London's *Daily Telegraph*. Arnold noted that a generation before he penned his poem, little or nothing was known in Europe of the faith then followed by nearly 500 million people. "Most other creeds are youthful compared with this venerable religion," Arnold wrote in his introduction. Not everyone was pleased with Arnold's poem, which began:

> *The Scripture of the Saviour of the World,*
> *Lord Buddha—Prince Siddartha styled on earth—*
> *In Earth and Heavens and Hells Incomparable,*
> *All-honoured, Wisest, Best, most Pitiful;*
> *The Teacher of Nirvana and the Law.*
> Thus came he to be born again for men.

Devout Christians balked at his parallels between Jesus and the Buddha, and scholars quibbled over aspects of his interpretation. But the public loved it. The work even spawned a Broadway show in 1928, with leading US actor Walter Hampden as the Buddha. The adaptation was less than successful, though, and the show was panned as "amateurish and shallow slop."

By then the life of the Buddha had gone well beyond the cloistered world of Western scholars into the popular and artistic imagination. The German composer Richard Wagner attempted an opera on the subject. He read widely on Buddhism and drafted *Die Sieger,* or *The Conquerors,* about an incident in the life of the Buddha. He never completed the work he toyed with for two decades, although some of its ideas fed into his other operas, especially *Parsifal.*

The Theosophists, an influential and at times eccentric group of thinkers and mystics, took an interest in the world's religions, including Buddhism. But the great popularizer of Buddhism in the West during the first half of the twentieth century was a Japanese layman, D.T. Suzuki. He first arrived in America at the turn of the century, and he taught in universities there and in Japan throughout his life. He espoused Zen Buddhism—a form of Buddhism in which the Diamond Sutra is esteemed. He did so especially after he studied Pelliot's Dunhuang manuscripts in Paris at the beginning of the twentieth century.

Suzuki was a bridge between East and West, between an ancient tradition and a modern phenomenon. He was a prolific and accessible writer who had studied the Christian mystics of the past, including Emanuel Swedenborg and Meister Eckhardt. He was also in tune with the times and engaged with the emerging discipline of psychology. Carl Jung, the influential Swiss analytical psychologist, was among those who admired Suzuki's work. Suzuki's *Zen and Japanese Culture* spawned a series of Zen-related books in the West. Soon the Zen name was linked to everything from flower arranging to motorcycle maintenance.

In the 1950s, less than a decade after Stein died, the words of the Diamond Sutra made an impact in an unlikely place: amid a group of post-war American artists who looked toward Buddhism for inspiration. The Beat Generation was hardly a monastic order, but a radical, hedonistic group of writers and poets. They shook the literary scene in the 1950s and laid a path for sixties counterculture. The writings of Allen Ginsberg, Jack Kerouac, and Gary Snyder in particular alerted a young generation to spiritual traditions of the East.

As a young man, Snyder was drawn to Chinese and Japanese landscape painting and poetry. He had already begun his inquiries into Buddhism when, in about 1950, he came across a book that contained the Diamond Sutra. "I read it as poetry. I was taken with that particular kind of logic: x is not x, therefore we call it x," says the Pulitzer Prize–winning poet. "It's not philosophy, it's not normal poetry. It's a very special kind of literature. It's a strange kind of literature. It's a wonderful, magical, poetic text that you're not sure if you understand or not."

Snyder packed a copy of the sutra in his rucksack when, in the early 1950s, he spent a summer as a fire lookout on a mountain on the Canadian border. It was a short translation contained in D.T. Suzuki's *Manual of Zen Buddhism*. Soon after, he went to Japan for a decade to study Zen Buddhism, which he continues to practice. His teachers there advised against intellectually analyzing the Diamond Sutra and its teaching on emptiness. "They told me, 'Don't read that, you'll get the wrong ideas. Emptiness cannot be understood that way.' So they make you stay away from trying to philosophically grasp something like the *Prajnaparamita* sutras, except to just chant them. The tradition I am in does not debate or discuss something like the Diamond Sutra or the Heart Sutra—not until you are very, very far along in your practice."

None of the Beat poets was as affected by the Diamond Sutra as Snyder's friend Jack Kerouac. From the time he borrowed— and never returned—an anthology of Buddhist writing from San Jose Public Library in 1952, the Diamond Sutra became Kerouac's favorite Buddhist text. He studied the sutra almost daily for several years, and few writings influenced him more.

Kerouac also spent two months alone as a fire lookout, at Desolation Peak on the Canadian border in 1956. He studied one verse of the Diamond Sutra each day and gathered his thoughts for his spiritual odyssey, *The Dharma Bums*. The novel, in which Snyder appears as central character Japhy Ryder, refers repeatedly to the Diamond Sutra and echoes its paradoxical language—including in its opening pages which find the narrator sleeping rough on a California beach and contemplating, Subhuti-like, the grains of sand.

On his mountain lookout, Kerouac, dissatisfied with the ponderous rendition of the Diamond Sutra he had with him, began writing a more accessible version. He was also unhappy with the sutra's English name. He knew "Diamond Sutra" was a shorthand and considered it inaccurate. But "The Diamond Cutter of God's Wisdom" and "The Diamond Cutter of the Wise Vow," alternative names he toyed with, are considerably less catchy than another phrase he coined: "Beat Generation."

As Kerouac was publishing *The Dharma Bums*, British author Aldous Huxley was also drawing on the Diamond Sutra, alluding to it in his final novel, *Island*, in which a cynical journalist is shipwrecked on a utopian island inhabited by Buddhists. It was the favored reading matter of characters in J.D. Salinger's 1961 novel *Franny and Zooey*. More recently, the sutra has inspired other artists. In 1999, German artist Thomas Kilpper incorporated aspects of it in a 4,300-square-foot woodblock carved into the parquet flooring of an abandoned building in London's Blackfriars. The building, since demolished, was the former home of the British Library's Oriental and India section, guardian of Stein's printed Diamond Sutra. In 2009, an avant garde opera titled *Ah!*, based on the Diamond Sutra, was performed in the Walt Disney Concert Hall complex in Los Angeles.

ॐ

In the Bay Area of San Francisco, the city associated with Kerouac and the Beats, another man has looked closely at the words of the Diamond Sutra. For the past decade, Paul Harrison, Professor of Religious Studies at Stanford University, has been working on a new translation. His detailed study is a far cry from Kerouac's freewheeling approach, but Harrison shares a concern about the sutra's name. Harrison prefers the Sanskrit title *Vajracchedika*, rather than either the Diamond Sutra or Diamond Cutter as it is generally translated—or mistranslated, he argues. The name is based on two Sanskrit words *vajra*, usually translated as "diamond," and *cchedika*, usually translated as "cutter."

"The main problem for me is the diamond bit," he says. "*Vajra* isn't really a diamond." *Vajra* refers to a mythical weapon, a thunderbolt. It is the weapon wielded by powerful deities in various traditions: by the Norse god Thor in the West, by Indra in Hinduism and Vajrapani in Buddhism. This fierce protector is often depicted in Buddhist art standing beside the Buddha like a bodyguard and wielding a thunderbolt—as he is in the Diamond Sutra's block-printed frontispiece. (The figure appears in the upper left.) In some Gandharan sculptures, with their fusion of classical and Indian images, he resembles a club-wielding Hercules.

But *vajra* has another meaning. It refers to a mythical, indestructible substance, harder than anything else in the universe. Because a diamond is the hardest material known, that is how *vajra* has been translated. For Harrison, this is not just semantics. The mistranslation affects how the sutra is understood.

"It's not that it cuts things with fine precision, it actually smashes. If I was to translate it into colloquial English, I would call it the Thunderbolt Buster rather than the Diamond Cutter," he says. "What's important is not its precision cutting but its destructive capacity . . . It just smashes any preconception you might have had, or false view, of how the world works."

The title Diamond Sutra is now so entrenched in the West that any change is unlikely, as Harrison freely concedes. Yet it highlights the problems a translator faces. Rendering an ancient sacred text into English is more complicated than translating one modern European language into another. The German literary critic and translator Walter Benjamin encapsulated the difficulty when he wrote that "all great texts contain their potential translation between the lines; this is true above all of sacred writings."

"I think people regard it as a mechanical exercise," Harrison says. "It's easy enough to translate a French novel into English, so translating a Buddhist sutra must be the same only with a different language . . . But if you roll the clock back 2,000 years, in a different cultural context of which you are only dimly aware, the difficulties multiply."

In working on his translation, Harrison combed through numerous early versions, including Sanskrit, the language in which it was first written, as well as Chinese and Tibetan. And he found something curious. From the outset, China and Tibet took different paths with this text. When Kumarajiva made the first translation into Chinese around the year 400, he made choices the Tibetans did not. Kumarajiva's choices have been repeated in translations ever since, including into English. Harrison believes this has resulted in misunderstandings. In his view, the Tibetan translators got it right. "Kumarajiva did a lot of very interesting and creative things with the text," he says. "[Yet] it's so unfaithful to the original." Nonetheless it has been the most popular translation.

The first English translation, by Max Müller in the 1880s, and a later one, by Edward Conze in 1957, have been highly influential. Yet they have reinforced the sutra's reputation in English as being opaquely mystical and beyond comprehension, Harrison believes. He is keen to correct what he sees as their misinterpretations and to aid understanding of the text. He also wants to move away from the odd, unnatural style of language that infuses many English translations of Buddhist texts, not least the Diamond Sutra. "They're often highly inaccurate, they misunderstand the text, and they're couched in this weird kind of language that isn't English," he says. Translations of Buddhist sutras into English still have a long way to go, he believes.

Harrison likens the Diamond Sutra to a piece of music that must be heard to be appreciated or a play that needs to be witnessed. Simply reading the sutra like a novel can be a puzzling experience, given its twists and repetitions. "If you just approach the text with a logical mind expecting things to be done in sequence and no repetitions to occur, it seems very weird," he says.

Memorizing or reciting the sutra might be an entirely different experience, he suggests. "These texts are not meant to be read the way we read books, where we scan pages for information. Unless we're reading poetry, we don't read for the sound of things. We just want to get the plot and find out what's happened or extract some bit of information. I don't think religious texts in a number of traditions work like that. They are meant to be deeply internalized," Harrison says.

There are many levels at which the Diamond Sutra can be understood, says Robert Thurman, one of the best-known exponents of Buddhism in the West. As an author, lecturer, and Professor of Indo-Tibetan Buddhist Studies at Columbia University in New York, Thurman has pioneered a Western way of teaching Buddhist philosophy, combining scholarly discipline and contemporary parlance. He was the first Westerner to be ordained a monk in the Tibetan Buddhist tradition after he traveled to India in the early 1960s. He later returned to lay life, married and became a father (one of his children is Hollywood actress Uma Thurman). Throughout, he has retained his commitment to the religion he encountered in the Himalayan foothills. Thurman, who is fluent in Sanskrit and Tibetan, says that at their core all the *Prajnaparamita* genre of sutras, including the Diamond Sutra, deal with the same question.

"The essential part of the *Prajnaparamita* teachings is the relativity of everything. People get excited about the idea of emptiness, and they think that's something very, very deep and the world must disappear," he says. It doesn't. Rather, it means that contrary to our everyday assumptions, everything in our lives, including ourselves, constantly changes. "People think there's something in me that is *really* me, that is always unchanging. They think it was there when I was sixteen and it will be there when I'm sixty or seventy. They have this sense of a solid being there. But we're empty of that thing. That doesn't mean we don't exist. It doesn't mean we are empty of existence. We exist, but we don't exist in a non-relational way that we feel that we do."

He cautions against equating emptiness with nihilism and a view that life is meaningless. This is a misunderstanding many Westerners make, he says. "The word emptiness is not wrong, voidness is also not wrong. But a more interesting one for us in a modern time would be the word 'freedom.' We are not frightened of that word because we hear politicians rattling on about it," he says. "When you say sugar-free or salt-free or trouble-free, you mean lacking those things."

Thurman, who shares Harrison's concern over the adequacy of English translations of Buddhist texts, says our habit of seeing the world and ourselves as unchanging has unfortunate consequences. "It leads to an exaggerated sense of self-importance. This brings one into terrible conflict with the world, because the world will not agree that one's self is so important," he says. People get frustrated because they think others are getting more than their share, and then become mired in aggression, fear, and greed. "Everything is stressful when one is unrealistic about one's relationship to things."

ᏒᎯᎧ

When Thurman first arrived in India, he did so just as Buddhism was making one of the most remarkable journeys in its 2,500-year history: a return to the land of its origin. Buddhism was wiped out in India around the twelfth century by the spread of Islam and the ascendancy of Hinduism. Although Buddhism flourished in China, Japan, and much of South-East Asia, the religion vanished from its birthplace.

After an absence of almost a millennium, Buddhism's revival in India in the past fifty years has been carried largely on a tide of human suffering. Refugees fleeing China's invasion of Tibet in 1959 have made the dangerous mountain crossing over the Himalayas into India ever since. Many have settled in the northern Indian town of Dharamsala, now the center for the Tibetan government-in-exile and the seat of its spiritual leader, the Dalai Lama. Monasteries, temples, and other Buddhist institutions have been established in the former Raj-era hill station, as they have elsewhere on the subcontinent.

No figure has drawn the West's attention to Buddhism more than Tenzin Gyatso, the fourteenth Dalai Lama. Since he fled Tibet half a century ago, the Nobel Peace Prize winner and the world's best known refugee has traveled the globe to deliver Buddhist teachings about tolerance and compassion. In late 2009, the Dalai Lama arrived in Sydney for a series of public talks, discussions with scientists and meetings with religious leaders.

For the first of his public talks—in an arena more associated with rock stars than red-robed monks—the stage was decked with flowers, colored brocade, iconic paintings, and a central throne. At its feet sat several dozen monks in maroon and saffron robes, their heads shaved, who quietly chanted as they awaited the figure they regard as the incarnation of the Buddha of compassion. The scene was redolent of the Diamond Sutra's frontispiece.

Nearby, in an anteroom decorated with white curtains, a white sofa and a couple of potted plants, the Dalai Lama took time for a private interview in which he reflected on the Diamond Sutra, speaking in English, although it is not his first language. The importance of the Diamond Sutra lies in what it says about the nature of reality, he explains. In particular, its insistence that nothing—and no one—has an unchanging, independent existence. "That does not mean [there is] no existence. Existence is there, but the very nature of existence is due to many other factors, not independently." Reality exists, but not in the way we habitually think of it.

"For example, when you look at me, you consider you are meeting or talking with the Dalai Lama," he says. "So it appears [there is] some almost independent self. You feel Dalai Lama's body is such and such, Dalai Lama's mind is such and such. You feel there is some absolutely independent Dalai Lama. That is ignorance, that is misconception. There is no such Dalai Lama. When I look at you, it's a combination of European body and white hair. There is this person, there is no doubt. I'm talking to this person. But if I investigate where is the person, I can't find [you]. That means absence of independent self."

Understanding this is not merely an abstract exercise. Humanity's problems stem from this mistaken view of reality, he says. "Why that theory is relevant is all these destructive emotions, such as attachment, anger, hatred, are based on ego, 'I.' The stronger the feeling of an independent 'I,' the more possibility of attachment: [we say] 'I love this, I like this, I don't want this,' that kind of thing. The less self-centered the ego, the weaker these destructive emotions automatically become . . . Positive emotions are not based on these misconceptions. Destructive emotion, in most cases, is based on misconception. Because of that [insight], this sutra becomes important and relevant."

Understanding how our view of reality can affect our emotions is of such importance that the Dalai Lama reflects on it each morning. "My daily prayers do not include Diamond Sutra, but [I] meditate on that meaning," he says. "My main practice, daily practice, as soon as I wake up, I investigate: Where is 'I'? Where is Buddha? You can't find him. Every day, as soon as I wake up, I think [about] that."

ॐ

Before dawn nearly every morning in New York City, about twenty men and women assemble at a single-story suburban home. Once inside, they remove their shoes and walk down a set of steps into the heated basement where they sit on the floor and recite the Diamond Sutra. A reading takes about forty minutes, and when they have reached the sutra's final verse, they start again.

Depending on when they begin—some days they rise at 3 a.m., others at 4 a.m.—the group chants the Diamond Sutra in unison up to seven times. Afterwards they repeat the name of the Future Buddha known as Buddha Maitreya for half an hour. And then the members get up from their lotus and half-lotus positions and head off into the early morning light for their homes, to school or to work.

The Diamond Sutra Recitation Group is more than twenty years old, says a current member, Yoon S. (Robert) Han, a Seoul-born lawyer who specializes in maritime law and disputes about construction projects. The group is part of the Korean community in the Queens neighborhood of Flushing, one of America's most religiously diverse communities.

For its readings of the Diamond Sutra, the group uses the Chinese translation by Kumarajiva, the same as Stein's printed version. The words, though, are spoken using a Korean pronunciation of the Chinese characters. Despite this potential language barrier, not every member of the Diamond Sutra Recitation Group is Korean. An Italian man, a pharmaceutical company executive, is among the group's long-time members. The group does not restrict membership to the Korean community, nor does it recruit people. Those who come find it either by word of mouth or through the group's small website, diamondsutra.org.

In the basement room where they assemble, the words of the Diamond Sutra fill an entire wall, and a copy of the sutra is placed atop two cushions that adorn a golden lotus-shaped seat. This reverential treatment is derived from the sutra's text. "The Diamond Sutra specifically states that wherever this sutra is located, there will be a Buddha or his disciples. So the Diamond Sutra, to our understanding, is the Buddha himself," Han says.

Despite their familiarity with the text, the Diamond Sutra Recitation Group does not memorize the sutra's words. Rote learning the Buddha's words would be seen as lacking respect. "We recite it very reverently," he says. "The mindset we have is as if we are in front of the Buddha more than 2,000 years ago, actually listening to his lecture, the dialogue between Buddha and Subhuti."

Throughout the day, members practice what they call "house-keeping of the mind" in an attempt to avoid cultivating self-importance. "As I go through my daily routine, I see a lot of things arising in my mind as I face my adversary, as I face my client," the New York attorney says. "The practice is about training your mind in each of those situations."

Such acts are a continuation of practices that saw Wang Jie commission his printed Diamond Sutra of 868 for the merit of his parents. But intervening centuries and geography have not diminished the sutra's relevance. In Australia, forty minutes from central Sydney, in a building sandwiched between high-rises, the sacred text continues to be used to create merit for the dead.

The Nan Tien temple is an offshoot of Australia's largest Buddhist temple, located in Wollongong, New South Wales. But this modest center, in suburban Parramatta, serves a community of mostly Asian migrants who have settled in the city's sprawling western suburbs. Aside from a pair of lion statues that guard the entrance, the white building has little to distinguish it. But about once a month, nuns, monks, and lay members convene to chant the Diamond Sutra.

The Sunday morning ceremony begins with an offering of incense to a white ceramic Buddha that sits on a platform at the front of the room. Under a ceiling of angelic apsaras that would not look out of place on the walls of the Mogao Caves, the congregation then sits on red velvet cushions and begins chanting.

Led by two nuns and accompanied by a steady staccato beat tapped out on a wooden block, the group of about fifty people recites the sutra in Mandarin. For about forty minutes, the text reverberates hypnotically off the wooden floor and walls that are covered with miniature bas-reliefs of the Buddha.

When the sutra's recitation is finished, the assembly chants the Buddha's name and slowly weaves single file between the rows of red cushions several times, their palms pressed together in reverence. Then the lights are dimmed. A gong, a bell, and a drum sound. Finally, they dedicate the merit of their act for the deceased.

⁎

Just as Buddhism has evolved as it has traveled, adapting to local cultures and conditions, the Diamond Sutra is also being discovered, recited and studied in the West today beyond the traditional confines of temples.

A Sydney lawyer, Andrew Fisher, began reading the Diamond Sutra before high-pressure legal cases. A Buddhist friend suggested he do so to calm intense anxieties Fisher felt ahead of complex judicial proceedings. It was an unorthodox introduction to the Diamond Sutra. But Fisher, who died in 2008, never charted a conventional course. As a young man in London he had worked for the influential 1960s underground magazine *Oz*, which became the subject of an infamous obscenity trial. He later wrote a play about those turbulent years, *A Taste of Oz*, which was produced at Britain's National Theatre. His career also saw him venture into film, publishing, and television presenting, but

Fisher was in his sixties before he embarked on his unusual way to cope with professional pressures.

"Andrew started reading the Diamond Sutra and made a strong connection with it. He found it actually did calm him down," says Fisher's widow, Renate Ogilvie. He particularly liked the figure of Subhuti in the Diamond Sutra, the disciple said to have had an ungovernable temper before he encountered the Buddha. Fisher continued reading the sutra even when he was not preparing for difficult cases. Ogilvie, a German-born psychotherapist and Buddhist teacher who married Fisher in 2000, read the sutra daily as part of an orderly practice. Fisher's approach was different.

"He read it in a completely unstructured way," Ogilvie says. "He read it in the evening in bed before he went to sleep. It is true to say it was his only Buddhist practice."

Fisher continued to enjoy reading the Diamond Sutra until Alzheimer's claimed his ability to do so. Yet it remained a part of his life until the end. As his long illness worsened, he fell into a coma and it was clear he had only days to live. Ogilvie moved into his hospital room to tend to her husband around the clock. Friends came to visit, and her students performed Buddhist rituals. But afterwards, when Ogilvie and Fisher were alone in the quiet room filled with flowers and candles, she returned to a familiar practice.

"He was in a coma, but as Buddhists we assume that the consciousness, the mind can freely communicate. I talked to him all the time and so on, but I also read the Diamond Sutra for him each day," Ogilvie says. "That was very soothing for me as well, because it was my practice anyway. But it was also something Andrew really loved and appreciated. So it was a very powerful thing to do. I remember it really quite fondly, reading this particular sutra in the circumstances. I thought there really could be nothing better than the Diamond Sutra."

Fisher died peacefully in Ogilvie's arms a few days before Christmas 2008, aged seventy. Ogilvie considered how best to prepare a funeral that would be attended by close friends and family, few of whom were Buddhist. She wanted to create a ceremony that was delicate and meaningful but not overtly Buddhist. After the eulogies were delivered, she read the final eloquent lines of the Diamond Sutra.

"Reciting that verse, which is the essence of the Diamond Sutra because it describes *shunyata* [emptiness] in these beautiful poetic images, was a discreet and tactful way of actually introducing the essence of Buddhist wisdom teachings," she says. "I thought just reading the verse was meaningful to him and me. And to the others, it was just a poem."

18

Shifting Sands

The eyes of the Diamond Sutra's reverential monks have focused on the Awakened One for more than a thousand years. But behind the locked door of the British Library's conservation department the robed figures have been joined in their devoted attention by Mark Barnard. As manager of the library's conservation section, he has come to know every fiber and wrinkle along the sixteen-foot five-inch document while undertaking the single greatest conservation effort in the scroll's long life.

On an April afternoon in 2009, he interrupted his labors to explain the work. Much of it has involved undoing the well-intentioned efforts of the past century since the scroll arrived in London. Those attempts to strengthen the scroll, including adding a border and linings, actually increased strain on the Diamond Sutra as the different papers pulled against one another each time the sutra was rolled.

Near a wall map of the terrain explored in Stein's epic travels, Barnard recounted how he had already devoted more than 600 hours to removing the early linings, concentrating on the sections of the scroll that contain the words of the Buddha rather than his image, working his way inch by inch across the text. He turned to a long wooden bench on which lay a square maroon box about the size of a family-sized pizza carton. He raised the lid and folded back a protective paper. Lying flat within was the illustrated frontispiece of the Diamond Sutra. He had saved work on the iconic image until last.

The tools of Barnard's trade were a mix of high-tech and low, and looked as if they would be equally at home in an operating theater or a beauty parlor. An ultrasonic humidifier capable of emitting a fine mist sat beside round-nose scissors, a magnifying glass, tweezers, blades, and a row of four fine paintbrushes. But his most vital tool was invisible. It was patience. Just moistening sections of the scroll evenly before work could begin took up to four hours.

The roots of the conservation work go back more than twenty years. Since then, experts have analyzed every aspect of the scroll's creation, including the wheat starch glue that held the sheets together, the mulberry paper on which it was printed and even the dye that colored it yellow. This laid the groundwork for the hands-on conservation.

Conserving the scroll has also involved separating it into its seven sheets, just as when the sutra was printed from woodblocks. Keeping the sections flat makes them easier to work on and, more importantly, it removes strain on the scroll caused by repeated rolling and unrolling.

The Diamond Sutra of 868 was once a well-used scroll. To Barnard's trained eye, the evidence is apparent in wear along the middle where ties once prevented it from unrolling. Damage is also evident on the innermost portion, where the scroll has been wrapped tightest, and on the exposed exterior, which contains the frontispiece. Before it was stored in the Library Cave, the sutra had already been patched to prolong its life. Those repairs from centuries ago are visible in the earliest photograph of the sutra, published in Stein's *Ruins of Desert Cathay*.

"If you look very closely, there's evidence of patches on the verso [back] of the scroll," Barnard says. "It was fractured in places and repaired, which implies it was actually slightly worn, which is hardly surprising."

Also visible in that first photograph is a water stain that darkens part of the illustration, including the Buddha's face. Before the scroll's first exhibition in London, the frontispiece was separated from the rest of the scroll and washed. The disfiguring stain and the ancient patches were removed and the first lining was added.

Barnard has removed at least four linings applied between 1909 and the mid-1960s. In the years since the last lining was added, conservation skills and knowledge of materials have changed substantially. Conservation now involves techniques considerably more sophisticated than gluing one paper to another. However, the question of whether or not to line has been a source of debate. Current thinking is that unlined scrolls fare better. In addition, unlike Chinese calligraphy and paintings, religious scrolls such as the Diamond Sutra were not lined in antiquity. So leaving the Diamond Sutra unlined is consistent with its original form.

For many years after World War II, the scroll was on permanent display in the King's Library of the British Museum. (Appropriately for the Diamond Sutra, that space is now called the Enlightenment Gallery.) While ceramics, bronzes, and other objects can be displayed without harm for long periods, books, with their sensitivity to light, need rest. Ideally, such sensitive material should occasionally be taken off exhibition.

Yet the renown of the world's oldest dated printed book made it difficult to remove the Diamond Sutra from permanent exhibition, says Dr. Frances Wood, head of the British Library's Chinese section. The scroll was on permanent display when she joined the library in 1977, but was removed in 1995, around the time the library prepared to move from Bloomsbury to its current purpose-built home at St. Pancras. "It was always something people asked for and it was therefore difficult to take it off display," she says. "So it had been on display for, we felt, too long."

Whether the scroll will be reassembled is still to be decided. But Wood does not favor this. "I don't think we should put it back as a scroll, because the endless rolling and unrolling is what does damage. If we can keep the sheets separate, if you wanted to exhibit it, you could put them back together to look as if it was a scroll."

In May 2010, after nearly 1,000 hours of conservation work, the sutra was on temporary display as the centerpiece of a British Museum exhibition. The five-month show, The Printed Image in China, covered 1,300 years of the artform's development. The scroll is unlikely to go on permanent exhibition again. But that does not mean the public can no longer see it. Online ways of viewing the scroll have become available in recent years. These reveal the Diamond Sutra in detail not possible for someone peering at it in subdued light through the glass of a display cabinet. An interactive version allows people to scrutinize the entire document. Viewers can pause at the illustrated frontispiece where, with the click of a mouse, it is possible to zoom in on the downcast eyes of the Buddha and the wrinkles on Subhuti's neck. Even the creases that have accumulated as the scroll has been wrapped and unwrapped over the centuries are apparent. Along the scroll, the Chinese characters of the Buddha's teaching and the colophon that gives its date are all visible. This is part of the British Library's Turning the Pages project, which lets viewers inspect some of the most precious works among the library's 150 million items. William Blake's notebook, sketches by Leonardo da Vinci, Mozart's musical diary, and Lewis Carroll's original *Alice's Adventures Under Ground* are other gems that can be viewed this way. Just a few years ago, this method of enjoying a literary treasure would have seemed as fanciful as a caterpillar smoking a hookah pipe. For some, it will never replace the experience of viewing the real object. But if the Diamond Sutra's life is to be extended, it offers a way to appreciate the scroll without causing harm—guiding principles of conservation and Buddhism.

For much of the twentieth century, even experts were unable to readily see the treasures of Dunhuang's Library Cave. The scattering of the objects posed geographic obstacles. The Cold War and the Iron Curtain posed political ones. Even after China opened its door and *perestroika* thawed Russia, deep pockets were still needed to examine relics as far apart as London and St. Petersburg or New Delhi and Beijing.

Now the contents of the Library Cave are being reunited in cyberspace. The Dunhuang manuscripts, paintings, and other Silk Road discoveries are accessible through a unique digital archive. The International Dunhuang Project (IDP), based at the British Library, was established in 1994 and grew out of the first meeting of conservators from the various international collections. When the specialists gathered, they recognized a common problem, says IDP's director, Dr. Susan Whitfield. "Everybody in all the collections felt a bit anxious, as if they hadn't done enough with this material and it wasn't accessible enough," she says. "It was quite a cathartic experience for everyone. It was like confession time and now let's work together."

Whitfield suggested one way to improve access was by digitizing the material and putting it online. It was a radical suggestion in the mid-1990s with the internet in its infancy. "Everybody looked at me as if I must be mad. 'There's no way the web is ever going to do that. There's too much material. It will be too slow,'" Whitfield said. Nonetheless, the work proceeded. The result is an extensive digital archive, among the largest of its kind in the world.

The website (http://idp.bl.uk) has information on manuscripts, textiles, and paintings as well as historic photographs. By the middle of 2012, the online archive had digitized more than 125,000 of these items and contained more than 350,000 images—all freely available. From Stein's journeys alone, the website holds everything from his hand-drawn maps of the Mogao Caves to a portrait of the forger Islam Akhun and a mountain panorama taken the day Stein suffered frostbite. There is even information about Stein's dynasty of dogs named Dash.

The resource, available in seven languages, continues to grow. The aim is to have 90 percent of the Dunhuang collection online by 2015. The search for Silk Road antiquities may have been characterized by international rivalry and hostility, but today there is collaboration between cultural institutions—including the National Library of China, the Bibliothèque nationale de France in Paris, and the Institute for Oriental Manuscripts in St. Petersburg—to understand, conserve and make the material available to scholars and the public. IDP has received funding from the European Union as well as the Mellon and Ford foundations. But another way of financing the work has not changed since the days of the Diamond Sutra's merit-making patron Wang Jie. Individuals, or groups, can sponsor a sutra. The sponsored document is copied—through digital photography, not hand-copying—and made available online for free. The woodblock-printed Diamond Sutra is among those that have benefited from this program.

⊱⊰

Much of what is known about the Silk Road and Buddhism's migration along it has its roots in Stein's epic journeys, his scholarship, and his stamina. He brought tangible evidence of how present-day Muslim Central Asia rests on Buddhist foundations. It is impossible to comprehend contemporary Central Asia—and its increasing importance in world events—without understanding the Silk Road. Stein is the thread that makes that possible.

He uncovered some of the only surviving records of daily life as it was more than a millennium ago—poignant letters by lonely soldiers, an angry missive from an abandoned wife. With his Persian Buddha, hymns to Jesus, and images of Eros, Heracles and Athena, Stein returned from the desert with sacred treasures from possibly the world's greatest and certainly least-known cultural melting pot. He showed that among the Silk Road's sands lie a magnificent lost Buddhist civilization, epitomized in the Diamond Sutra. In a world today riven by sectarian conflict, his discoveries remind us of the existence of places where people of different cultures and beliefs once coexisted peacefully and give hope that they may do so again.

Stein's resourcefulness is beyond doubt. His ability to plan and execute his epic journey over towering mountains and parched deserts and to organize teams of men and supplies is all the more remarkable given it was done without today's communication lifelines: satellite navigation, the internet, cell phones. At times, he had nothing more than a hand-drawn map to guide him, at others, not even that. But as much as his dedication and determination can be admired, his actions are more problematic. From today's perspective, the removal of manuscripts and murals is alarming, his treatment of Abbot Wang seems calculating and manipulative. But these were not the standards of his era, and it is facile to judge one era by the values of another. Stein worked in an era when Western powers viewed the cultural objects of others as theirs for the taking and jockeyed for the right to do so. It was a time when the West claimed "superior" knowledge and argued it alone could care for the world's treasures. Not even the bones of indigenous people were safe, as Australia's Aboriginal people know.

While the Romantic poet Robert Byron railed against Lord Elgin, who made off with the Parthenon marbles, and writer Victor Hugo against Britain and France's looting of Beijing's Summer Palace, few Western voices were raised against Stein in his lifetime. One who did protest was Sinologist Arthur Waley, the translator of the Xuanzang-inspired *Monkey*. Waley asked people to "imagine how we should feel if a Chinese archaeologist were to come to England, discover a cache of medieval MSS [manuscripts] at a ruined monastery, bribe the custodian to part with them, and carry them off to Peking." His words recalled criticism of Stein made by China's National Commission for the Preservation of Antiquities in the 1930s. Not that Waley had any sympathy for Abbot Wang, the "precious old humbug" as he called him. Stein well knew the Chinese were interested in their remote past, according to Waley. "But I was never able to convince him that the Chinese scholars who in the eighteenth and nineteenth centuries wrote about the geography and antiquities of Central Asia were anything more than what he called 'armchair archaeologists.'"

Waley's dissenting voice aside, Stein died a hero in the West. But not so in China, where he has long been reviled as the greatest pirate to have crossed the ocean of sand, far worse than France's Paul Pelliot, America's Langdon Warner, Russia's Sergei Oldenburg or Japan's Count Otani. Of all the material Stein removed, the Dunhuang manuscripts have attracted the most ire. Certainly more than the murals he cut from desert shrines and which arguably caused greater damage and despoiled what remained. Perhaps part of the reason for this anger is because the manuscripts were removed from within the confines of China itself, rather than Turkestan. China continues to feel aggrieved at being deprived of these records of its culture. A recent Chinese government book about the caves describes Stein as a looter and defrauder. Visitors to the Mogao Caves, or Peerless Caves, today receive a brochure that refers to the "theft" of the documents and concludes: "We hope that later generations will learn from this lesson." But the lesson of the Library Cave is ambiguous and raises questions about what the fate of its scrolls might otherwise have been.

When Abbot Wang broke open the cave, he could elicit little interest from local authorities in its contents. By the time Stein arrived, Wang had already given away some manuscripts to ingratiate himself with local officials. Stein's fear was that the rest would face a similar fate and be destroyed or lost. Wily and exploitative as Stein undoubtedly was in his treatment of Wang, there is no doubt his aim was to save the scrolls for the future and to better understand the past.

Personal gain and enrichment were never his motives. He lived frugally and his most treasured home was his tent. His appetite for work and his eagerness to reveal the past never dimmed. His will provided for a fund to encourage Central Asian exploration. To see Stein simply as either hero or plunderer is simplistic, the reality is more nuanced. However one views the ethics of his actions, the consequences are that the Diamond Sutra and the other scrolls he took have been well cared for in one of the world's finest institutions. They have been documented and are increasingly available in ways unimaginable a century ago. Stein removed the scrolls when to do so was not illegal and China had neither laws nor advocates to prevent this. Certainly that had changed by the time Stein pig-headedly persisted three decades later in the face of Chinese protests.

It is possible China may one day seek the return of the Diamond Sutra and other Dunhuang treasures. China was weak and racked by political upheaval when Stein took them. Today it is a global player with the world's fastest-growing economy. As its

power has increased, so has its interest in the fate of cultural treasures removed from its soil. So far this has focused on objects
plundered from the Summer Palace. China estimates about 1.5
million items were stolen when French and British troops under
the command of Lord Elgin—whose father acquired the Elgin
Marbles—sacked and burned the palace in 1860 during the Second Opium War.

In early 2009, China attempted to stop the auction of two
bronze heads belonging to the late fashion designer Yves Saint
Laurent that once adorned a fountain at the Summer Palace. The
Paris auction by Christie's went ahead, but then the buyer refused
to pay. He later identified himself as Cai Mingchao, an adviser to
China's National Treasures Fund, which seeks to retrieve treasures from abroad. A few months after the auction, China asked
the British Museum, the Metropolitan Museum in New York,
and other institutions in the UK, the United States, and France
to allow its teams to document the artifacts looted from the Summer Palace. In 2010, on the 150th anniversary of the sacking of
the Summer Palace, Chinese authorities called for the return of
the looted artefacts.

These moves come as other countries are increasingly seek-
ing the return of iconic objects, reigniting debate about restitu-
tion and the repatriation of cultural treasures. Greece has long
demanded that the British Museum return the Elgin Marbles
and has built a museum in sight of the Parthenon to house them.
Not that this has altered Britain's resolve to retain the statues.
The British Museum argues the sculptures are part of everyone's
heritage and transcend cultural boundaries. More recently Egypt
has demanded Nefertiti's bust from Berlin's Neues Museum and
the Rosetta Stone from the British Museum.

The argument that only the West can adequately care for
cultural items is less tenable than it was even a few decades
ago. Yet so is the argument that the Dunhuang documents are

not available for study. Some argue that objects belong to the cultures that produced them. But even that is not clear-cut with the Dunhuang manuscripts. Most of them are in Chinese, including the Diamond Sutra, but others are in a range of languages. Where, then, should the Manichean hymns go? Or the Sogdian letters?

Most countries today are more protective of their heritage with laws preventing the removal of their cultural objects. The ancient pilgrim Xuanzang could not openly venture from China to India now, intent on removing religious scrolls. Nor could he readily give objects to a major gallery or museum. Aware that acquiring antiquities can encourage looting, many museums no longer buy them without proof they left their country of origin legally. Yet despite international laws and museum ethical codes, the black market trade in looted antiquities has mushroomed. As ancient treasures are reefed from the soil or chipped off monuments without study or documentation, their history and context are lost. The illegal trade has been fuelled in part by buyers' ignorance. Others have deliberately turned a blind eye to the most basic question: where did this come from and how did it get here?

One area especially vulnerable to looting is the Gandharan art Stein so admired. The war in Afghanistan has taken a tragic human toll, but the continued conflict has meant the region's ancient culture is at risk of systematic destruction, according to the International Council of Museums, which has issued a "red list" of items at risk. Among the targets of the illicit trade are ancient manuscripts on palm leaf, birch bark, and vellum, as well as fragments of Buddhist wall paintings and figures.

Even as its art is at risk, knowledge of the Silk Road's 2,000-year history grows. Since the turn of the millennium, exhibitions in cities as far apart as London, Kyoto, Hong Kong, and St. Petersburg attest to the burgeoning interest. The romance of the Silk Road may have gone, but its imaginative power endures.

Tourism has stimulated curiosity about an area off-limits to foreigners for much of the twentieth century. So has politics. As rival powers again compete for influence in Central Asia, and oil, not silk, becomes the coveted commodity, some speak of a new Great Game.

19

Scroll Forward

Traveling the Silk Road today no longer means facing the hazards the ancient caravans endured—not least hunger, thirst, and attack by bandits—nor even the privations faced by Stein just a century ago. The old walls of Kashgar, along which Stein groped his way in a dust storm, have gone. They have fallen victim to the wrecker's ball that has reduced much of the old city to rubble in the past decade. But tucked away behind two high-rise hotel buildings bearing its name, Chini Bagh still stands. The former British consulate is a Chinese restaurant today. Diners fill the tables on a shady veranda beside the main entrance, through whose welcoming doorway over the years have passed Stein and Dash, Chiang, Father Hendricks, the formidable Russian consul Petrovsky, Australian journalist and correspondent for *The Times* G.E. Morrison, and writers Peter Fleming and William Dalrymple.

The castle-like ramparts, familiar from old photographs, and their whitewash and ochre exterior paintwork remain. But there are no traces of the shady orchard and gardens Mrs. Macartney so lovingly created, just a small vegetable patch beside some al fresco tables. Inside, the walls have been elaborately plastered and gilded, creating a baroque atmosphere in the light-filled rooms. From the rear, the view is no longer of a river, fields and the Russian cemetery where Father Hendricks' friends kept a candle burning on his grave, but of buildings and construction sites.

A fifteen-minute walk from Chini Bagh, the former Russian consulate also still stands. The once lonely outpost of the rival empire is similarly surrounded by Chinese hotel buildings. The original austere brown-and-grey-brick residence is less welcoming than Chini Bagh. In a rear room, a mural stretches the width of one wall. The painting depicts a classical landscape in which a brave Greek soldier wrestles a bull by its horns, a florid reworking of Carle van Loo's *Theseus, Vanquisher of the Bull of Marathon*. The French artist's name—in Russian script—appears in the corner. How long the mural has been there and who really painted it is unknown. Perhaps Petrovsky dined under it and saw in the mural an allegory of Great Game rivalries in which Imperial Russian force subdued the British beast. A more recent hand—perhaps of Chini Bagh's plasterer—has been at work, covering the Russian consulate's walls too in ornate curlicues. The building, known as the Seman, is not open to the public, but houses the office of a property company. The Russian Cossacks once stationed there, whose airs Stein could hear from Chini Bagh, would today be inaudible over the horns of taxis and buses that in the past two decades have replaced donkey carts as the main form of transport.

The yellow-and-white Id Kah Mosque still calls the faithful to prayer and within its walls the shady poplars are a peaceful refuge from the bustle of the night market, flashing neon and a billboard advertising a forthcoming Kashgar attraction—a golf course. Men with wispy beards and green embroidered hats sell circular bread cooked in clay ovens. Elderly women, faces veiled for modesty in coarse brown fabric, nonchalantly raise their dresses to reveal ample bloomers in which they keep their money.

From Kashgar, the southern oases through which Stein passed still see few foreigners. The route lacks the more impressive remains of Xinjiang's Buddhist past that dot the northern oases. At Yarkand, there is no sign of the *yamen* where Chiang lived before joining Stein and eventually becoming Macartney's secretary at Chini Bagh. No doubt Chiang knew of Yarkand's female poet, Aman Isa Khan, who died in childbirth in the sixteenth century and whose tomb remains the town's landmark. In its nearby bazaar, metal workers hammer tin into chests and the onion-domed barbecues used by street hawkers, the customers all locals. Yarkand was once a Silk Road crossroads, filled with travelers from Tibet, Afghanistan, and Ladakh and its population bigger than Kashgar. Today it is a backwater where the presence of foreigners sparks good-natured attention.

Farther east, jade is still the mainstay of Khotan, known today as both Hotan and Hetian. The stone extracted from its mountain-fed rivers, especially the white "mutton fat" variety, continues to be highly prized among the Chinese. High-end shops attract the cashed-up while street traders display lumps of stone of dubious value on shabby cloths.

Stein once dreamed of a museum in Hotan to house the treasures of Rawak Stupa, whose sculptures he reburied only to discover jade hunters had destroyed them in a futile search for treasures concealed within. The city does have a museum that displays remains of Hotan's Buddhist past, including statues and two mummies, but nothing can undo the damage to Rawak.

A camel across the sea of sand dunes was the only way to reach the stupa, until the recent opening of a road. Yet few visitors appear to travel along it. About ten miles from Rawak is the shrine of a Muslim saint where Stein once camped under a full moon. Each May pilgrims from far afield, including Sufi musicians, pay homage to the Islamic martyr. On a late summer day it is silent and devoid of pilgrims. But a soft cooing penetrates the still air. Behind the shrine, the sacred pigeons are better housed in their brick coop than when Stein offered them a handful of grain.

The princess who brought to Hotan silkworm eggs concealed in her headdress—and hence the means to make silk—may be largely forgotten, but a compound of silk-makers still spins and weaves the fabric just outside the oasis. A young woman, baby in her lap, sits before a bath of silkworm cocoons. She teases out a few threads and passes them to a man seated behind a large wheel, who hand spins the gossamer thread. It will be transformed into ikat-dyed fabric with a bold pattern favored by local women for clothing. On the edge of Hotan, an elderly man keeps another ancient tradition alive. He has been dubbed the last mulberry paper-maker of the Taklamakan. Within his family's mud-brick compound he pounds the tree's bark to a pulp. When it is the consistency of watery porridge, he pours it into a mold and leaves it to dry in the sun. The result is a strong creamy paper—the same type of paper on which the Diamond Sutra was once printed.

In Hotan's main square, the disparate influences of its recent past are evident. Beneath a statue of the late Chairman Mao, looming paternalistically over a former Uyghur leader, an evening concert begins. A man crooning pop songs vacates the stage for a group of Cossack-style dancers who perform a Cinderella story as they compete to fit a young maiden with a pair of red shoes. The streets teem with donkey carts next morning for the weekly Sunday market. The scents of cardamon, cumin, and rose flowers fill the air in a corner of the bazaar where merchants pound drums full of spices. Elsewhere, a man whittles wooden spoons, another sells metal-spiked brushes that create the swirling pattern on the circular naan bread. The old constantly bumps up against the new: two musicians perform on traditional Uyghur instruments to mark the opening of a whitegoods store.

The Taklamakan Desert itself has been tamed. Near the Thieves' Road, where Stein and his party almost died of thirst in search of the Keriya River, a sealed cross-desert highway links the northern and southern oases. Traders, travelers, and troops no longer have to take the slow, circuitous route to reach the far side of the desert, but can cut straight across it. Along each side of the road, mass plantings of rice straw in a neat grid attempt to hold back the moving sands—and the demons once conjured by this realm of deadly illusion. Trucks and buses now convey goods and people in about twelve hours along the once-trackless wastes. Passengers on a bus from Hotan to Kucha pass the hours watching dubbed Turkish soap operas, except for an elderly Uyghur man who quietly performs his prayers to Mecca in the aisle.

Across the desert on the old northern Silk Road the work of Albert von Le Coq is evident. At the Kizil Caves near Kucha, the German sawed off many murals. But he is not the only one to have left a destructive mark there. Treasure hunters have removed gold leaf from the robes and haloes of the Buddhas painted on the walls. Muslim iconoclasts have scratched the eyes and mouths from the sacred images. The caves, some older even than those at Mogao, were still used as dwellings until the 1980s, a guide explains, and evidence of cooking and heating is apparent on some soot-blackened paintings. Nonetheless, many murals remain. Outside the caves, a statue of Kumarajiva honors the great translator who was born in Kucha and whose translation was used for the Diamond Sutra of 868.

The Kizil Caves contain more surviving murals than at Bezeklik near the oasis of Turfan. Von Le Coq, who daubed "Robbers' Den" over his accommodation near Bezeklik, stripped these domed caves more thoroughly. Also near Turfan are the ruins of the ancient Buddhist city of Gaochang. Donkey carts convey visitors a mile or so along its hot, dusty length. In the once-thriving city, Xuanzang was detained by its king before being released to make his epic trip to India and back, returning via Dunhuang.

〜

In Dunhuang's open-air market, Muslim hawkers grill sticks of mutton over charcoals, a Tibetan in a cowboy hat sells "medicinal" dried snakes, animal horns and paws, while a Han Chinese artist etches images of angels onto gourds. The town remains a cultural crossroads, but it is far removed from the dusty garrison where Stein struggled to find someone to cut up his silver horseshoes for currency. Now he would queue at an ATM. With shop windows full of leather goods, fashion, and electronics, Dunhuang looks like any other prosperous Chinese town, although few anywhere are surrounded by towering sand dunes that creep ever closer.

As in the days of the Silk Road, Dunhuang's life blood is visitors from afar. But today's travelers are the result of a recent phenomenon: global tourism. Travelers to Dunhuang no longer arrive on plodding camels or bumpy donkey carts, but by planes, trains, and private cars. They come to see the Jade Gate, the ruined clay fort through which so many Silk Road caravans traveled. And they come to see Crescent Lake, nestled in a hollow and surrounded by towering dunes. Stein once wished to be buried by its tranquil banks. Perhaps it is just as well his wish was never realized. There is little solitude by the lake today, where tourists ride brightly decked camels and hire toboggans to slide down the dunes. But the Ming Sha dunes no longer rumble. Pollution, not least from so many visitors, has affected the sands and since the early 1980s they have fallen silent.

Above all, people come to Dunhuang to see the Mogao Caves. And they arrive not once a year for an annual pilgrimage, but daily. Today, a paved path to the caves crosses a footbridge over the dry bed of the Daquan River, near where Stein camped. The poplars Abbot Wang planted along the river banks still provide welcome shade from the summer heat. The caves remain a place of pilgrimage for some. A visiting brown-robed priest lights incense sticks near a central pagoda, places them in a large incense holder and bows three times. Other visitors follow his example, although most simply pose at the photogenic spot. The rickety ladders to the caves have been replaced by steps and walkways. The once-exposed entrances to the honeycombed grottoes that reminded Stein of troglodyte dwellings have been fitted with metal doors. It is no longer possible to wander unescorted from cave to cave, as Stein did.

On a clear autumn day, a guide unlocks a door to one of the grottoes. She walks ahead down a narrow passage that opens onto a dark chamber. She flashes her torch on the wall. After the dazzling sunshine outside, our eyes adjust to the mute light, and murals in azure, lapis, and ochre emerge from the darkness. Row upon row of painted Buddhas adorn every inch of the walls. The ceiling is covered in images of celestial musicians and dramatic hunting scenes that include a galloping horse invested with the energetic confidence of a Picasso. The magnificence of this grotto alone—like a Buddhist Sistine Chapel—is overwhelming. It is just one of 492 remaining painted caves in the world's greatest gallery of Buddhist art.

Unlike the Sistine Chapel, the artists who painted these are unknown. So many hands have taken part in their creation. First came laborers who chipped and hollowed each cave out of conglomerate rock. Others hauled mud from the Daquan River in front of the cliff, mixed it with straw and lined each cave wall. This created a "canvas," a smooth surface—finished with a thin layer of plaster—over the lumpy rock interiors. Next came the artists who, under the direction of a senior monk, drew and then painstakingly painted the walls and ceilings. Traces of gold and precious stones still adorn some of the images. By the flickering light of oil lamps, they must have looked especially magnificent.

Artists also created the painted clay statues of fierce temple guardians, jeweled bodhisattvas and Buddhas of the past, present and future. More than 2,000 statues remain.

We re-emerge, blinking, into the sunlight, and the guide leads the way to another cave behind a nine-story pagoda facade. Inside we are dwarfed by a 116-foot Buddha, the largest of three colossal Buddhas at the caves. Elsewhere are an eighty-five-foot seated Buddha of the future, Maitreya, and a fifty-one-foot sleeping Buddha. A smaller sleeping Buddha, forty-seven feet long, is surrounded by statues of seventy-two disciples. Each face reveals a different reaction as they observe the Buddha entering *parinirvana*—the final nirvana—on the point of physical death.

Paintings on some of the walls are like storyboards on which unfold morality tales and legends of the Buddha. A sixth-century cave depicts a prince being devoured after he offers his body to a tigress so she can feed her hungry cubs. The final scene depicts the prince's brothers making their gruesome discovery and fleeing, their hair raised in horror. Painted when few could read, even an illiterate ancient peasant could grasp this story—a modern-day manga cartoon could not tell it more vividly.

No two caves are alike. Each differs in size and decoration. Some evoke the interiors of tents, their high tapered ceilings painted like the drapery of richly patterned fabric. Yet many share an identical layout—a narrow hallway that opens onto a square chapel with a central altar. Most of the images are Buddhist, but there are also images of everyday life: a butcher cutting meat while three hungry dogs wait expectantly nearby, an artisan making pottery, even a man defecating. There are scenes that recall the ancient travelers from afar who ventured along the Silk Road, including images of big-nosed foreigners. Others portray an ever-present peril that faced Silk Road merchants—bandits. We enter a cave where the evidence of a more recent foreigner is evident. A rectangle on the wall is devoid of the murals that fill the rest of the chapel. The aftermath of Langdon Warner disfigures like a wound.

At the northern end of the cliff is the cave all visitors want to see. Behind its door a narrow passageway leads to a large cave containing statues. On the right of the passage, about four feet above the ground, is the opening to an antechapel. The painted figures of two attendants—one holding a fan, the other a pilgrim's staff—decorate the antechapel's far wall. They flank two painted Bodhi trees whose leafy branches frame the statue of a seated monk. The figure is Hong Bian, once the most revered Buddhist dignitary west of China's Yellow River. His statue, removed to make room for the scrolls, has been restored to the chapel built in his honor more than 1,000 years ago. The statue of Hong Bian and the painted figures of his two attendants are all that remain within the chapel. The Diamond Sutra and the 50,000-plus scrolls that once filled it from floor to ceiling are spread around the world. The mural and the statue within the niche can't match the splendor of others at the caves. But this empty grotto is the site of one of the Silk Road's most dramatic episodes and the place that has transformed our understanding of a culture unlike any other.

What occupies today's guardians, however, is not what has gone from the caves but how to safeguard what remains. For well over a millennium, the caves survived desert winds, earthquakes, invasion, refugees, pilgrims, and vandals. But their greatest threat in the twenty-first century is from tourism. The trickle of visitors who arrived in the late 1970s, when the caves were first opened to the public, has turned into a torrent. More than 650,000 people arrive each year, eager to see the Silk Road's most magnificent site, and the numbers continue to soar. It seems incredible now that the caves could ever have been abandoned and forgotten. As improbable as the art of the Louvre and the books of the British Library slipping from memory and into a sleep lasting centuries.

But having awoken, the danger now is that the caves will be loved to death.

Many of the sacred caves are small, some no bigger than a sub-urban bedroom. They were never designed to hold large numbers of people. Locals refer to some of the tiny chapels as the "falling-down caves." This is not a reference to Stendhal syndrome—the sense of being overwhelmed by the beauty of art—although it is impossible not to be transported by the exquisite images. Rather, it is the result of too many people in too small a space breath-ing too little air, especially in summer when most tourists arrive. Every humid breath expelled by visitors risks damaging the wall paintings. So does the rush of air that changes the temperature each time a cave door is opened. Both activate salt—the caves' great enemy—within the walls. Salt causes the paint to flake and peel from the murals—wiping far more than the sublime smile from the Buddha's face.

How best to deal with so many visitors is a concern for the Dunhuang Academy, the prestigious research institute which since 1943 has served as guardian of the caves. Juggling the com-peting demands of mass tourism and conservation is tricky, the academy's deputy director, Dr. Wang Xudong, acknowledges. "One of the most challenging issues we face is the rapid increase in tourists and the influence created by people," he says. "Although the site is large overall, the space in the individual caves is quite small. So the capacity is definitely limited. One needs to balance enabling visitors to come and enjoy the site, but at the same time not having any destructive influence on it. This is easy to say but difficult to do."

His office is a fifteen-minute walk from the caves and close to the main entrance through which visitors arrive all day, every day. Remoteness was once the caves' great natural protector. Dun-huang was still difficult to reach even two decades ago when Wang Xudong first arrived after an arduous journey from his hometown four hundred miles away. "The economy was not as developed when I was younger, and it was a long way for us. When I came to work here in 1991, I had to change buses twice and have one overnight stop. Now you have the train and freeways," he says.

Better transport and a prosperous Chinese economy have led to a huge increase in domestic visitors, who comprise about 90 percent of today's overall numbers. The Dunhuang Academy has been working with international specialists, including the Getty Conservation Institute in Los Angeles, to strike a balance between conservation and tourism. The Getty's conservation scientist Dr. Neville Agnew, one of the first foreign scientists to work on protecting Chinese heritage sites, says this has involved looking at how many visitors the caves can cope with and how to manage them. After a long day working in the caves, Agnew and his team of specialists gather back at the Dunhuang Academy, where amid laptops and charts, they discuss the day's findings and consider how best to protect the caves for the future.

Agnew explains that China's best-known tourist attractions—Beijing's Forbidden City and Xian's Terracotta Warriors—receive many more visitors than Mogao, but the nature of the caves is different. "The Terracotta Warriors have a big shed over them and people can walk around. Many of the cave temples are relatively small with a narrow entrance . . . The tourist industry says, 'Why don't you take more visitors? Take more visitors.' But you can't do that. The site is very, very sensitive."

Visitors see inside about a dozen caves during a two-hour tour, but plans are underway to limit further the time people spend in the World Heritage–listed caves. There is no suggestion the caves will be closed, as has occurred at France's Lascaux Cave with its prehistoric animal paintings. Closure might be in the best long-term interest of the Buddhist caves, but tourism brings much-needed revenue into Gansu, one of China's poorest provinces.

Tourism is not the only threat to the caves; there is the ever-encroaching sand. The movement of the dunes is imperceptible but relentless. On a ridge above the caves, a fence helps reduce the amount of sand blown over the cliff and into the caves. But no fence can stop the advance of the sands which have reclaimed so many Silk Road towns and treasures over the years. The desert, less than three miles from Dunhuang, is expanding by an estimated twelve feet a year. Rivers have run dry, crops have died and even Crescent Lake has shrunk to a fraction of its former size. The water table has fallen as Dunhuang's thirsty population has expanded from 40,000 to 200,000 in the past fifty years.

Walking along a flat sandy expanse above the grottoes, there is an unearthly silence on a windless day. The visitors to the caves are out of sight and earshot in the valley below. Not a breath rustles the scant vegetation, not an insect hums. It is a silence rare in the modern world with the unceasing throb of traffic, aircraft, computers, and cell phones. Perhaps there was a similar silence when the monk Lezun arrived in 366 and, inspired by his golden vision of a thousand Buddhas, carved the first grotto here. It is not hard to imagine why the Caves of the Thousand Buddhas were created in this place of terrifying beauty on the edge of two great deserts, the Taklamakan and the Gobi. One direction is pancake flat, the other sees rolling dunes that stretch to the horizon. People once came to the caves to pray for their own survival. Perhaps the greatest miracle is that the caves themselves have survived.

ﹸﹰ

Picture this: monks sit cross-legged before a long, low table. The smoke of fragrant incense and the sound of resonant chanting fill the room. The monks' gaze shifts from the golden statues around them to small screens held in the hand of each robed figure. "Thus I have heard . . ." It is hardly as romantic as the image of a monk slowly unrolling a long paper sutra. But far-fetched? Just as handwritten scrolls gave way to printed ones such as the Diamond Sutra, so the book and the printed word are undergoing change every bit as dramatic.

Portable devices such as the Kindle and the iPad are transforming how we read. Will the printed book go the way of cassette tapes, video recorders, pay phones, and manual typewriters? And will the book-lined study become as quaintly old-fashioned as an overstuffed Victorian parlor? It may be premature to write the obituary of the printed book. Theaters have not emptied with the advent of film, nor have paintings been rendered redundant by digital art.

And yet, so many vital elements in the life story of the Diamond Sutra—printing, libraries, reading, even the use of paper—are undergoing profound change. Paper was once a precious resource. In the year 700, a Dunhuang official lamented that paper was so scarce he could not fulfill his promise to copy a sutra. Today, much of the world's paper is thrown away the same day it is printed. But as forests dwindle and as books and other documents increasingly begin life on screen, it is possible that paper and the printed book may become more valued again.

There's no doubt the future will be digital. Libraries are at the frontline in the shift from print as their collections are digitized and made available in cyberspace. How best to achieve this is still being debated. As centers of learning and understanding, libraries have always been far more than simply storehouses of books. They are keepers of cultural memory that hold safe what we know and encourage further inquiry.

What is changing is how that cultural memory is accessed. The so-called "Heavenly Library" that exists in the cloud of the internet may make available more works than any single "real" library could hold. The move by Google to scan the collections of the world's great libraries and make them available online remains controversial. Advocates compare the move to the development of Gutenberg's printing press, arguing that it will have a democratizing effect. But critics question whether responsibility for digitizing the world's books should rest with a private company, rather than a public non-profit organization. The political and social consequences of the technology are not yet apparent as the Gutenberg Age gives way to the Google Age. Yet if the past is a guide, these will be far-reaching.

Wading through the reams of Stein's correspondence, so carefully preserved in the Bodleian Library in Oxford and on microfilm in the British Library, the handwritten letter already seems a relic of a bygone era. Perhaps today Stein would blog to keep his friends and backers apprised of his journey, or SMS his friend Fred Andrews for a new pair of spectacles. Even Stein's neat cursive script seems beyond the ability of many of us who are more likely to tap, tweet or text a message on a keypad than pick up a pen. Some might wonder, who needs handwriting in an age of the keyboard? But if we don't need it, how long might it be before the ability to read the handwritten word becomes a rare skill, its form as incomprehensible to an average reader as ancient Sogdian?

The knowledge that everything changes is at the heart of the religion that produced the Diamond Sutra. The scroll itself has undergone so many changes, passed through countless hands and survived potential catastrophes. It outlived a 1,000-year entombment on the edge of the Gobi Desert, it evaded the looting of Dunhuang, it could so easily have been lost in a mountain stream, sunk at sea en route to Britain or burned in the bombings of World War II. Miraculously, it survived these trials by earth, fire, water, and air. Of all the paradoxes associated with the Diamond Sutra, none is greater than the endurance of this text about impermanence. Having survived its elemental trials, the Diamond Sutra has fulfilled a 1,300-year-old promise: that it be freely available to all.

Postscript

Percy Allen became president of Corpus Christi College, Oxford. Stein was a frequent visitor to his home. An Erasmus scholar, Allen traveled extensively in Europe, where he visited libraries great and small. He died in 1931.

Fred Andrews built a house in Srinagar from where he could see across a valley to Stein's camp at Mohand Marg. He returned to England in 1929. He was technical adviser on his brother George Arliss's 1936 film *East Meets West*. He died in 1957, aged ninety-three.

Chiang-ssu-yeh (Jiang Siye) remained in Kashgar, where he died in the spring of 1922. Stein felt deeply the loss of his devoted companion and helped pay to transport Chiang's body back to his home in Hunan.

Dash the Great remained in Oxford with the Allens. Aged about fourteen, Stein's favorite fox terrier was run over by a bus in Oxford in 1918.

Florence Lorimer spent three years in Kashmir before returning to London. The "Recording Angel" became a buyer of Oriental carpets for a London department store and later assistant librarian at the Royal Asiatic Society. Aged forty-five she married a retired civil servant. She died in 1967.

George and Catherine Macartney left Kashgar in 1919. They retired to Jersey in the Channel Islands. Lady Macartney penned a memoir of her Kashgar years, *An English Lady in Chinese Turkestan*. Knighted in 1913, Sir George died on Jersey in 1945, Lady Macartney nearly six years later.

Aurel Stein's grave was tended for nearly thirty years by an Afghan man named Rahimullah, along with the graves of other foreigners buried in the British Cemetery in Kabul. The elderly caretaker died of natural causes in March 2010. His son Abdul Samay has taken on the role.

Abbot Wang Yuanlu spent the rest of his life at the Caves of the Thousand Buddhas. He died in 1931. His burial stupa is at Mogao, where visitors pass it daily on their way to his beloved caves.

Acknowledgments

A journey across more than a thousand years and several continents doesn't happen without great kindness, memorable encounters and eureka moments. It is a journey that began when a scruffy backpacker set down her rucksack in the shabby surrounds of Kashgar's Chini Bagh in 1989. But the seeds for the book might never have ripened without a fleeting computer image of the Mogao Caves glimpsed during a visit to the Getty's Conservation Institute in Los Angeles in 2005.

Since then it has become a shared journey during which we have crossed the dunes of the Taklamakan Desert atop reluctant camels, spent quietly thrilling days absorbed in Aurel Stein's letters in the British Library and Bodleian Library and been captivated by the painstaking work to conserve the Diamond Sutra.

His Holiness the fourteenth Dalai Lama made time in his schedule of teachings to discuss the Diamond Sutra. Others also shared their understanding of Buddhism, including Robert Thurman, Paul Harrison, Gary Snyder, Robina Courtin, Wai Cheong Kok and Yoon S. Han. The Nan Tien temple in western Sydney welcomed us to hear practitioners chant the Diamond Sutra. Renate Ogilvie graciously related her moving personal story.

At the British Library, Susan Whitfield and Frances Wood were generous in their time and knowledge, illuminating in their responses to queries and made invaluable comments on an early draft of the manuscript. That said, any errors are our own. Mark Barnard opened the door of his conservation studio to us. Lynn Young pointed us to archival gold, and staff of the Asian and African studies reading room were endlessly helpful.

At the British Museum, Helen Wang shared her expertise on Stein and Florence Lorimer; and Marjorie Caygill her wartime knowledge. Archivists Stephanie Clarke and Julia Flood were enthusiastic in their support.

We are indebted to Colin Harris at the Bodleian Library and Julian Reid, archivist at Merton and Corpus Christi Colleges, Oxford. Stein's biographer Annabel Walker offered insights into the explorer's life. Medi Jones-Jackson and other staff at the National Library of Wales unlocked their secret wartime tunnel for us, and even provided the hard hats.

In Dunhuang, Wang Xudong, Neville Agnew and his colleagues from the Getty's Conservation Institute explained their work at the Mogao Caves, as did Sharon Sullivan, Kirsty Altenburg and Peter Barker.

In Australia, Edmund Capon, former director of the Art Gallery of New South Wales, opened his personal library. Gallery curators Jackie Menzies and Liu Yang shared their expertise, as did Lindie Ward from the Powerhouse Museum. Alan Oakley, former editor of *The Sydney Morning Herald*, gave the precious gift of special leave to work on the book, which Peter Fray kindly extended.

Anne Coombs provided wise counsel and incisive comments on the manuscript, as she has during three decades of friendship. Brenda O'Neill's eye for detail was meticulous. Julian Droogan and Mark Rossiter read portions of the manuscript and suggested improvements. We drew on the specialist knowledge of Victor H. Mair, Lukas Nickel, Mark Allon and Judith Snodgrass. Barbara Harper, Linda Mors, Bob Smillie, Susan Varga, Rae Bolotin,

Isabelle Li, Tony Twiss, Philippa Drynan and Sasha Anawalt helped in miraculous ways.

At Lyons Press, Holly Rubino and her team have been enthusiastic in their support. Our agents, Pamela Malpas and Lyn Tranter, have been energetic champions. We are grateful to all who helped us weave together the threads of this Silk Road story.

Endnotes

A note on spellings:
There are numerous possible renderings of Chinese and Turkic names into English. We have generally used the spellings Stein adopted in his books and letters for events set in his day. (The key exceptions are Dunhuang and Xuanzang.) Elsewhere we have favored contemporary spellings for people and places.

CHAPTER 1: THE GREAT RACE
Page
6   "more like a log": Aurel Stein, *Ruins of Desert Cathay*, vol 1, p 24.
6   "incapable of facing prolonged hard travel": ibid., vol 1, p 9.
12 "Sadiq now in Chinese prison": Bodleian Library, Oxford University, Stein MS 3, Macartney telegram, April 10, 1906.

Chapter 2: Signs of Wonder
Page

22 "I wonder whether you have seen": Bodleian, Stein MS 90, John Lockwood Kipling to Stein, May 16, 1902.

26 "It was a melancholy duty": Aurel Stein, *Ancient Khotan*, vol 1, p 502.

30 "A great many of the grottos": Bodleian, Stein MS 294, application of September 14, 1904.

30 "It seems scarcely possible": ibid.

30 "The wide-spread interest": ibid.

31 "center of intellectual sunshine": Jeannette Mirsky, *Sir Aurel Stein: Archaeological explorer*, p 210.

31 "A bold demand": ibid., p 212.

32 "Rejoice": ibid., p 217.

Chapter 3: The Listening Post
Page

35 "There is a piece of news": Bodleian, Stein MS 96, Macartney to Stein, January 20, 1905.

35 "another poacher on your preserves": Bodleian, Stein MS 296, Macartney to Stein, October 16, 1905.

36 "The sooner you are on the field": ibid.

37 "The absence of the Professor": ibid., October 19, 1905. Extract from Macartney's confidential report dated October 18, 1905.

37 "There is a good deal": ibid., November 10, 1905.

37 "Good morning, old fat-head": Albert von Le Coq, *Buried Treasures of Chinese Turkestan*, p 76.

38 "I have never believed": Bodleian, Stein MS 297, Stein to Macartney, February 6, 1906.

38 "Grünwedel is ill": Bodleian, Stein MS 296, Macartney to Stein, December 29, 1905.

38 "My own plan now": Bodleian, Stein MS 3, Stein to Allen, January 20, 1906.

39   "The true race": ibid., January 6, 1906.

40   "the most timid, unenterprising girl": Lady (Catherine) Macartney, *An English Lady in Chinese Turkestan*, p 2.

42   "living newspaper": Aurel Stein, *Ruins of Desert Cathay*, vol 1, p 122.

43   "Wolves, leopards, and foxes": Catherine Macartney, *An English Lady in Chinese Turkestan*, p 40.

43   "Baby had three falls": Bodleian, Stein MS 96, Macartney to Stein, May 7, 1904.

44   "They tell me": Catherine Macartney, *An English Lady in Chinese Turkestan*, p 38.

44   "I sometimes suspected": ibid., p 131.

45   "easy-going slackness": Bodleian, Stein MS 3, Stein to Allen, June 25, 1906.

45   "It cost great efforts": ibid.

45   Bactrian camels are so critically endangered today that fewer than a thousand remain in the wild. See iucnredlist .org and edgeofexistence.org.

46   "inordinate addiction to opium": Aurel Stein, *Sand-Buried Ruins of Khotan*, p 116.

46   "captivating Khotan damsel": ibid., p 466.

46   "shrivelled up with the cold": Bodleian, Stein MS 3, Stein to Allen, June 2, 1906.

47   "a hardy plant": Bodleian, Stein MS 37, Stein to Andrews, January 31, 1907.

47   "lively ways": Aurel Stein, *Ruins of Desert Cathay*, vol 1, p 116.

48   "They may turn up": Bodleian, Stein MS 3, Stein to Allen, June 19, 1906.

48   "The rush past": ibid.

49   "a cave by the seashore": Aurel Stein, *Ruins of Desert Cathay*, vol 1, p 124.

CHAPTER 4: THE MOON AND THE MAIL

Page

51   "One may invade the house": Aurel Stein, *Sand-Buried Ruins of Khotan*, p 184.

52   "He has told me many little secrets": Bodleian, Stein MS 4, Stein to Allen, March 5, 1907.

52   "I never could look": Aurel Stein, *Ruins of Desert Cathay*, vol 1, p 143.

53   "It was a piece of real good fortune": ibid., p 117.

53   "To peep into every house": Bodleian, Stein MS 261, part 1 of 2. Undated extract of personal narrative.

54   "She looked as if rising from the sea": Aurel Stein, *Sand-Buried Ruins of Khotan*, p 221.

56   Indian surveyors disguised: Peter Hopkirk, *Trespassers on the Roof of the World: The race for Lhasa*, pp 20–36.

57   "After an event like that": Bodleian, Stein MS 40, Lionel Dunsterville to Stein, August 28, 1912.

57   "My care in burying these": Aurel Stein, *Serindia*, vol 1, pp 127–28.

58   "There is thus every reason": Bodleian, Stein MS 3, Stein to Allen, September 20, 1906.

59   "All Charklik is being ransacked": Bodleian, Stein MS 3, Stein to Allen, December 3, 1906.

60   "I shall make a depot": ibid.

61   "Had he not always tried": Aurel Stein, *Ruins of Desert Cathay*, vol 1, p 373.

61   "a handful when things are easy": Bodleian, Stein MS 261, part 1 of 2. Undated extract of personal narrative.

62   "I felt the instinctive assurance": Aurel Stein, *Ruins of Desert Cathay*, vol 1, p 358.

62   "One longs for helpers": Bodleian, Stein MS 3, Stein to Allen, December 14, 1906.

62 "The odours were still pungent": Aurel Stein, *Ruins of Desert Cathay*, vol 1, pp 393–94.

63 "The ink is beginning to freeze": Bodleian, Stein MS 3, Stein to Allen, December 27, 1906.

Chapter 5: The Angels' Sanctuary

Page

67 "How sorry I am": Bodleian, Stein MS 4, Stein to Allen, January 7, 1907.

69 "sweepings from the hearth": Aurel Stein, *Ruins of Desert Cathay*, vol 1, p 439.

70 "I sometimes wondered": ibid., p 517.

70 "the slightest capacity": ibid., p 446.

71 "What had these graceful heads": ibid., p 457.

71 "In one chapel": Bodleian, Stein MS 4, Stein to Helen Allen, February 2, 1907.

71 "I had longed for finds": ibid., Stein to Allen, February 17, 1907.

72 "For my eyes": Aurel Stein, *Ruins of Desert Cathay*, vol 1, p 484.

73 "Truly this part of the country": Bodleian, Stein MS 4, Stein to Helen Allen, February 2, 1907.

74 "This sounds hopeful": ibid., Stein to Allen, February 17, 1907.

76 "a drearier sight": ibid., March 5, 1907.

76 "My unmusical ear": ibid.

76 "When travellers are on the move": Marco Polo, *The Book of Ser Marco Polo*, vol 1, p 197.

77 "have to make the best of his solitude": Bodleian, Stein MS 4, Stein to Allen, March 5, 1907.

80 "It amused me": Aurel Stein, *Ruins of Desert Cathay*, vol 2, p 13.

81   Magistrate Wang Ta-lao-ye and Stein's passport: Wang Jiq-
     ing, "Stein and Chinese Officials at Dunhuang," Interna-
     tional Dunhuang Project (IDP) newsletter, No. 30, Spring
     2007.
81   "I instinctively felt": Aurel Stein, *Ruins of Desert Cathay*,
     vol 2, p 14.

CHAPTER 7: TRICKS AND TRUST
Page
102 "It gave me the first assurance": Aurel Stein, *Ruins of Desert
     Cathay*, vol 2, p 22.
102 "'The Caves of the Thousand Buddhas'": ibid., p 23.
104 "I had told my devoted secretary": ibid., p 28.
104 "I always like to be liberal": ibid., p 30.
104 "The gleam of satisfaction": ibid., p 31.
105 "the craziest crew": ibid., p 41.
105 "Across an extensive desert area": ibid., p 64.
106 "I would rather be a dog's or a pig's wife": Susan Whitfield
     and Ursula Sims-Williams, *The Silk Road: Travel, trade, war
     and faith*, p 185.
106 "I feel at times as I ride along": Bodleian, Stein MS 4, Stein
     to Allen, April 26, 1907.
107 "He had spent many a hot day": ibid.
107 "If they are people": ibid., May 18, 1907.
108 "mental distemper": Aurel Stein, *Ruins of Desert Cathay*,
     vol 2, p 71.
108 "So I have learned at last": Bodleian, Stein MS 4, Stein to
     Allen, May 18, 1907.
109 "The trees bent": Catherine Macartney, *An English Lady in
     Chinese Turkestan*, pp 115–6.
109 "Overtaken by violent sand storm": Bodleian, Stein MS 204,
     Stein diary, April 11, 1907.

110 "with the strength of a hidden magnet": Aurel Stein, *Ruins of Desert Cathay*, vol 2, p 164.

110 "The skill of man": Mildred Cable and Francesca French, *The Gobi Desert*, p 63.

110 "There could be no more appropriate place of rest": Bodleian, Stein MS 4, Stein to Allen, May 18, 1907.

111 "sound like that of distant carts": Aurel Stein, *Ruins of Desert Cathay*, vol 2, p 161.

111 "divine sweeping": ibid., p 162.

111 "My brave [Chiang]": Bodleian, Stein MS 4, Stein to Allen, May 18, 1907.

112 "He looked a very queer person": Aurel Stein, *Ruins of Desert Cathay*, vol 2, p 165.

113 "To rely on the temptation of money alone": ibid., p 167.

114 "[But] this was not the time": ibid., p 167.

114 "There rose on a horseshoe-shaped dais": ibid., p 168.

114 "I could not help feeling": ibid., p 168.

115 "saintly Munchausen": ibid., p 170.

115 "Would the pious guardian": ibid., p 170.

116 "There was nothing for me": ibid., p 171.

CHAPTER 8: KEY TO THE CAVE
Page

118 "The sight of the small room": Aurel Stein, *Ruins of Desert Cathay*, vol 2, p 172.

119 "There can be little doubt": ibid., p 187.

120 "Such insignificant relics": ibid., p 188.

121 "No place could have been better adapted": Aurel Stein, *Serindia*, vol 2, p 811.

122 "It would have required a whole staff": Aurel Stein, *Ruins of Desert Cathay*, vol 2, p 175.

123 "temple of learning in Ta-Ying-kuo": ibid., p 191.

124 "Should we have time": ibid., p 174.

124 "embarras des richesses": ibid., p 195.

125 "Independence": Bodleian, Stein MS 4, Stein to Allen, June 9, 1907.

125 "Very tired with low fever": Bodleian, Stein MS 204, Stein diary, June 10, 1907.

125 "gloomy prison of centuries": Aurel Stein, *Ruins of Desert Cathay*, vol 2, p 193.

126 "He had already been gradually led": ibid., p 190.

127 "I secured as much as he possibly dared to give": Bodleian, Stein MS 37, Stein to Andrews, June 15, 1907.

128 "We parted in fullest amity": Aurel Stein, *Ruins of Desert Cathay*, vol 2, p 194.

CHAPTER 9: THE HIDDEN GEM

Page

133 "Thus shall you think": A.F. Price (translator), *The Diamond Sutra.*

136 On the earliest known woodcut illustration: Clarissa von Spee, *The Printed Image in China from the 8th to the 21st Centuries*, p 15.

138 "this ox may personally receive": Lionel Giles, *Descriptive Catalogue of the Chinese Manuscripts from Tunhuang in the British Museum*, p 32.

138 On an official and a homesick woman who copied the Diamond Sutra: ibid., p 26.

139 On the woman pierced with knives: John Kieschnick, *The Impact of Buddhism on Chinese Material Culture*, pp 169–170.

140 "fragrant," and "believing heart": Lionel Giles, *Descriptive Catalogue of the Chinese Manuscripts from Tunhuang in the British Museum*, pp 32–33.

140 On the elderly man who mixed blood and ink: Stephen F. Teiser, *The Scripture on the Ten Kings and the Making of Purgatory in Medieval Chinese Buddhism*, p 126.
140 On the monk who drew blood to copy scrolls: ibid., p 127. For more on blood writing, see John Kieschnick's article "Blood writing in Chinese Buddhism." *Journal of the International Association of Buddhist Studies*, (2000) 23.2, pp 171–194.
140 On the grumpy scribe: John Kieschnick, *The Impact of Buddhism on Chinese Material Culture*, p 184.

CHAPTER 10: THE THIEVES' ROAD
Page
149 "trotted up gaily": Bodleian, Stein MS 205, Stein diary, October 5, 1907.
150 "The single ancient Sanskrit MS": Bodleian, Stein MS 4, Stein to Allen, October 14, 1907.
151 "Ram Singh's rheumatism has disappeared": ibid., Stein to Allen, July 28, 1907.
151 "asking him to keep his own body": Bodleian, Stein MS 205, Stein diary, October 14, 1907.
153 "like excavating in one's own garden": Aurel Stein, *Ruins of Desert Cathay*, vol 2, p 360.
153 "Robbers' Den": Albert von Le Coq, *Buried Treasures of Chinese Turkestan*, p 91.
154 "Somewhat in despair": ibid., p 106.
154 "How much greater would be the chance": Aurel Stein, *Ruins of Desert Cathay*, vol 2, p 361.
155 "How often I have thanked you": Bodleian, Stein MS 5, Stein to Allen, January 11, 1908.
156 "robbers and others": Aurel Stein, *Serindia*, vol 3, p 1,241.
156 "I must confess": Aurel Stein, *Ruins of Desert Cathay*, vol 2, p 376.

156 "precious but embarrassing impedimenta": ibid., p 376.

157 "He gave it with more ceremony": ibid., p 383.

158 "Nowhere in the course of my desert travels": Aurel Stein, "Dr Stein's Expedition in Central Asia," *The Geographical Journal*, vol 32, no 4 (October 1908), p 350.

158 "My secret apprehension": Aurel Stein, *Ruins of Desert Cathay*, vol 2, p 392.

158 "How the camels held out so far": Bodleian, Stein MS 205, Stein diary, February 10, 1908.

CHAPTER 11: AFFLICTION IN THE ORCHARD

Page

164 "I could not help smiling": Bodleian, Stein MS 37, Stein to Andrews, March 6, 1908.

165 "On one occasion": Bodleian, Stein MS 5, Stein to Allen, June 10, 1908.

166 "I shall be more than ever bound to the collection": ibid.

167 "It is sad to think that I shall have to leave Dash": ibid., January 26, 1908.

167 "Disgust at having to employ such a scoundrel": Bodleian, Stein MS 205, Stein diary, July 17, 1908.

168 "You can imagine the trouble": Bodleian, Stein MS 5, Stein to Allen, June 23, 1908.

168 "He suffered awful pains": ibid., July 27, 1908.

168 "Marmite turned to use at last": Bodleian, Stein MS 205, Stein diary, July 23, 1908.

169 "You can imagine my feelings": Bodleian, Stein MS 5, Stein to Allen, June 23, 1908.

169 "You have nothing to reproach yourself with": Bodleian, Stein MS 205, Stein diary, July 6, 1908.

171 "Presented by Dr M.A. Stein to Chiang-ssu-yeh": Bodleian, Stein MS 37, Stein to Andrews, May 17, 1907.

172 "Often as I look back": Aurel Stein, *Ruins of Desert Cathay,* vol 1, p 117.

172 "Then, as I rode on": ibid., vol 2, p 439.

CHAPTER 12: FROZEN

Page

175 "He recognized me when I stroked him": Aurel Stein, *Ruins of Desert Cathay,* vol 2, p 467.

175 "What he succumbed to": Bodleian, Stein MS 5, Stein to Allen, October 16, 1908.

177 "The world appeared to shrink": Aurel Stein, *Ruins of Desert Cathay,* vol 2, p 480.

178 "The aid of an experienced surgeon": ibid., p 483.

178 "so gorged they could hardly move": David Fraser, *The Marches of Hindustan: The record of a journey in Thibet, Trans-Himalayan India, Chinese Turkestan, Russian Turkestan and Persia,* p 264.

179 "Here fell Andrew Dalgleish": Charles Murray, Earl of Dunmore, "Journeyings in the Pamirs and Central Asia," *The Geographical Journal,* vol 2, no 5 (November 1893), p 386.

179 On the disputed territory of the Siachen Glacier: Tim McGirk and Aravind Adiga, "War at the Top of the World," *Time Asia,* May 4, 2005.

180 "Dr [Schmitt] assures me": Bodleian, Stein MS 5, Stein to Allen, October 16, 1908.

181 "I never thought of such a communication": ibid., November 16, 1908.

181 "If you have a chance": ibid., October 26, 1908.

182 "Things might have fared a great deal worse": Bodleian, Stein MS 37, Stein to Andrews, November 14, 1908.

183 On Stein's health in India: Annabel Walker, *Aurel Stein: Pioneer of the Silk Road,* p 187.

184 "May kindly divinities protect them": Bodleian, Stein MS 5, Stein to Allen, December 17, 1908.

CHAPTER 13: YESTERDAY, HAVING DRUNK TOO MUCH . . .

Page

189 "the value of a domestic slave": Lionel Giles, *Six Centuries at Tunhuang*, p 36.

190 "Chief of the hundred plants": ibid., p 28.

191 "Yesterday, having drunk too much": ibid., pp 33–34.

191 "Yesterday, Sir, while in your cups": ibid., p 34.

191 "Even if Heaven and Earth collapse": Lionel Giles, "Dated Chinese Manuscripts in the Stein Collection," *Bulletin of the School of Oriental and African Studies*, University of London, vol 11, no 1 (1943), p 160.

192 "What had this neat, almost calligraphic manuscript": Aurel Stein, *Ruins of Desert Cathay*, vol 2, p 187.

192 "Jesus the Buddha": Tsui Chi (translator), "The Lower (Second?) Section of the Manichean Hymns," *Bulletin of the School of Oriental and African Studies*, University of London, vol 11, no 1 (1943), pp 174–219.

193 "Nestorian Christians could safely address their prayers to": Bodleian, Stein MS 91, Stein to von Le Coq, March 14, 1926.

194 "Iron snakes belched fire": Victor H. Mair, *Tun-huang Popular Narratives*, pp 87–88.

195 Extensive work on the Dunhuang medical manuscripts has been undertaken by Wang Shumin. See http://idp .bl.uk/4DCGI/education/ medicine_society/abstracts.a4d.

196 On the importance of almanacs: Susan Whitfield and Ursula Sims-Williams, *The Silk Road: Travel, trade, war and faith*, p 82. See also: Susan Whitfield, "Under the Censor's Eye: Printed Almanacs and Censorship in Ninth-Century China," *British Library Journal*, vol 24, part 1, 1998, pp 4–22.

197 On the Dunhuang star chart: Jean-Marc Bonnet-Bidaud, Françoise Praderie and Susan Whitfield, "The Dunhuang Chinese Sky: A Comprehensive Study of the Oldest Known Star Atlas," *Journal of Astronomical History and Heritage*, vol 12, no 1 (March 2009), pp 39–59.

199 On the painted silk banner retrieved by Paul Pelliot: Joseph Needham, *Science and Civilisation in China*, vol 5, part 7, pp 222–23.

200 On paper flowers: Susan Whitfield and Ursula Sims-Williams, *The Silk Road: Travel, trade, war and faith*, p 268.

CHAPTER 14: STORMY DEBUT
Page

201 "I am afraid you will find": Jeannette Mirsky, *Sir Aurel Stein: Archaeological explorer*, p 87.

202 "In the course of my explorations": British Museum archives, CE 32/23/23/2, Stein letter, May 20, 1909.

203 "The cellar has been made": Bodleian, Stein MS 37, Andrews to Stein, August 11, 1909.

203 "He has true British terrier blood": "Dog Explorer: Adventures of a Fox Terrier," *Daily Mail*, May 26, 1909.

203 The story of Stein's camp chair: George Macartney, "Explorations in Central Asia, 1906–8—Discussion," *The Geographical Journal*, vol 34, no 3 (September 1909), p 265.

204 For more on Florence Lorimer, see Helen Wang's article "Stein's Recording Angel—Miss F.M.G. Lorimer," *Journal of the Royal Asiatic Society*, series 3, 8, 2 (1998), pp 207–228.

204 For more on the manuscripts sent to Pelliot in Paris, see Frances Wood's article "A Tentative Listing of the Stein Manuscripts in Paris 1911–1919." In *Sir Aurel Stein, Colleagues and Collections*. British Museum Research Publication Number 184, 2012. www.britishmuseum.org/pdf/12_Wood%20 (Tentative%20listiing).pdf.

205 "extravagant multiplication of limbs": *Festival of Empire, 1911, Guide Book and Catalogue,* Bemrose & Sons, London, 1911, p 17.

205 "epoch-making importance": "Buddhist Paintings at the Festival of Empire," *The Times,* September 7, 1911.

206 "Greatly delighted was I": Aurel Stein, *Ruins of Desert Cathay,* vol 2, p 189.

206 Stein captions his photograph: "Roll of block-printed Buddhist text with frontispiece from wood-engraving, dated 864AD." Elsewhere he refers to the scroll with "a date of production corresponding to 860AD." See *Ruins of Desert Cathay,* vol 2, fig 191 and p 189.

206 "Late last night": Bodleian, Stein MS 8, Stein to Allen, June 17, 1912.

206 "Many congratulations": Bodleian, Stein MS 12, Allen to Stein, June 1912.

207 "I cannot express on paper": Bodleian, Stein MS 96, Chiang to Stein, July 30, 1912.

207 "Mr. Macartney has been kind to me": ibid.

207 "Deaf as he is": Bodleian, Stein MS 96, Macartney to Stein, October 14, 1912.

207 "Chiang-ssu-yeh can't quite make up his mind": Bodleian, Stein MS 41, Macartney to Stein, February 12, 1913.

208 "Massacres of Chinese officials": Bodleian, Stein MS 96, Macartney to Stein, May 24, 1912.

208 "Finally there is the substantial printed roll": British Library archives, Or 13114, "Correspondence with M. Pelliot regarding Chinese documents," October 2, 1912. This information courtesy of Dr. Frances Wood.

209 "The more I see of this glorious land": Bodleian, Stein MS 40, Stein to Andrews, May 6, 1912.

209 "In a way I am sorry": Bodleian, Stein MS 42, Stein to Andrews, June 29, 1913.

210 "the Queen wore a hat": "The King and the Museum," *The Times*, May 8, 1914, p 4.

211 "The King and Queen": "The British Museum: The New Edward VII Wing," *Manchester Guardian*, May 8, 1914.

211 "His two greatest finds": "Wonders of the East: Exhibits in the British Museum Extension," *The Times*, May 7, 1914, p 5.

211 "There was a succession": Bodleian, Stein MS 94, Lorimer to Stein, May 8, 1914.

212 "He is better qualified": Bodleian, Stein MS 89, Stein to Kenyon, June 30, 1913.

212 "If you should prefer": British Museum archives, CE32/23/50/1, Barnett to Kenyon, August 11, 1913.

213 "It is from every point of view desirable": British Museum archives, CE 32/23/49, Stein to Kenyon, July 1, 1913.

214 "The museums in this country": British Museum archives, CE32/23/54, Government of India, August 20, 1914.

214 "Mr Andrews's disadvantages in the matter": British Museum archives, CE 32/23/82-2, Binyon to Kenyon, November 25, 1916.

CHAPTER 15: TREASURE HUNTERS
Page

222 "as jovial & benign": Bodleian, Stein MS 11, Stein to Allen, March 27, 1914.

223 "Honest Wang, the priest": ibid., April 3, 1914.

224 "There was nothing to do but gasp": Langdon Warner, *The Long Old Road in China*, p 211.

224 "Across some of these lovely faces": Langdon Warner, *Langdon Warner Through His Letters*, edited by Theodore Bowie, Warner to his wife, Lorraine Roosevelt Warner, p 115.

224 "My job is to break my neck": ibid., p 116.

224 "As for the morals of such vandalism": ibid., Warner to Hamilton Bell, p 118.

225 "Each one visits the caves": ibid.

225 "No vandal hand but mine": Langdon Warner, *The Long Old Road in China*, p 220.

225 "neither of whom could ever come back and live": Langdon Warner, *Langdon Warner Through His Letters,* edited by Theodore Bowie, Warner to Lorraine Roosevelt Warner, p 128.

227 "Otherwise it is no longer scientific archaeology": British Museum archives, CE32/24/25, National Commission for the Preservation of Antiquities, Beijing, China. Received by British Museum January 5, 1931.

227 "still in the stage of grinding": "China and her Treasures. Hampering the Scientist," *The Times,* March 30, 1931, p 11.

CHAPTER 16: HANGMAN'S HILL

Page

229 On World War II: The authors have drawn on the following sources, which proved invaluable in reconstructing wartime events. P.R. Harris, *A History of the British Museum Library, 1753–1973;* John Forsdyke, "The Museum in War-time," *The British Museum Quarterly,* vol XV (1952), pp 1–9; Jacob Leveen, "The British Museum Collections in Aberystwyth," *Transactions of the Honourable Society of Cymmrodorion,* 1946; David Jenkins, *A Refuge in Peace and War: The National Library of Wales to 1952,* National Library of Wales, Aberystwyth, 2002; N.J. McCamley, *Saving Britain's Art Treasures From the Nazis.* See also Joyce Morgan's article "The Stein Collection and World War II." In *Sir Aurel Stein, Colleagues and Collections.* British Museum Research Publication Number 184, 2012. www.britishmuseum.org/pdf/14_Morgan%20REV.pdf.

237 "suicide exhibition": Marjorie Caygill, "1939: Evacuating the BM's treasures," *British Museum Society Bulletin,* no 62, Winter 1989, p 21.

239 "Stein Sahib is some kind of supernatural being": C.E.A.W. Oldham, "Sir Aurel Stein 1862–1943," obituary from the *Proceedings of the British Academy*, vol 29 (1943), pp 453–65.

239 "but his age of 60 shows": quoted in Jeannette Mirsky, *Sir Aurel Stein: Archaeological explorer*, p 546.

240 "I have had a wonderful life": "Sir Aurel Stein," *The Times*, November 4, 1943, p 7.

240 "As Marco Polo is regarded": C.E.A.W. Oldham, "Sir Aurel Stein 1862–1943," obituary from the *Proceedings of the British Academy*, vol 29, pp 453–65.

240 "the last of the great student-explorers": Percy M. Sykes, "Sir Aurel Stein," *Journal of the Royal Central Asian Society*, 1944, vol 31, part 1, p 5.

240 "He brought to light": "Obituary, Sir Aurel Stein," *The Times*, October 28, 1943.

241 "Like Odysseus": Lionel Barnett, "Explorations in Central Asia, 1906–8—Discussion," *The Geographical Journal*, vol 34, no 3 (September 1909), p 265.

242 "One cannot help feeling": Peter Hopkirk, *Foreign Devils on the Silk Road*, p 229.

CHAPTER 17: FACETS OF A JEWEL
Page
246 "amateurish and shallow slop": Geddeth Smith, *Walter Hampden, Dean of the American Theatre*, p 230.

247 "It's not philosophy": Gary Snyder, interview by Joyce Morgan, March 24, 2010.

250 "The main problem for me": Dr. Paul Harrison, interview by Joyce Morgan, August 25, 2009.

250 "all great texts": Walter Benjamin, "The Task of the Translator," in *Selected Writings, vol 1, 1913–1936*, p 263.

252 "The essential part": Professor Robert Thurman, interview by Joyce Morgan, September 30, 2009.

254 "That does not mean": His Holiness the Fourteenth Dalai Lama, interview by Joyce Morgan, December 1, 2009.
257 "The Diamond Sutra specifically states": Yoon Han, interview by Conrad Walters, August 3, 2010.
259 "Andrew started reading": Renate Ogilvie, interview by Joyce Morgan, June 28, 2010.

CHAPTER 18: SHIFTING SANDS
Page
263 "If you look very closely": Mark Barnard, interview by authors, April 7, 2009.
264 "It was always something": Dr. Frances Wood, interview by authors, March 16, 2009.
265 "Everybody in all the collections": Dr. Susan Whitfield, interview by Joyce Morgan, March 10, 2009.
268 "imagine how we should feel": Arthur Waley, *Ballads and Stories from Tun-huang,* pp 237–38.
268 On Stein as a looter: Gansu Provincial People's Government Information Office, *Dunhuang sees Great Changes over the Years,* p 141.

CHAPTER 19: SCROLL FORWARD
Page
282 "One of the most challenging issues": Dr. Wang Xudong, interview by Joyce Morgan, October 26, 2007.
283 "The Terracotta Warriors": Dr. Neville Agnew, interview by Joyce Morgan, November 20, 2007.

Select Bibliography

Allen, Charles, *The Buddha and the Sahibs*, John Murray, London, 2002.

Almond, Philip C., *The British Discovery of Buddhism*, Cambridge University Press, Cambridge, 1988.

Arnold, Edwin, *The Light of Asia*, Echo Library, Teddington, 2008 (1879).

Atwood, Roger, *Stealing History*, St. Martin's Griffin, New York, 2004.

Barrett, T.H., *The Woman Who Discovered Printing*, Yale University Press, New Haven, 2008.

Benjamin, Walter, *Selected Writings, vol 1, 1913–1926*, edited by Marcus Bullock and Michael W. Jennings, Harvard University Press, Cambridge, Massachusetts, 1996.

Boulnois, Luce, *Silk Road: Monks, Warriors and Merchants*, translated by Helen Loveday, Odyssey Books, Hong Kong, 2008.

Cable, Mildred, and French, Francesca, *The Gobi Desert*, Readers Union, London, 1950 (1944).

Ch'en, Kenneth, *Buddhism in China*, Princeton University Press, Princeton, New Jersey, 1964.

Conze, Edward, *Buddhist Wisdom Books Containing the Diamond Sutra and the Heart Sutra*, Allen & Unwin, London, 1975 (1957).

Cuno, James, *Who Owns Antiquity?*, Princeton University Press, Princeton, New Jersey, 2008.

Dalrymple, William, *In Xanadu*, Flamingo, London, 1990.

Febvre, Lucien, and Martin, Henri-Jean, *The Coming of the Book*, translated by David Gerard, Verso, London, 1976 (1958).

Fleming, Peter, *News from Tartary*, Macdonald Futura, London, 1980 (1936).

Fraser, David, *The Marches of Hindustan: The record of a Journey in Thibet, Trans-Himalayan India, Chinese Turkestan, Russian Turkestan and Persia*, William Blackwood and Sons, Edinburgh and London, 1907.

French, Patrick, *Younghusband*, Flamingo, London, 1995.

Gansu Provincial People's Government Information Office, *Dunhuang Sees Great Changes over the Years*, China Intercontinental Press, Beijing, 2007.

Gelber, Harry G., *The Dragon and the Foreign Devils*, Bloomsbury, London, 2007.

Giles, Lionel, *Descriptive Catalogue of the Chinese Manuscripts from Tunhuang in the British Museum*, Trustees of the British Museum, London, 1957.

———. *Six Centuries at Tunhuang*, The China Society, London, 1944.

Greenfield, Jeanette, *The Return of Cultural Treasures*, Cambridge University Press, Cambridge, 2007 (1995).

Harris, P.R., *A History of the British Museum Library, 1753–1973*, The British Library, London, 1998.

Hedin, Sven, *My Life as an Explorer*, translated by Alfhild Huebsch, Kodansha International, New York, 1996 (1925).

Hopkirk, Peter, *Foreign Devils on the Silk Road*, University of Massachusetts Press, Amherst, 1984.

———. *The Great Game*, John Murray, London, 1990.

———. *Trespassers on the Roof of the World: The Race for Lhasa*, John Murray, London, 2006 (1982).

Huili, *The Life of Hiuen-Tsiang by the Shaman Hwui Li*, translated by Samuel Beal, Routledge, London, 2000 (1888).

Kapr, Albert, *Johann Gutenberg*, translated by Douglas Martin, Scolar Press, Brookfield, Vermont, 1996.

Keay, John, *Explorers of the Western Himalayas 1820–1895*, John Murray, London, 1996.

Kerouac, Jack, *The Dharma Bums*, Paladin, London, 1992 (1959).

Kieschnick, John, *The Impact of Buddhism on Chinese Material Culture*, Princeton University Press, Princeton, New Jersey, 2003.

Kipling, Rudyard, *Kim*, Vintage Books, London, 2010 (1901).

Ledderose, Lothar, *Ten Thousand Things: Module and Mass Production in Chinese Art*, Princeton University Press, Princeton, New Jersey, 2000.

Lo, Vivienne, and Cullen, Christopher (eds.), *Medieval Chinese Medicine: The Dunhuang medical manuscripts*, RoutledgeCurzon, London, 2005.

Lopez, Donald S. (ed.), *Curators of the Buddha*, University of Chicago Press, Chicago, 1995.

Lowenthal, David, *Possessed by the Past*, Free Press, New York, 1996.

Macartney, Lady (Catherine), *An English Lady in Chinese Turkestan*, Oxford University Press, Hong Kong, 1985 (1931).

Mair, Victor H., *Tun-huang Popular Narratives*, Cambridge University Press, Cambridge, 1983.

McCamley, N.J., *Saving Britain's Art Treasures from the Nazis*, Leo Cooper, Barnsley, 2003.

Menzies, Jackie (ed.), *Buddha: Radiant Awakening*, Art Gallery of New South Wales, Sydney, 2001.

Meyer, Karl E., and Brysac, Shareen Blair, *Tournament of Shadows*, Basic Books, New York, 2006 (1999).

Mirsky, Jeannette, *Sir Aurel Stein: Archaeological Explorer*, University of Chicago Press, Chicago, 1998 (1977).

Needham, Joseph, *Science and Civilisation in China*, Cambridge University Press, Cambridge, 1987 (1954).

Nhat Hanh, Thich, *The Diamond That Cuts Through Illusion*, Parallax Press, Berkeley, 1992.

Pine, Red, *The Diamond Sutra: Text and Commentaries Translated from Sanskrit and Chinese*, Counterpoint, Berkeley, 2001.

Polo, Marco, *The Book of Ser Marco Polo*, translated and edited by Sir Henry Yule, 3rd edn, John Murray, London, 1903 (1871).

Price, A.F. (translator), *The Diamond Sutra*, Buddhist Society, London, 1955.

Shaw, Robert, *Visits to High Tartary, Yarkand and Kashgar*, Oxford University Press, Hong Kong, 1984 (1871).

Shuyun, Sun, *Ten Thousand Miles Without a Cloud*, Harper Perennial, London, 2003.

Skrine, C.P., and Nightingale, Pamela, *Macartney at Kashgar*, Oxford University Press, Hong Kong, 1987 (1973).

Smith, Geddeth, *Walter Hampden, Dean of the American Theatre*, Associated University Presses, New Jersey, 2008.

Stein, Aurel, *Ancient Khotan*, Clarendon Press, Oxford, 1907.

————. *Innermost Asia*, Clarendon Press, Oxford, 1928.

————. *On Ancient Central-Asian Tracks*, Macmillan, London, 1933.

————. *Ruins of Desert Cathay*, Macmillan, London, 1912.

————. *Sand-Buried Ruins of Khotan*, Asia Educational Services, New Delhi, 2000 (1903).

————. *Serindia*, Clarendon Press, Oxford, 1921.

Suiter, John, *Poets on the Peaks: Gary Snyder, Philip Whalen & Jack Kerouac in the North Cascades*, Counterpoint, Washington, D.C., 2002.

Sutin, Lawrence, *All Is Change: The Two-thousand-year Journey of Buddhism to the West*, Little, Brown, Boston, 2006.

Teiser, Stephen F., *The Scripture on the Ten Kings and the Making of Purgatory in Medieval Chinese Buddhism*, University of Hawaii Press, Honolulu, 1994.

Twitchett, Denis, *Printing and Publishing in Medieval China*, Wynkyn de Worde Society, London, 1983.

Von Le Coq, Albert, *Buried Treasures of Chinese Turkestan*, translated by Anna Barwell, George Allen & Unwin, London, 1928.

Von Spee, Clarissa (ed.), *The Printed Image in China from the 8th to the 21st Centuries*, The British Museum Press, London, 2010.

Waley, Arthur, *Ballads and Stories from Tun-huang*, George Allen & Unwin, London, 1960.

————. *The Real Tripitaka and Other Pieces*, George Allen & Unwin, London, 1952.

Walker, Annabel, *Aurel Stein: Pioneer of the Silk Road*, University of Washington Press, Seattle, 1998.

Waller, Derek, *The Pundits: British Exploration of Tibet and Central Asia*, University Press of Kentucky, Lexington, 1990.

Warner, Langdon, *Langdon Warner Through His Letters*, edited by Theodore Bowie, Indiana University Press, Bloomington and London, 1966.

————. *The Long Old Road in China*, Arrowsmith, London, 1927.

Waxman, Sharon, *Loot: The Battle over the Stolen Treasures of the Ancient World*, Times Books, New York, 2008.

Wenbin, Zhang (chief ed.), *Dunhuang: A Centennial Commemoration of the Discovery of the Cave Library*, Morning Glory Publishers, Beijing, 2002.

Whitfield, Roderick, *Dunhuang: Caves of the Singing Sands*, Textile & Art Publications, London, 1995.

————. *The Art of Central Asia*, Kodansha International in co-operation with the British Museum, London, 1982.

Whitfield, Roderick, and Farrer, Anne, *Caves of the Thousand Buddhas*, British Museum Publications, London, 1990.

Whitfield, Roderick, Whitfield, Susan and Agnew, Neville, *Cave Temples of Mogao*, Getty Conservation Institute and the J. Paul Getty Museum, Los Angeles, 2000.

Whitfield, Susan, *Aurel Stein on the Silk Road*, The British Museum, London, 2004.

————. *Life along the Silk Road*, John Murray, London, 2000.

Whitfield, Susan, and Sims-Williams, Ursula, *The Silk Road: Travel, Trade, War and Faith*, The British Library, London, 2004.

Whitfield, Susan, and Wood, Frances (eds), *Dunhuang and Turfan: Contents and Conservation of Ancient Documents from Central Asia*, The British Library, London, 1996.

Winchester, Simon, *Bomb, Book and Compass: Joseph Needham and the Great Secrets of China*, Penguin, London, 2009.

Wood, Frances, *The Silk Road: TwoThousand Years in the Heart of Asia*, University of California Press, Berkeley, 2002.

Wood, Frances, and Barnard, Mark, *The Diamond Sutra: The Story of the World's Earliest Dated Printed Book*, The British Library, London, 2010.

Wriggins, Sally Hovey, *The Silk Road Journey with Xuanzang*, Westview Press, Boulder, 2004.

Wu, Ch'eng-en, *Monkey*, translated by Arthur Waley, Penguin, London, 2006 (1941).

Xuanzang, Si-Yu-Ki, *Buddhist Records of the Western World*, translated by Samuel Beal, Routledge, London, 2000 (1884).

Yule, Henry, *Cathay and the Way Thither*, Asian Educational Services, New Delhi, 2005 (1866).

Index

INDEX

About the Authors

Joyce Morgan has worked as a journalist for more than three decades in London, Sydney, and Hong Kong. Her writing has appeared in *The Sydney Morning Herald, The Australian, The Guardian,* and *The Bangkok Post.* She has written on arts and culture since 1994. Joyce is a senior arts writer at *The Sydney Morning Herald* and a former arts editor. She has also worked as a producer with ABC Radio. Born in Liverpool, England, she has traveled extensively in Asia, including India, Pakistan, China, Tibet, and Bhutan.

Conrad Walters has worked in the media for more than thirty years in the US, where he won awards for investigative journalism, and Australia. In 1999, he joined *The Sydney Morning Herald,* where he has worked as a feature writer and book reviewer. He is now an editor on the paper's iPad edition. Conrad was born in Boston, educated in Europe and the Middle East and has lived in seven countries. He has a master's degree in Creative Writing from the University of Technology, Sydney.

They live in Sydney with a vial of sand from the Taklamakan Desert on their mantelpiece.

www.journeysonthesilkroad.com